Human Services
at Risk

Politics of Planning Series

Barry Checkoway, Editor

Human Services at Risk

Administrative Strategies for Survival

Edited by
Felice Davidson Perlmutter
Temple University

LexingtonBooks
D.C. Heath and Company
Lexington, Massachusetts
Toronto

Library of Congress Cataloging in Publication Data
Main entry under title:

Human services at risk.

    Includes index.
    1. Social work administration—United States.
2. Social work administration—United States—Case
studies.   I. Perlmutter, Felice Davidson, 1931–
HV95.H76 1984   361.3′068   84–928
ISBN 0–669–07813–1

Second printing, June 1985

Published simultaneously in Canada

Printed in the United States of America on acid-free paper

International Standard Book Number: 0–669–07813–1

Library of Congress Catalog Card Number: 84–928

To my children, Shira, Saul, and Tova,
who continue their grandparents' coupling
of personal caring with social concern

Contents

Foreword

It is perhaps trite to write of history repeating itself, but it was only a decade or so ago under President Nixon that "cut-back-management" was highly popularized. And here we are again, but this time there is no "Watergate" in sight, and a staggering Federal deficit is in place. Thus the current flurry of conferences, journal articles, popular press coverage, and this comprehensive volume are more on target.

For the human services industry, several simultaneous strategies are evidenced. One group with a larger perspective focuses on replacing the conservatives in Washington with more altruistic, elected officials. Voter registration, campaign fund raising, and support of compatable candidates are the principle means to this end. Lobbying current officials is another tack. We still have friends in Congress. The social actionists are likely to act on both fronts. Other groups seek to isolate their cause and their unique interests from the mainstream. These groups are different. They demand more favorable treatment. Some groups may succeed, given the right political connections or a favorable accident of timing. Their cause may be currently popular. Others fight over the diminishing financial pie. They have found competitors, and these are other voluntary programs.

Still another approach to survive the present difficult situation is fostered by those who engage in intraorganizational thrusts. They seek to "manage with less."

Fund raising and the stimulation of new income sources are cited as the approach by another school.

These approaches are not totally incompatible. Several themes may be acted on simultaneously.

This book of thirteen chapters sets forth the alternatives well. Although it does not consider the merit of interorganizational conflict among the various organizations, it does consider comprehensive general coping. It covers topics from an overview of the political history of American social welfare and the requisite political role of the social administrator to an examination of the new strategies for executive performance. These roles are arrayed against both public and private organizations, and both strategic and tactical alternative activities are described. Case histories provide specific examples of the many options. They provide hope to the beleaguered practicing administrator. The tone of the book is pragmatic.

My task in introduction will be to highlight the various options and to examine the impact of the recent Federal budget cuts.

Assuming a smaller relative pie, in constant dollars, and the unlikely major shift of public policy during the next several years, continued retrenchment is likely. The goal is to survive without immobilizing organization, frustrating clients, and embittering staff. Several classes of activities can be identified, not necessarily in order of importance. They are linked in a general fashion. The first link is management. The objective is to make the organization more effective and more efficient. Several means are suggested to reach this objective: program budgets, zero-based budgets, accrual accounting, improved financial management, and cost containment. All are directed toward the financial side of the organization. Client and management information systems tied either to the budget or to staff productivity are also recommended tools. The business of personnel administration, improved productivity, tightened management, and improved supervison are also discussed. Pre- and in-service training are responsible options, as are work innovation and pilot projects. Fully consistent with survival goals are renewed emphasis on planning, need assessment, and priority setting.

In both public and private organizations, the role and composition of councils, commissions, trustees, and boards are reexamined. Public-sector agencies need volunteers with political contacts, competence, and motivation. Aggressive promotion of the agency and its objectives are necessary. In the voluntary not-for-profit sector the same political contacts and skills are necessary, especially in agencies with a large investment in public funding. But also of importance are board members with effective contacts to key actors in foundations, large donors, local business, organized labor, and the United Way. Thus for the voluntary sector a bimodal distribution of board member competencies may be advisable. Careful screening, recruitment, selection, and board training and reinforcement are all suggested.

More and more agencies are getting into the fund-raising procedure. But not all agencies have suffered from Federal budget cuts. Some have enjoyed increased income. Thus client fees on the one hand and old-fashioned fund raising on the other are potential sources of support. Getting to know local businesses, foundations, and wealthy individuals is necessary. The use of special fund-raising events and direct-mail solicitation is increasing. Market research and well-trained, committed, and energetic volunteers are essential.

Just as volunteers become more essential in lobbying, policy making or advising roles, and fund raising, so is there renewed emphasis on their role with clients. All of this occurs in an era in which some in the feminist movement have decried the role of women as volunteers and many more women have entered the labor market. Among organizations recording such matters (e.g., the Family Service Association of America), volunteers have generally played a less active role in the last decade.

Another very popular means to deal with all crises—including the present one—is to reorganize. Many agencies have done so in the last two or three years.

Interorganizationally, shared purchasing and training, client exchange, service integration, technical assistance, and contracting are all being tested.

The second-order choices include firing staff, reducing the quantity and/or quality of services, restricting admissions, eliminating functions, closing branch offices and operating with a deficit budget. The final option is to close the agency.

Reducing the Federal support of social, rehabilitation, legal, and employment services appears to be a rather straightforward measure. Drastic budget cuts are generally effective ways to bring pressure on the agencies.

In health, however, the matter has not been as simple. For more than two decades various measures have been implemented to control the rapid growth in health expenditures. For example health planning, certificates of need, rate setting (fee schedules), facility cost control, utilization review, peer review, health maintenance organizations, self-insurance and now DRG are only a sampling of the organized efforts. Most recently DRG has been coupled with improving the cost-consciousness of consumers, providers, and insurers, and the encouragement of the entry of competitors in the marketplace.

The result of this long-standing campaign has been that health costs have generally risen at about twice the rate of inflation. Without such controls the growth may have been larger. I seek not to improve or disapprove of the growth but to note only that cost control in a complex environment is fraught with difficulty.

Dr. Margaret Gibelman and I* recently completed an analysis of the Reagan budget cuts. We examined the effect on the voluntary, not-for-profit human service sector as a major test of the results of the budget reductions. We found various strains. Regarding changes in Federal support for the voluntary sector, the Urban Institute** using a 1980–86 frame, forsees a decrease (in constant 1980 dollars) of 52 percent in social services, 48 percent in community development, 27 percent in education/research, 9 percent in health care, 24 percent in international activities, and 60 percent in the arts. (Our analalysis confirmed the past Federal budget reductions.) Nor do we see any reason to doubt the institute's forecasts about future cuts. But we also discovered great variation among the voluntary providers. Some agencies

---

*Demone, H.W., Jr., and Gibelman, M. "Reagan Budget Cuts: Response of the Voluntary Not-For-Profit Sector." *1983 National Association for Social Workers Professional Symposium,* November 1983, Washington, D.C.

**The Urban Institute. *Serving Community Needs: The Nonprofit Sector in an Era of Governmental Retrenchment.* The Urban Institute, September 1983.

are weathering the storm quite well. Others are holding their own. Some are severely hampered and some have closed down.

We concluded that the variable response was due to several reasons. Few funds go directly from the Federal treasury to the private sector. They are customarily mediated by other levels of government. Block grants currently highlight the transition. Lower-level governments have their own priorities and service delivery systems. Many also possess taxing powers. For fiscal year 1984, 45 of the states increased their spending over 1983. Thirty eight of the states raised at least one tax. By the end of 1983 several states found themselves with unexpected surpluses because of their new taxes and economic recovery. Morgan Guaranty Trust Company of New York forecast that state and local governments will have an overall surplus of $15 billion in fiscal year 1982.†

Thus some flexibility in response is still possible. Some states are more committed to services. Some are committed to the public delivery of services. Others make greater use of the contractual mechanism.

The agencies vary too. Some are well established, with multiprograms based on solid community linkages. These agencies appear to have fared better.

Influencing all of these developments are priorities. Given the realities of the world-wide economic situation, conflicting ideologies, and the rapid growth of the human service industry in recent years, we have become much more visible and more vulnerable. This book of readings will assist in the delineation of coping strategies and tactics.

Harold W. Demone, Jr.
Dean of the School of Social Work
Rutgers, The State University of New Jersey

---

†Herbers, J. "States Discover Large Surpluses in Their Income." *New York Times,* December 4, 1983, pp. 7, 26.

Preface

We live in puzzling times. The past no longer serves to inform the present administration of the human services, either in its philosophical underpinnings or in its professional practices.

Everything is up for grabs. Everything is changing. Who can read the following questions without a nod of recognition?

1. Is there a *value base or ideology* that protects the provision of human services?

2. Are there *roles and responsibilities* that one can expect from the public sector? Didn't the federal government set standards and raise expectations among all of us?

3. When legislation was passed and public policy enunciated, could we not assume that this provided a *stable and permanent base* for human services?

4. Were not *voluntary agencies* the backbone of the social-service system in our society? Were they not respected for their unique contributions to the social good?

5. Was not the *demonstration project* intended as an occasional mechanism to provide ongoing programs with a defined, delimited, and occasional opportunity for innovation of professional services?

6. Was not *professional expertise* the respected basis for movement into management on the assumption that an understanding of, and competence in, the services being provided was a sin qua non for executive leadership?

As we all know, these questions cannot be answered in the affirmative nor are there any simple answers to them. In fact, these questions breed more questions—and few solutions.

The effect of these ambiguities upon administrators working in the human services has been serious, occasionally catastrophic. Everyone in a leadership position, from the middle manager to the chief executive officer, is continuously at risk. Not only are the job pressures enormous, but they now include stressful time deadlines, fiscal constraints, and political pressures. Not only is there enormous competition for the scarce jobs from other human-service professionals, but MBAs are now swarming in to capture the market. Not only is professional competence required, but technical expertise, ranging from financial management to management information systems and computer technology, is expected. Is it surprising to find that burnout is reaching epidemic proportions and an industry dealing with burnout is emerging?

As we spoke with administrators in an array of human-service settings, it became clear that it was difficult for the harried executives, often dealing with organizational survival, to obtain the conceptual, analytical, technical, and interractional tools to help them meet the new realities inherent in their work. The need for some "bread and butter" approaches, available in one accessible volume, was dramatically apparent, as was the need for material on organizational issues. Consequently, this volume addresses the *whys, whats,* and *hows* of human-services administration.

This book is designed for managers at all levels of our human-service systems who are struggling to protect our services and keep them alive and healthy. Our intent is to familiarize practitioners with the political basis for executive performance in order to broaden their potential repertoire of administrative responses.

This book of original contributions is organized into three sections. In part I, "Understanding Why," the two chapters focus on the political process from both societal as well as professional perspectives. Thus, Stern's discussion of the politics of American social welfare argues that the need of the 1980s is consistent with our American intellectual heritage and that the New Deal and the Poverty Program were in fact unusual periods that should not be expected to return. Gummer examines the political dimension of executive leadership and suggests that the effective administrator must link political skill with professional competence.

Part II, "Understanding What," outlines new professional developments and indentifies new strategies for executive performance. In discussing cutback management, Weatherley differentiates between the roles of the executive as technician and as statesman and illustrates preferable approaches to this administrative nightmare. Aware of the threat to voluntary agencies, Kahn examines the political realities these agencies must face and provides the executive with an armamentarium with which to proceed. Closely coupled to Kahn's political agenda is Bevilacqua's discussion of the rapprochement between state government and the human-service system. This chapter, which notes that the state role in human services has been legitimized, examines the constraints within the system and the implications for executives who must learn to deal at the state level. As any game plan must include a broader arena than the public sector, Lohmann discusses a broader base of resource development. Vosburgh and Perlmutter present an approach to understanding and dealing with the political realities of demonstration projects, on the assumption that the demonstration project is here to stay as an ongoing instrument of public policy, albeit with short-term objectives. The final chapter in part II is a provocative and informative discussion of administrative responses to information management. Not only does it address technical issues but, more important, it provides an ethical framework for professional responsibilities and links information systems utilization with problems of social change.

Part III moves us from the *whys* and *whats* to the *hows;* it presents five case studies that focus on administrative leadership in the human services. The case studies illustrate practical problems, issues, constraints, and opportunities: Perlmutter focuses on child welfare; Kutza describes a program in aging; Friesen and Austin discuss mental health; addictions are dealt with by Weiner; Richan is concerned with public welfare. These experiences from different fields illustrate the principles of administrative strategy.

It is our hope that this book will be of practical use to those committed and critical actors in the human services—the executive suite.

Special appreciation is expressed to the contributors to this volume who worked diligently, patiently and with good humor through the numerous drafts and revisions. Special acknowledgement is made to Ms. Lillian Gibson who provided valuable secretarial assistance. And special affection to my husband Daniel who always is there to make things possible!

Part I
Understanding Why:
Conceptual Foundations for
Administrative Leadership

1

The Politics of American Social Welfare

Mark J. Stern

The election of Ronald Reagan and his attack on the federal government's domestic programs has sent shock waves through the social-welfare community. Not since the Great Depression have those involved in human services faced such a tremendous change in the context and prospects of their field. This sudden shift calls for explanation, for only by understanding the origins of the present crisis can we chart a coherent path for the future.

In pursuing this goal, however, we must be conscious of what there is to be explained. For many in the social-welfare community, habituated to the incremental increase in the social-welfare system over the past five decades, all that needs to be explained is Reagan's ascendancy. Yet this takes for granted that the slow expansion of the welfare system is a "natural" occurrence and that Reagan's domestic program is therefore an unnatural deviation from the path of progress. I believe, however, that Reagan's success was *not* a deviation from the natural development of social welfare. Rather, his victory was the culmination of a four-decade process that first witnessed the greatest expansion of social welfare in American history and then the destruction of the political and social realities that made that expansion possible. The elections of 1982 notwithstanding, the realities of social welfare in the United States will never be the same.

The reasons for this fundamental change in American society are complex. Stated briefly, the expansion of social welfare in the United States was based on two critical coalitions: an electoral coalition, which provided long-term general support for the growth of the federal government's role in social welfare, and a coalition *within* government composed of administrators, legislators, and lobbyists at the federal level that took advantage of the stable electoral situation to expand the system. The electoral coalition was the New Deal consensus; the internal coalition I will call *administrative politics*.

During the 1960s and 1970s both of these coalitions fell apart. It was these breakdowns that fueled the counterattack on the welfare state and set the stage for Reagan's victory. Although it is doubtful that Reagan will accomplish all of his avowed goals with respect to the

3

welfare state, it is equally doubtful that the New Deal and administrative politics coalitions will regain their former power.

The New Deal Consensus

The American social-welfare system during the past fifty years has operated within the political limits set by the New Deal. During the administration of Franklin Roosevelt the role of the federal government was fundamentally altered. At the same time, the political bases of the New Deal, the character of its ideological justification for government action, and the nature of its policies imposed severe limits on social welfare. Particularly when compared to the social democratic regimes that established the welfare states of Europe at the same time, the limitations of the New Deal are as impressive as its accomplishments.

The basis of federal policy development during the 1930s was the New Deal coalition, the grouping of various political constituencies that provided the electoral support for Democratic policies. To some extent, the coalition was already emerging during the 1920s, as urban working-class constituencies increasingly became attached to the Democratic party, but more important, the final coalition was forged in the crucible of the Great Depression. This crisis and its repercussions brought together groups that in "normal" times could not be found in the same camp.

The chief centrifugal force built into the New Deal coalition was the tension between the southern and western wing of the party and the eastern, urban wing. During the 1920s these two wings had fought a fratricidal war, and Prohibition, anti-Catholicism, and personality conflicts had immobilized the party. Only the Depression, which moved the citizenry's attention from these "social" issues to economic concerns, allowed the two wings to work out their differences. In addition, the magnitude of the Depression brought many groups into the New Deal coalition, some with unswerving loyalty (black Americans), others with more tentative support (small businessmen and midwesterners).

The strength of the Democratic party was also its weakness. Although it swept into power during the 1930 and 1932 elections, it did so without any mandate. Its power derived from two sources, the interests of the party's various constituencies and the willingness of the electorate and politicians to experiment in the face of the Depression. Thus, after experimenting with a probusiness policy during the "first hundred days," Roosevelt had the political ability to turn around and endorse a totally different policy during the "second hundred days" of 1935.

This split between politics as usual and the extraordinary powers provided by the emergency situation imposed stringent limits on the extent of government action in social welfare. Ever mindful of political realities, even after he committed himself to social security, Roosevelt rejected disability and health insurance. The Social Security Act that did emerge was conservative in its adherence to actuarial principles, its delegation of power to the states, and its restrictions on coverage. Furthermore, as the emergency situation subsided and politics as usual again asserted itself, the ability of the Democrats to unite behind social-reform legislation vanished; by 1938 the coalition of Republicans and conservative southern Democrats had brought the New Deal to an end.

The weakness of the political basis of the New Deal was also apparent in its philosophy, which can be called political capitalism. During the 1930s, the democracies of Europe and Australia had adopted a policy of encouraging the welfare state based on the tenets of social democracy and the political strength of a workers' party. Just as the Democratic party was not a workers' party, its philosophy was not social democratic. Rather than seeing the justification of state action in the rights of citizens to economic as well as political security (Marshall 1950), the New Deal viewed federal social-welfare legislation as either a response to an emergency or, in its more sophisticated version, as a corrective to the more glaring defects in capitalism caused by market forces. Thus, political capitalism's legitimacy is not based, as is social democracy's, on a critique of capitalism. Rather, it attempts to make minor corrections in a social system that is assumed "naturally" to work well.

Even this rather restricted view of the interventionist state is not particularly popular with voters in American political culture. In bad times, government action could gain public and congressional support because "something had to be done," but in better times, the appeals of self-reliance, the work ethic, and negative stereotypes of the poor made federal social-welfare actions less palatable.

The programs of the New Deal established the basic outlines within which the subsequent growth of the social-welfare system took place. Although the programs themselves were ground-breaking, the principles on which they were based were not; a distaste for direct relief, the use of social insurance as a preventive program, the stress on maintaining the distinction of the worthy and unworthy poor through the mix of social insurance and public assistance, and a mix of state and federal responsibility were the guiding principles established by the New Deal and preserved during subsequent administrations.

First, the idea of direct income maintenance had no legitimacy for the New Deal. Although the various relief programs of the New Deal—

FERA, WPA, PWA, CWA—were its most effective tools against the Depression, for Roosevelt and his followers relief was "a subtle destroyer of the human spirit." Relief was always conceptualized as a temporary, emergency step. Time and time again, Roosevelt's premature cutoff of a relief program caused undue dislocation and contributed to the depression of 1937 (Axinn and Levin 1982, p. 194).

Second, the passage of the Social Security Act was the culmination of the struggle for social insurance that had been fought by such partisans as I.M. Rubinow and the American Association for Labor Legislation since the early twentieth century (Lubove 1967). It represented the use of insurance principles as a means of preventing poverty and want. It was assumed that Old Age and Survivers Insurance and unemployment insurance would eliminate the need for direct assistance which accounts for the lack of attention given the categorical assistance programs for the aging, children, the disabled, and the blind. The notion that insurance programs would replace assistance programs has remained a dominant feature of the public and congressional perception of federal public-assistance programs.

The third element of the New Deal approach to public-welfare policy was the maintenance of the distinction between social insurance and public assistance, a distinction anchored finally in the old distinction between the worthy and unworthy poor. As Patterson points out, this emphasis was unique: "Other western nations developed a blend of social policies, including family allowances, health services, housing allowances, and assistance, that benefited the poor and nonpoor alike and obscured the distinction between social insurance and welfare. The separation of the two policies in the United States narrowed severely the scope of welfare . . . making the stigma for those who participated all the greater" (1981, p. 76).

Finally, with a few exceptions, the bulk of federal social-welfare programs were based on the states taking the leading role in welfare matters. To some extent, given the states' historical responsibility for welfare and the limitations imposed on Congress and the president by the Supreme Court, there was little choice but to do so. Still, this principle preserved a system of regional inequity in the American social-welfare system that has successfully withstood later attempts to correct it.

In summary then, in its political composition, its ideological base, and its programmatic principles, the New Deal set stringent limits on the development of social welfare in the United States. It did not address either the stereotypes of the poor or the suspicion of government action in the field of welfare. It did, however, provide the foundations of a structure that would steadily expand over the next forty years.

Administrative Politics

As Wilensky and Lebeaux have noted, social welfare is a fundamental element of advanced capitalist societies. In their terms, it is an "institutional," not a residual, element of the modern social order (1974). Although the welfare state is ubiquitous, its extent and nature vary from society to society.

The functions of the welfare state are two. First, it serves to increase the general functioning of the population and the economic system by minimizing the disruption caused by want and ignorance. Second, it serves to redistribute resources from the haves to the have-nots. Although it is often difficult to separate these two motives in most social-welfare legislation, the distinction is important. Those programs that increase general social functioning contribute to the better functioning of the economic and political system and therefore are fundamentally conservative. Redistributive programs clearly benefit the recipients and do not benefit those who pay for them.

In analysing the welfare state, Ira Katznelson has made a similar distinction between the *minimum* extent of social welfare "required to ensure the process of economic accumulation, and to give it broad social acceptance," and surplus social welfare, which goes beyond what is functionally necessary. As Katznelson notes:

> Under certain conditions, various political parties and social movements may succeed in utilizing the democratic process (including protests as well as elections) to push welfare state advances forward at a pace more rapid than that dictated by the emergence of manifest "problems." When such attempts succeed it makes sense to speak of a social policy *surplus* (1981, p. 317).

For Katznelson, the creation of a social-welfare "surplus" is usually the result of the success of a social democratic or radical political movement. Thus, in the conservative climate of American politics, "we may infer that the role of the state may be understood as being very close to the structural minimum necessary for system reproduction" (1981, pp. 318–19).

Although Katznelson is correct to stress the conservatism of the political system, he does not give sufficient attention to the role of forces *within* the government which independently can produce a social-welfare surplus. Administrative politics is such a system. In its heyday, from 1939 through the mid-1970s, it consisted of a system of actors that influenced the legislative process to bring about an expansion of the welfare system independent of the pressures of electoral politics.

The outcome of administrative politics was the expansion of social welfare throughout the postwar period. Although public assistance was constricted at the state level through eligibility and other restrictive regulations during the 1950s, the social security program was broadened through the addition of disability insurance, the addition of grants for parents under Aid to Dependent Children, and the increase in the federal share of assistance programs.

During the 1960s, this expansion continued; the Public Welfare Amendments of 1962 increased the federal stress on prevention through extensive grants for social services for welfare recipients and those "likely to become" recipients (Derthick 1975, p. 11); under Lyndon Johnson, Medicare and Medicaid were added to social security, bringing medical coverage to the aging and the poor; finally, the War on Poverty, with its stress on community participation, manpower training, and rehabilitation, dominated the political agenda briefly in the mid-sixties, leaving its legacy in programs like Headstart and an extensive body of research on poverty.

Yet it was during the 1970s that the greatest expansion of welfare took place. Although the family assistance plan was sidetracked, the food stamps program grew from a modest $550 million in 1970 to over $10 billion in 1981 (Institute for Research on Poverty 1981–82). The Public Welfare Amendments of 1962 reaped their harvest in the expansion of grants to states for social services; in 1968, $347 million were spent; in 1972, the amount had expanded to $1.7 billion (Derthick 1975, p. 8). The assistance titles of social security were consolidated into supplemental security income, which also was given an increase in benefits. But the biggest increases were in the social insurances: in 1965 income security and health consumed 23 percent of the budget; by 1981, the figure was 44 percent (Institute for Research on Poverty 1981–82).

What was the explanation for this expansion of social welfare? As we have seen, it was not an increase in the strength of the New Deal coalition. In fact, the biggest expansion, that of the 1970s, occurred with the acquiescence of Republican presidents. The only element of this entire expansion with clear political motives was the War on Poverty, which Johnson saw as a means of tying black voters more closely to the Democratic party (Piven and Cloward 1979). Even in this case, however, electoral politics was only a partial motivation.

The welfare explosion had a variety of demographic and political causes. The most important factor in welfare's expansion, however, was a set of relationships between the federal bureaucracy, Congress, state and local officials, and special-interest groups which can be called *administrative politics*. The primary goal of these groups as it was worked out in the postwar period was the steady, incremental expansion of social-welfare programs through a low-key strategy that attempted to remove the welfare debate from electoral politics. As Steiner (1966) has shown, whenever this strategy failed and welfare expansion did become a public issue, it almost invariably was blocked. Thus, although the electoral politics of the New Deal coalition set limits on the expansion of welfare, within these limits there was plenty of room for expansion.

This analysis is not conspiratorial; the various elements of the administrative politics coalition did not work in concert. For example, the special-interest groups, such as labor and the aging lobby, focused on the programs that concerned them. Taken together, however, this coalition proved durable and effective for three decades.

The key role in administrative politics was played by federal officials in the Department of Health, Education, and Welfare and in the Social Security Administration. As Martha Derthick (1979) has demonstrated, program administrators used their intimate familiarity with the programs of HEW and the SSA to develop proposals that generally appeared inoffensive and incremental and to insulate these programs from the control of the president and his cabinet.

Although it was orchestrated by administrators, two elements were necessary for administrative politics to be put into law: a set of executive-legislative liaisons that served to tailor proposals to congressional tastes and a congressional leadership willing to work with the administrators. Thus, administrative politics depended on effective leadership both in the bureaucracy and in Congress.

The role of liaison was played most often by Wilbur Cohen, who from his early years on the staff of the Committee on Economic Security until his retirement as secretary of health, education, and welfare in 1969, served as the ideal bridge between the technical masters in the bureaucracy and Congress. A host of other "program executives," including the commissioners of the Social Security Administration, also served as advocates and liaisons (Derthick 1979, pp. 17–37). Such continuity was not uncommon in the bureaucracy; a group of professionals learned their lessons well in the fights over the amendments of 1939, the Wagner-Murray-Dingall Bill of 1943, disability insurance, Medicare, and the expansion of benefits. The adoption of the incremental philosophy of administrative politics developed as the experts in the executive branch learned to make proposals that were palatable to Congress.

On the congressional side, administrative politics were facilitated by the stability of leadership and the constrictions imposed on debate. In his long tenure as chairman of the House Committee on Ways and Means, Wilbur Mills served as the leader of congressional action. Furthermore, through the expansion of the "closed rule" Mills prevented floor debate from challenging the work of Ways and Means. The pride of proprietorship that developed on the Ways and Means Committee and the desire of committee members to have some function other than raising taxes provided the legislative momentum for administrative politics (Derthick 1979, pp. 45–46).

Special-interest groups served as support for congressional action. For social security during the 1950s and 1960s, labor was the most consistent supporter. Led by Norman Cruikshank of the AFL-CIO, organized labor worked so closely with program executives and legislators that it was difficult to distinguish them. As Derthick notes, although its role as pressure group was significant, labor served primarily to support the executives in their work and "left no distinguishing marks on the program" (1979, p. 110). During the 1970s, the role of lobbying was increasingly taken over by the aging interests. As Patterson concludes, in the 1930s "old age lobbies such as the Townsendites had seemed a little zany to younger Americans. By the late 1960s, old people began to be called senior citizens. Their 'gray lobbies,' increasingly well organized and financed, reflected 'senior power.' Without the force of such lobbies, Medicare . . . would not have been passed in 1965" (1981, p. 167).

The final element of the coalition for administrative politics was the co-optation of state and local officials. During the early postwar period, they fought a losing battle to protect their control and influence. With the expansion of social services, however, they decided if they could not beat the Feds at their game, they would join them. Through the creative use of the amendments of 1962, which obligated the federal government to pay 75 percent of the costs of social services provided for anyone "likely to become" a welfare applicant, state officials, with the encouragement of some federal administrators, exploited the clause to pay for a host of social services for both poor and middle-income groups. When Congress moved to stop this expansion, it enacted Title

XX, which served to bond state officials more closely to the goals of administrative politics.

The expansion of public welfare then was not a result of a massive change in the beliefs or politics of the American people. Indeed, in 1977, as administrative politics reached their peak, a *New York Times–CBS* poll found that 58 percent of Americans disapproved of "most Government-sponsored welfare programs" and 54 percent thought "most people who received money from welfare could get along without it" (Patterson 1981, p. 202).

The benefit and the liability of administrative politics were the same: isolation from popular opinion. Had social welfare depended on the support of politicians and voters, it would not have expanded very far. Yet the success of welfare measures was never used to mobilize public support for or understanding of the function and structure of the American welfare state. Thus, when the special conditions that insulated administrative politics from electoral pressures fell apart, its vulnerability became clear.

The Decline of the New Deal Consensus

The New Deal consensus had been the result of a convergence of a number of historical circumstances. In the four decades that followed, however, the dynamics of American society undermined that consensus and produced a set of social problems that the New Deal had not been designed to accommodate. Most important were the changing class and ethnic stratification of American society and the changing role of women in the economy and society.

One of the most cherished ideals of postwar America was the notion that social class had become obsolete. *Fortune* declared confidently: "The union has made the worker . . . a middle class member of a middle class society," while the historian Eric Goldman declared: "New Dealism . . . had created a nation of the middle class" (quoted in Hodgson, 1976, p. 82). Indeed, in the glow of the 1950s, it often appeared that there never had been social classes in the United States. Yet, by the end of the 1970s, the role of social class and ethnic stratification had never been so obvious.

The history of social class over the last century in the United States is a story of increasing complexity. In mid-nineteenth-century America, both in objective fact and in the consciousness of most citizens, society had been divided fairly clearly into the business class and the working class (Katz, Doucet, and Stern 1982). Yet by the beginning of World War I, this simple class structure had begun to change dramatically. In the business class, the rise of the corporation had brought about the rise of a "new" business class composed of professionals and business employees, groups that had been rather small in the entrepreneurial society of the nineteenth century (Stern 1979). In the working class, during the early twentieth century, a split had developed in the labor market between a primary labor market composed of workers with stable, relatively well-paying jobs and a secondary market composed of those with unstable, poorly paying jobs (Edwards 1979, Piore 1979).

In the 1940s and 1950s prosperity returned to the upper tier of the working class as the combination of low unemployment and rising wages lifted a large portion of the working class out of poverty. Between 1940 and 1960 the poverty rate fell from nearly a third of the population to under a quarter, largely as a result of general economic growth. These "affluent" workers, many of them newly protected by the mass-production labor unions (auto workers, steel workers, rubber workers, mine workers) and the first generation covered by old age, survivors, and unemployment insurance, hoped to construct a firm economic foundation for the security of themselves and their children.

Yet the general improvement of the economy failed to pull many of those in the lower tier of the working class out of poverty. Although by the mid-1970s the official poverty rate had fallen below 12 percent or, when in-kind transfers were included, to around 6 percent, much of this improvement was the result of the welfare state. Whereas economic growth had brought the upper tier of the working class out of poverty in the 1940s and 1950s, the same could not be said for the lower tier. For those in the unskilled, insecure, and low-paying jobs it was not the capitalist economy but government action that led to a reduction in poverty (Institute for Research on Poverty 1981–82).

Furthermore, this split in the experience of the upper and lower tiers of the working class was reinforced by ethnic divisions. By the 1970s, the upper tier was predominantly white, the descendants of immigrants to northeastern and midwestern cities from Europe and rural America. The lower tier was increasingly composed of nonwhite groups. These included black Americans, who had shifted from a predominantly rural and southern to a predominantly urban and northern population in less than a generation, Puerto Ricans, whose migration had increased during the late 1950s and early 1960s, and a new wave of immigrants from southern and eastern Europe, Latin America, and Asia, who entered after the revision of the immigration law in 1965. Most of these groups entered and remained in the secondary labor market (Piore 1979).

The other major group to enter the labor force during these years was women. After a mass exit from the labor force at the end of World

War II, women again began to enter in greater numbers during the 1960s and 1970s; in 1960 approximately 30 percent of adult women were working; by 1980, the proportion had increased to more than 50 percent (Smith 1979; Axinn and Levin 1982, p. 284). The motives for this massive change varied according to social class and ethnicity. For black women, wage labor was not a new experience; in the nineteenth century, women's work had been an essential element of black families' struggle for survival. For women of the business class, entry into the labor force during marriage was a result of increasing education, the attractiveness of extra earnings, and the impact of the feminist movement. For the white working class, women's work was almost totally the result of economic need. As the economy slowed down after 1965, the increasing labor-force participation of women became a means of continuing the rise of family income. Because of occupational segregation, women were confined to secondary-labor-market jobs with low wages and little security. Despite the Civil Rights Act's ban on sexual discrimination in employment (Title VII), by 1980, women still earned about 60 cents for each dollar earned by men.

The divergence of the experience of the white upper tier of the working class and the nonwhite lower tier during the postwar era led to overt conflict between these groups in the 1960s and 1970s. For the white working class the promise of affluence was only partially kept. After 1965 the gains of the immediate postwar period did not continue; increasingly, wage increases were offset by inflation. What increase blue-collar families did experience was a product of increases in the number of two-earner households, as millions of working-class wives entered the work force. Thus, while not poor, the better-off blue-collar workers could no longer look forward to automatic increases in their standard of living.

These macroeconomic changes had serious consequences for the families of the white and the black working class. Among whites, the expectations of the postwar period—a full-time housekeeping wife, college for the children, homeownership, and a consistently rising standard of living—receded. For blacks, although absolute income rose, the dependence on uncertain government support did not allow for the shedding of their traditional family strategy, based on extended kin relations, economic reciprocity, and short economic horizons (Stack 1974). Thus, both for blacks and whites, the late 1960s and 1970s were a time of frustration and disappointment, if not of outright crisis.

Furthermore, these social trends produced a set of social problems unforeseen when social security was enacted in 1935. As the nonwhite underclass of the city emerged, Aid to Families with Dependent Children became the largest assistance program; the increasing number of independent women, coupled with the low level of female wages, threatened the "feminization of poverty." Finally, with the rise of black militancy and anger, the deferential, obsequious behavior that was expected of welfare recipients gave way; increasingly, the poor demanded welfare as a right (Piven and Cloward 1979). This led to increases in the percentage of eligibles who applied for and received welfare (Patterson 1981, p. 179).

This combination of no progress for white workers and partial, government-sponsored increases for nonwhite workers was an explosive mix. The blue-collar revolt against the goals of liberal and social welfare was a product of the resentment, frustration, and betrayal felt by these families. As one commentator put it:

> Working-class people had to bear the brunt of the pressures, in ordinary life, caused by the great in-migration of blacks: competition for jobs, the disruptions caused by block-busting and changing neighborhoods, and all the fear that the great change caused. They had to live through these strains at a time when the strongest traditional working class institutions—the family, the parochial school, the labor union, and the political machine—were all either declining or undergoing transformation that made them less able to cope.
>
> Nothing about the political history of the 1950s was more eerie than the silence of the American working class while the liberal intellectuals proclaimed contentment to the world (Hodgson 1976, pp. 483–84).

The changing nature of the social structure had an impact on the political order as well. By the late 1970s, the bonds that had held the New Deal coalition together could no longer contain the centrifugal forces that were pulling it apart.

During the late 1940s and early 1950s, antiradical campaigns swept American society, from the movie studios of Hollywood to the factories of Toledo to the campuses of the Ivy League. Although often referred to as McCarthyism, this campaign was much wider than the paranoid crusades of the junior senator from Wisconsin. Throughout American society, its impact was to remove from the political arena a set of groups that had consistently pushed the centrist New Deal coalition to the left.

The most enduring damage, perhaps, was done to the labor movement. After unprecedented gains during World War II, the movement to organize American workers stalled during the late 1940s as the Taft-Hartley Act severely restricted the ability of unions to organize. Yet, just at the time when its enemies were gaining strength politically, organized labor was swept by an internal, antiradical campaign. In industry after industry, anticommunist campaigns were used either to attack radical unions outright, as in the case of the United Electrical

Workers, or to purge radicals from within unions, as with the United Auto Workers (Green 1980, pp. 198–209; Brody 1980, pp. 224–29). Combined with the anticorruption attacks on organized labor in Congress, which led to the Landrum-Griffen Act, the antiradical campaign permanently capped the gains of organized labor and led to its progressive decline as a force in American politics.

For a time, the declining power of the unions was offset by the increasing militancy and mobilization of the black movement. Although a part of the New Deal coalition, blacks had served as a decidedly junior partner during the 1930s and 1940s, as the interests of the Solid South held sway in Democratic party policy; Roosevelt even refused to endorse a federal antilynching bill (Leuchtenberg 1963, p. 186). Yet, after the convention battle of 1948 led to the adoption of a civil-rights plank and the exit of Strom Thurmond and the Dixiecrats, blacks gained increasing power within the party.

During the 1950s, the Democrats suffered a decline in black support, for Adlai Stevenson refused to take up the fight for civil rights, but in the wake of Kennedy's dramatic intervention in the jailing of Martin Luther King during the 1960 election, black votes provided the winning margins for the Democratic candidate. Indeed, the need to retain black support was one of the factors influencing Johnson's initiation of the War on Poverty (Piven and Cloward 1979).

Yet these shifts in the Democratic coalition could not be contained for long. The interests of blacks and southern die-hards could not be reconciled. In addition, the Vietnam War served to heighten the contradictions between prowar elements of the party, including most of organized labor, and the antiwar elements. This led in 1968 to the charge of "Gestapo tactics" from the podium of the party convention and in 1972 to the forced or voluntary exclusion of the representatives of the blue-collar ethnics—union leaders and city bosses—from the party.

The morphology of conservatism also changed during the period. In the 1950s, the locus of Republican conservatism was the country clubs and Rotary clubs of the Midwest and the boardrooms of New York and Chicago, and Senator Robert Taft of Ohio, author of the Taft-Hartley Act, was its champion. This was the base the party had retained in the 1930s, and it guaranteed the Republicans a permanent minority status. But during the 1960s and 1970s, conservatism diversified. In the growing states of the Sun Belt, a conservatism with an antiestablishment ring found its voices in Barry Goldwater and Ronald Reagan. In the South, George Wallace represented a more belligerent antiestablishment conservatism, which in 1964 and 1968 was able to mobilize surprising support in the industrial North.

The political wild card during the late 1960s and 1970s, however, was something called "populism." It represented a general revolt against dominant trends and a reaffirmation of "traditional" social values. Yet its voices ranged from Wallace on the right through Jimmy Carter in the middle to George McGovern and Fred Harris on the left, and its constituency was the southern working class, the ethnic voters of the North, and transplanted westerners. It was what Richard Nixon, with consummate political skill, called middle America. As Hodgson points out: "It was not intrinsically conservative. . . . It was a revolt against the indifference and the condescension of the liberal elite" (1976, p. 421). Yet it was conservatives who successfully captured this vote during the 1970s and 1980s.

The New Deal and its legacy were based on a political base that was contradictory in composition and philosophy. Over the entire post-war period, those contradictions increased: the left was silenced, blacks pressed their demands, and the white blue-collar vote pulled back. At the same time, conservatism found a new political voice and a new strategy to reenter the political mainstream. These are the political legacies of the last forty years.

The End of Administrative Politics

In the 1970s, a number of events undermined and ultimately subverted administrative politics. When these events merged with the social and political trends of the preceding three decades, they fundamentally redefined the politics of welfare in America.

The most important event was the performance of the economy during the late 1970s and early 1980s. In rapid succession, America experienced recessions in 1974–75, 1980, and 1981–82. Even in the recovery from 1975 through 1980, inflation and America's deteriorating position in the world economy contributed to a feeling of unease about the economy. The economy sent shock waves off in a number of directions.

The federal budget became a focus of concern. An old conservative theory—that federal spending was the central cause of inflation, de-clining productivity, and lack of investment—gained new legitimacy in the hands of the supply side and monetarist economists. At the same time, the tax revolt, symbolized by Proposition 13 in California, pre-vented legislators from using revenue increases to lower deficits.

The aftermath of the Vietnam War also shaped federal fiscal policy. As the war deescalated between 1967 and 1973, defense spending's share of national income fell from 11.1 to 7 percent. Thus, the large increases in domestic spending during these years did not lead to either new taxes or increased deficits (Janowitz 1976, p. 45). By the late 1970s, the post-Vietnam decline in spending was over and the Reagan administration sought to increase defense, veterans', and international affairs spending from 29.5 to 40.1 percent of federal spending between 1981 and 1986. In such a situation, welfare increases could not be depoliticized.

The continuing economic malaise placed increasing pressure on the working class. The weakening of the unions and the rise of populist calls "to send a message to Washington" led to an increasing deterioration of blue-collar support of New Deal policies. In 1980, over 50 percent of blue-collar workers voted Republican (Burnham 1981).

The economy was not the only problem. The prestige of the social sciences had been on the wane for over a decade. As Patterson points out, the War on Poverty "accentuated doubts about the capacity of social science to plan, and government to deliver ambitious programs for social betterment" (1981, p. 152). Vietnam and Watergate simply served to underline a growing distrust of the activist state and its academic cadres.

This disillusionment was related to real structural disruptions within the political system. In electoral politics, the declining identification with party and the deterioration of grass-roots political organizations greatly complicated the political system. Although some talked of a realignment of party coalitions, to Burnham this indicated a "dealignment" in which no durable coalition could be forged (1981, p. 98). The electoral instability that resulted meant that politicians became increasingly aware of the possible political impact of every action (Janowitz 1976, pp. 95–99). This too undercut the depolitical basis of administrative politics.

Finally, the passing of time led to a breakdown of the set of accommodations on which administrative politics were based. The congressional reforms brought about in the wake of Watergate weakened the ability of committee chairmen to control dissent both inside and outside committee. At the same time, the personnel that ran the system departed; Cohen retired, and a new generation of administrators replaced him. Wilbur Mills, who had dominated social security legislation for so long, was forced to resign in the wake of scandal. The people and institutions that had maintained the system lost their power.

Thus, before the 1980 election delivered the coup de grace, the system of administrative politics had been mortally weakened. Its legitimacy was openly questioned, and since its success was based on its depolitical character, to question it was to destroy it. It was left to Jimmy Carter to play out the final scene. Indeed, in its initiatives and retreats on family policy, welfare reform, and health insurance, Carter underlined the impact of changes in social class on the politics of welfare. The white working class could no longer be held in the New Deal coalition by the promise of increased government programs. Yet, as Carter moved to hold this group's loyalty by abandoning his own proposals, the forces in society and the electorate that still supported government action—particularly liberals and black leaders—withdrew their support. The social basis of politics left the Carter administration no room to maneuver.

The election of 1980 was the final chapter. The advent of a Republican Senate and the departure of a host of liberal supporters of administrative politics, the end of a working majority in the House, and Reagan's election suggested that no short-term revival of the administrative coalition was in the offing. Although analysis of the election makes it clear that Reagan did not have a conservative mandate from the electorate, Reagan, like Roosevelt fifty years earlier, certainly had the political room and power to exercise his own ideological preference.

Implications

The 1982 elections, in which the Democratic party made sizable gains in Congress and in state elections, gave the appearance of a return to "normalcy" in national politics. Yet the revitalization of the Democrats should not be misinterpreted. The shift in politics signalled by Reagan's election is still very much in place, and it will continue to impede efforts to create a more just and humane society.

As we have seen, in the United States, a set of coalitions between groups within the executive and legislative branches of the federal government, supported by state and local officials and special-interest groups, which I have called administrative politics, brought about an expansion of the American social-welfare system above that which electoral politics or social necessity would have required. In Katznelson's terms, administrative politics created a "surplus" of social legislation.

During the 1970s, the elements fell into disrepair, while at the same time the strength of the electoral coalition that had supported administrative politics declined. Thus, with breathtaking speed, the advances of the early 1970s were followed by the reversals of the 1980s.

What are the possibilities for a revival of administrative politics? As we have noted, this coalition was based on two elements: a durable administrative network and broad electoral support. An examination of the current state of both of these elements must lead us to a pessimistic answer regarding the possibilities of revival.

The internal administrative network was based on long-term knowledgeable employees who staffed the executive bureaucracy and strong congressional leadership, epitomized by Wilbur Mills. While it is certainly possible that a new generation of administrators will emerge, the revival of congressional leadership is less likely. The post-Watergate congressional reforms, the "dealignment" of the electorate, and the pressure exerted by the structural budget deficits of the coming decade will prevent the emergence of such leadership in the legislative branch.

Even less likely is a reemergence of the New Deal coalition. Although the Democrats picked up substantial blue-collar support in the 1982 election, they did so by a strategy that stressed "middle-income" issues (like social security), while at the same time agreeing to go along with the Republicans' continuing attack on programs for the poor in the 1983 budget. Although blacks and liberals were scared enough by Reagan's performance to support the policy, any return of Democratic initiative is likely to spark the same split between blacks and liberals, on the one hand, and white, blue-collar ethnics, on the other, which characterized the Carter administration. Any success could quickly kill the Democratic party.

Ultimately, the historical experience of the poor and nonpoor working class continue to determine their view of the future. The nonpoor working class experienced affluence as a result of the general economic growth of the 1950s and 1960s, while the improvement of the poor has resulted from direct government action. Thus, a fundamental division in strategy exists in the Democratic coalition which will continue to make it difficult to maintain a commitment to both groups.

This split between the poor and nonpoor affects not only the quantity of government spending but its type as well. The demands of the social security and health programs over the next several decades will make it extremely difficult to find the necessary funding for a renewed attack on poverty. Similarly, the racial antagonism that characterizes the relationship of black and white workers will continue to hamper the mobilization of both groups for a united program.

Social-welfare administrators are in for a long siege in this social environment, which requires a new set of skills to maximize agency goals and to minimize the adverse effect on client populations. Yet, if the only actions of social-welfare administrators is directed at these narrow goals, we will have won some battles and lost the war. Administrators must simultaneously focus on broader issues of social justice. As a first step toward reversal of present trends, it is necessary to rebuild the coalition of the well-off, white working population and the poor, nonwhite population. This will require imaginative program and policy development and an increased effort to understand and correct the crippling impact of racism on American society.

References

Axinn, June, and Herman Levin. *Social Welfare: A History of the American Response to Need,* New York: Harper and Row, 1982.

Berkowitz, Edward, and Kim McQuaid. *Creating the Welfare State: The Political Economy of Twentieth Century Reform.* New York: Praeger Books, 1980.

Brody, David. *Workers in Industrial America: Essays on the Twentieth-Century Struggle.* New York: Oxford University Press, 1980.

Burnham, Walter Dean. "The 1980 Earthquake: Realignment, Reaction, or What?" In Thomas Ferguson and Joel Rodgers, eds. *The Hidden Election: Politics and Economics in the 1980 Presidential Campaign.* New York: Pantheon, 1981.

Danzinger, Sheldon, and Robert Haveman. "The Reagan Administration's Budget Cuts: Their Impact on the Poor," *IRP Focus* 512 (Winter 1981–82):13–16.

Derthick, Martha. *Uncontrollable Spending for Social Service Grants.* Washington, D.C.: Brookings Institute, 1975.

———. *Policymaking for Social Security.* Washington, D.C.: Brookings Institute, 1979.

Dolgoff, Ralph, and Donald Feldstein. *Understanding Social Welfare.* New York: Harper and Row, 1980.

Edwards, Richard A. *Contested Terrain: The Transformation of the Workplace in the Twentieth Century.* New York: Basic Books, 1979.

Elder, Glen. *Children of the Great Depression.* Chicago: University of Chicago Press, 1974.

Green, James R. *The World of the Worker: Labor in Twentieth Century America.* New York: Hill and Wang, 1980.

Hodgson, Godfrey. *America in Our Times: From World War II to Nixon.* New York: Random House, 1976.

Institute for Research on Poverty. "Poverty in the United States: Where Do We Stand?" *IRP Focus* 512 (Winter 1981–82):1–10.

Janowitz, Morris. *Social Control of the Welfare State.* Chicago: University of Chicago Press, 1976.

Katz, Michael B., Michael J. Doucet, and Mark J. Stern. *The Social Organization of Early Industrial Capitalism.* Cambridge, Mass.: Harvard University Press, 1982.

Katznelson, Ira. "A Radical Departure? Social Welfare and the Election." In Thomas Ferguson and Joel Rodgers, eds. *The Hidden Election: Politics and Economics in the 1980 Presidential Campaign.* New York: Pantheon, 1981.

Leuchtenberg, William. *Franklin D. Roosevelt and the New Deal, 1932–1940.* New York: Harper and Row, 1963.

Lubove, Roy. *The Struggle for Social Security*. Cambridge, Mass.: Harvard University Press, 1968.

Patterson, James T. *America's Struggle Against Poverty, 1900–1980*. Cambridge, Mass.: Harvard University Press, 1981.

Piore, Michael J. *Birds of Passage: Migrant Labor in Industrial Society*. New York: Cambridge University Press, 1979.

Piven, Frances Fox, and Richard A. Cloward. *Poor People's Movements: Why They Succeed, How They Fail*. New York: Random House, 1979.

———. *The New Class War: Reagan's Attack on the Welfare State and Its Consequences*. New York: Pantheon, 1982.

Polenberg, Richard. *One Nation Indivisible: Class, Race, and Ethnicity in the United States Since 1938*. New York: Viking Press, 1980.

Rubin, Lillian B. *Worlds of Pain: Life in the Working Class Family*. New York: Harper and Row, 1976.

Smith, Ralph, ed. *The Subtle Revolution: Women in the Workplace*. Washington, D.C.: The Institute, 1979.

Stack, Carol. *All Our Kin*. New York: Harper and Row, 1974.

Steiner, Gilbert. *Social Insecurity: The Politics of Welfare*. Chicago, Rand McNally, 1966.

———. *The Futility of Family Policy*. Washington, D.C.: The Brookings Institute, 1981.

Stern, Mark J. "The Demography of Capitalism, Industry, Class, and Fertility in Erie County, New York, 1855–1915," unpublished Ph.D. dissertation, York University, 1979.

Thurow, Lester C. *The Zero-Sum Society: Distribution and the Possibilities for Economic Change*. New York: Basic Books, 1980.

Wilensky, Harold L., and Charles Lebeaux. *Industrial Society and Social Welfare*. New York: Free Press, 1958.

Witte, Edwin E. *The Development of the Social Security Act*. Madison: University of Wisconsin Press, 1962.

2 The Social Administrator as Politician

Burton Gummer

Social-welfare administrators frequently go through a series of career stages prior to attaining an executive position. Many begin as line service workers, move into supervisory positions, and then become program or unit managers before assuming the directorship of an agency or department. This process entails negotiating a number of occupational transitions. One such transition concerns the capacity and willingness of social administrators to acquire and exercise political influence as part of their work within their organizations and in their extramural dealings.

The past several years have witnessed a growing interest among social workers in the political dimension of organizational behavior and its implications for the qualities needed for effective practice (Wax 1971, Pawlak 1976, Gummer 1978, Hasenfeld 1980, Martin 1980, Murdach 1982, Lee 1983). While there is as yet no consensus as to the role political dynamics should play in our normative models of practice, there is growing awareness of their importance in the operations of social agencies. This awareness is heightened by what many see as the politicalization of the environment within which social agencies exist. The New Federalism and declining resources, in particular, are often singled out as factors contributing to growing political influences at all levels of social-service systems (Mott 1976, Terrell 1980, Schram 1981, Finch 1982).

The Nature of Organizational Politics

Any discussion of political behavior in organizations immediately faces two obstacles. The word *political* can have so many meanings that individuals using it rarely share a common understanding of what is meant, and in an organizational context, the term is often used pejoratively to describe deviations from the norm of rational, goal-directed behavior. To avoid these pitfalls, it is necessary to define how the term will be used here.

Organizational politics perform two related but different functions.

The first involves an approach to organizational decision making, and the second concerns the acquisition, maintenance, and use of power within an organization. Organizational politics provide a mechanism for making decisions about key organizational issues, such as the nature of goals, procedures for pursuing them, and how resources should be distributed. Political decision making can be expected to occur when there are *apparently irreconcilable conflicts* among organizational members over these issues. Political decision making acknowledges conflict as a normal part of organizational life and makes provisions for transforming potentially disruptive conflicts into negotiated settlements. These provisions are twofold: the establishment of "constitutions" and the creation of "decision arenas."

The primary function of organizational constitutions is to prescribe a set of norms regulating the adversarial behavior of individuals and groups within the organization (Zald 1970, pp. 81–82). Constitutions provide criteria for determining acceptable behavior on the part of contending parties and how conflicting claims are to be adjudicated. They can be formal documents (bylaws, charters of incorporation) written in painstakingly precise and unambiguous language or unwritten, informal agreements about "how things are done here." Regardless of their form, they all play the critical function of spelling out the "rules of the game" in terms of who can play, what plays are fair or foul, and how to determine when the game is over and who wins.

The notion of decision arenas has its roots in the observation of Norton Long that, in a political analysis of organizational behavior, "there is no right way for organizational policy to be decided, there are just various ways" (1962, p. 115). These "various" ways take the form of the preferences and interests of organizational members, as well as interested parties outside the organization. The conception of decision arenas is also informed by the idea of "policy arenas" developed by Francine Rabinovitz (1976, pp. 405–6) and her colleagues to describe the "web of individual and institutional interrelationships" that develops among the people and organizations concerned with a policy decision. Within an organizational context, this refers to conscious efforts on the part of organizational members to insure that in making important decisions, key interests are represented. Thus, membership on committees and task forces, attendance at meetings, and access to information are all viewed within an explicitly representational framework.

While constitutions and decision arenas provide the context for organizational politics, the driving force for political behavior is the

acquisition and exercise of organizational power. To engage in organizational politics, an individual must view the accumulation and use
of power in a positive light. For its most extreme practitioner—the
professional politician—power acquisition is valued over all other human endeavors. "If there is a political type," Harold Lasswell has
argued, "the basic characteristic will be the accentuation of power in
relation to other values within the personality when compared with
other persons" (1962, p. 22). While a politically oriented social worker
may not have to assume this extreme posture toward power, individuals
so inclined must, at a minimum, view the use of power as an integral
and legitimate part of their professional and organizational roles.

The use of political influence is not confined to the internal operations of social agencies. The environments of these organizations are
evolving in ways that increasingly demand political responses on the
part of administrators. Specifically, control of agency resources has
spread over several external bodies, while intense interagency conflict
over domain ("turf") continues unabated. The New Federalism has
been identified as a major force operating in the politicalization of the
social agency's environment. As decisions about the distribution of
federal dollars are increasingly made at state and local levels, the control
previously exercised by the more professional federal bureaucracies is
giving way to a diffuse system of control involving, in addition to professional bureaucrats, state and local politicians, community elites, and
any number of organized interest groups (Randall 1979, Terrell 1980,
Schram 1981). The organizational environment of the social agency has
become denser and more complicated, with the result that the successful
social administrator has had to develop the technical and political skills
needed for acquiring the information and formulating the negotiating
strategies upon which the survival of programs and agencies are increasingly dependent.

Administrators have had to adjust their ways of thinking about how
their organizations should deal with external matters. The usual view
of this started with the organization and, given its resources and capabilities, tried to identify what unique contribution it could make
toward addressing some community problem. In a more politicized
conception of this relationship, the definition of an agency's role is the
result of negotiations between the agency and significant elements in
its environment. This means that administrators have to become more
open to external influences, and they find themselves operating in arenas in which they have little formal control, and which require the same
political orientations and skills needed for internal administrative work.

Politicians: Good and Bad, but Never Indifferent

What qualities are needed to engage in organizational politics? More important, what are the qualities of a "good" politician? The two dimensions of organizational politics discussed above—the acquisition and exercise of power and the structuring of decision arenas—offer some preliminary answers to these questions. Theories about what motivates people to seek power range from those that view power seeking as an expression of psychopathology to those that view it as the quest of the mature personality to acquire the resources needed to influence an ever larger part of one's world. How a particular individual answers this question plays a central role in determining his or her willingness to engage in organizational politics. (How this question is addressed by social administrators, in particular, is a focus of the last section of this chapter.)

While the acquisition of power is a necessary condition for engaging in organizational politics, it is not, by itself, sufficient. More to the point, it *should not* be sufficient, for it is here that we must distinguish between "good" and "bad" politicians. For the good politician, the acquisition of power is an instrumental rather than a terminal activity. Power is used for accomplishing a larger purpose: the promotion of those policies, programs, and practices to which the politician is committed. The nature of this commitment, moreover, brings us to the second essential feature of the "compleat" politician.

In Max Weber's (1958, p. 95) classic essay "Politics as a Vocation," the politician is described as a person of intense convictions: "To take a stand, to be passionate . . . is the politician's element." Politicians can advocate positions not only when they *know* them to be right, but when they *believe* them to be so, thus enabling them to act when knowledge is lacking or inconclusive. Political decision making in organizations arises when other methods have proved inadequate. When both the *answer* to a question is not self-evident, and there is disagreement about the correct *means* for finding the answer—that is, when we don't know and can't agree on how to go about knowing—then the conditions for rational decision making are not present and alternatives must be sought (Thompson and Tuden 1959). Uncertainty plays roles of varying importance in different enterprises. As we move closer to science-based technologies, the degree of uncertainty diminishes and rational problem solving predominates. When one enters the world of valuations rather than facts, or subjective appraisals rather than objective analyses, the situation becomes ripe for politicalization.

This latter situation most accurately describes social-welfare activities. While some areas within social welfare lend themselves to technological certainty, they are limited in nature and often of minor importance. Many of them deal with housekeeping matters, such as inventory control, centralized purchasing, and the like. Even in areas where advanced technologies exist, their transferability to welfare operations is hindered or prevented by essentially political considerations. Thus, the sophisticated technology for distributing social security and veterans' pension checks has had only limited utilization in public assistance and food stamps, where, for a variety of political considerations, recipients are not permitted the benefits of these technologies. Similarly, queing theory and linear programming, advanced management techniques for deciding about the distribution of scarce resources, could conceivably be used to allocate scarce day-care or foster home slots. That they are not is less the result of technical difficulties as it is of decisions to allocate these resources through mechanisms that can be influenced and shaped by a variety of interests. The vast proportion of social-welfare activities involve questions of the "social health" of a society and, as such, are subject to intense debate and disagreement (Donnison 1955).

Moving from the issue of power to that of political decision making, a paradox arises in terms of desirable traits for the organizational politician. The distinguishing feature of political decision making is the importance of negotiation, bargaining, and compromise. The paradox arises when one compares the characteristics needed to engage in these activities with those associated with holding strong beliefs; they tend to work at cross-purposes. This produces what can only be called an existential tension, which must be present in all good politicians. Without that tension, we either have intransigent ideologues ("I'd rather be right than president") or amoral opportunists ("When I'm not near the goal I love, I love the goal I'm near"). To deal with this tension, the good politician must first recognize that it's there and won't go away. It is, in a very real sense, the price of professional integrity. In addition, the good politician must be scrupulously clear about which features of his or her position are essential and which marginal. This requires an understanding of policies, organizations, and programs which usually can only be acquired through hard-won experience.

The good organizational politician, in sum, must have a healthy respect for power and its uses; a set of beliefs about the purposes of his or her work that are well thought out and sufficiently part of his character to serve as the primary guide for professional actions; and an understanding of, and ability to engage in, the give-and-take of negotiation and compromise. A tall order, indeed!

Social Administrators and Political Behavior

We now turn to the question that initially prompted this essay: What factors seem to be associated with the willingness and ability of social administrators to exercise political influence as part of their professional roles? Before attempting an answer, it is necessary to note that people from a variety of backgrounds, and with a range of personal and oc-cupational characteristics, assume administrative roles in social agen-cies. Although the majority of social administrators were originally trained in clinical social work, there are other career paths leading to these positions, specifically bureaucratic advancement and specialized training in administration (Patti and Maynard 1978). However, because they make up the large majority of social administrators, the present discussion will focus on the clinician-turned-administrator, while rec-ognizing that some generalizations made may not apply to other groups.

Three aspects of administrative work seem to have a bearing on one's propensity to engage in organizational politics. They are, in rough order of importance: conceptions of the nature of the administrative role ("professional ideologies"), personal characteristics, and technical skills.

Professional Ideologies

Professional ideologies are "any body of systematically related beliefs held by a group of people . . . [which] crucially affect [their] profes-sional styles" (Strauss et al. 1964, p. 8). Social administration covers a range of activities from goal setting and program planning, to budgeting, coordination, supervision and staff development, and community and interorganizational relationships. Within certain limits, administrators have latitude in defining their particular jobs by assuming personal control over certain functions and delegating or ignoring others. Profes-sional ideologies can be expected to play a role in determining which aspects of work will be emphasized by a particular administrator and which will be downplayed or ignored.

The aspect of administrative work of particular concern here is the extent to which administrators desire to play a leading role in setting the policy goals that guide their agencies' work. For a variety of reasons, American social policies tend to be ambiguous, general, and insufficiently specified (Gummer 1979). When policy statements are cast in general terms ("pursuing economic and social self-sufficiency"), the organizations charged with their implementation are free to pursue a variety of programmatic strategies. Administrators, in turn, have a number of options as to how program strategies are to be selected. These range from ones in which the administrator acts as a neutral facilitator whose primary function is to promote consensus around a program, to ones in which the administrator assumes leadership and advocates a particular position. To the extent that administrators adopt the latter position, they must, of necessity, engage in active "politicking." Definitions of program goals and strategies tend to be the areas of greatest conflict in social agencies. When administrators become active participants in this process they become one of many interests, albeit a particularly powerful one, contending for a dominant role in influencing the organization's course.

Goal setting and goal implementation are highly interactive, and it is difficult to neatly categorize administrative actions as clearly one or the other. There is, nevertheless, an impression that administrators show a marked tendency to avoid questions of program goals and purposes and concentrate on the technical issues of implementation and control. Part of this is due, as Philip Selznick suggests, to "the wish to avoid conflicts with those in and out of the organization who would be threatened by a sharp definition of purpose, with its attendant claims and responsibilities" (1957, p. 25).

Another factor fostering an aversion to the political aspects of administrative work has to do with what is considered appropriate *professional* behavior. As administration gains legitimacy as a form of professional social-work practice, this issue becomes more pressing. Until recently, social administrators did not have a highly developed ideology. For most of this century, social workers performing administrative functions were seen as marginally connected to the profession (Patti 1983, pp. 1–20). Whatever negative consequences this may have had, it did allow for the development of a highly pragmatic approach to administrative work.

This situation changed significantly as the importance of administration in social welfare grew and administrators became increasingly concerned with their professional status. While professionalization of an occupation can have many positive effects, it can also have the negative consequence of promoting an apolitical attitude on the part of practitioners. Professionalism in American society has become characterized by an almost exclusive concern with the development of technical competence. Moreover, the great advances made by the powerful and prestigious science-based professions have been facilitated by freeing themselves "from the constraints of values and purposes" (Price 1965, p. 19). This lesson has not gone unheeded; for professions in general, the key to advancement has been through uncoupling their activities from political and social questions and concentrating on developing their unique technical competencies.

As social administrators find themselves under greater pressure to compete with other professionals for recognition, legitimacy, and influence in the management of social-welfare institutions, there have been accompanying pressures to jettison any "unscientific" approaches to practice and to adopt, wholesale, the new management technologies, particularly those derived from the "command and control" school of industrial and business management.

This position, however, ignores the fact that one of the unique features of social administration is its intimate connection with social policies as they are specified and operationalized in the process of service provision (Neugeboren 1979). The ideological issue facing social administration now, and in the future, is the development of practice models and philosophies that "hold the middle" between a purely technological approach to management and an abstracted policy analysis devoid of considerations of program implementation. To the extent that social administrators are active participants in making policy, both organizationally and within entire service systems, they will, perforce, have to deal with the basic political questions of "who gets what, when, and how."

Personal Characteristics

Given the importance of power in political behavior, the predisposition of individual administrators toward seeking and exercising power assumes paramount importance. In their study of psychiatrists who move into administrative roles, Levinson and Klerman offer some important insights into these predispositions. They suggest that these professionals have an attitude toward power similar to the Victorian view of sex:

> It is seen as vulgar, as a sign of character defect, as something an upstanding professional would not be interested in or stoop to engage in. . . . The *devaluation* of the interest in and use of power contributes heavily to the misuses and perversions of power that plague our organizational life (1973, p. 66; emphasis in original).

Research done on the transition of clinical social workers to administrative roles indicates that a similar attitude may also characterize this group of professionals (Patti et al. 1979).

A negative orientation toward power can come from at least two sources: the personal makeup of individuals who initially choose social work and/or the nature of their socialization into the profession. The question of whether social workers, as people, are innately averse to the use of power is difficult to answer, and there is little evidence one way or the other. There are, however, several indications that professional education plays a significant role in shaping the expectations of practitioners in a particular professional culture. The professional culture of social work, moreover, shows many signs of becoming increasingly apolitical and technical (Howe 1980, Austin 1983).

The historic division between "cause" and "function," between social activism and technical expertise, has diminished as the field pursues a fairly consistent strategy of endeavoring to secure its professional niche through the development of its core technologies of counseling and therapy. The curricula in schools of social work are overwhelmingly weighted in favor of psychosocial theory and treatment. What little attention is paid to political and organizational issues is either confined to the small number of students specializing in "macro" social work practice or is dealt with cursorily in introductory courses. Organizational and administrative issues are frequently presented as marginal concerns, and there is often the implicit or explicit assumption that the fee-for-service private practitioner is the ideal form for truly professional practice.

The effect of all this is to create a climate that, more than being apolitical, is, to use Harold Lasswell's more specific term, "antipolitical," an attitude that arises when "participation in the power process is actively opposed on the grounds of its alleged incompatibility with other values" (1962, p. 151). Individuals socialized into this kind of professional culture can be expected to have a generally negative orientation toward questions of organizational power and politics and their appropriate role in professional practice. In this respect, at least, clinical social-work training may create, as Rosemary Sarri argues, a "trained incapacity" for future effectiveness in administrative work (1973).

If these practitioners are to develop different attitudes as they move into supervisory and administrative roles, the transition from clinical practice to administration will have to be viewed as more than a change in job responsibilities. It will have to be seen as an occupational *transformation* in which individuals assume, in addition to new skills and responsibilities, new attitudes and values concerning the appropriate exercise of the role.

Administrators of social agencies will have to approach the selection and socialization of future administrators within a context that will facilitate such a transformation. One method is to create an occupational rite of passage during which the clinician literally leaves the agency in one capacity and returns in another. This could be done through leaves of absence to attend continuing education programs or through temporary transfers to other divisions of the agency where the prospective manager could serve an apprenticeship with a senior manager.

Technical skills

In a general sense, the skills needed to engage in political behavior and those possessed by most professional social workers may be the least problematic aspect of the present discussion. A principal asset for political effectiveness is what Charles Merriam called "facility in group combination." Professional social workers, like politicians, are adept at developing relationships among people. Both are equally conversant with the processes of coalition formation, the bases of power and influence in interpersonal relationships, and the sources of group cohesion.

Other similarities are found in the communication skills that both possess and in their typical work settings. Social workers, like politicians, place a premium on the ability to use words to convey ideas, sentiments, and beliefs and to persuade and convince others. Both are highly developed in their ability to focus on what people say and subsequently do as a basic source of information. "Listening with the third ear" is as accurate a description of how politicians go about eliciting the intentions and interests of their friends, foes, and constituents, as it is of the social worker's approach to probing the thoughts and feelings of clients.

Finally, both groups work in and deal with complex bureaucratic organizations. Political power is organized power, and politicians are inseparable from their political and governmental organizations. Social work, like the other human-service professions, has been an integral part of large organizations since its beginnings in the Charities Organization Societies of the last century. Like teaching and nursing, the practice of social work takes place almost exclusively within large organizations, and, even though many would be uncomfortable admitting it, effective social-work professionals have to develop bureaucratic and organizational skills on a par with their service skills.

Skills become an issue, however, when their purposes are in question. Politicians use their skills to advance their policies, programs, and themselves at the expense of others. This requires what George Brager calls "artful" behavior, "the conscious rearranging of reality to induce a desired attitudinal or behavioral outcome." He goes on to argue:

> The values of social workers allow reality rearrangements when the fact is shared with those affected. . . . It is when the arrangements are secret or ill defined that negative prescriptions are involved and the action is called "manipulation" (1968, pp. 8–9).

Manipulation is a critical issue because it figures so prominently in all political behavior. Politics take place in a context of conflict. While compromise is usually the ultimate solution to a dispute, before that point is reached politicians endeavor to advance their positions by the most effective means available. Dissembling, involving the manipulation of information, committee compositions, meeting times, public announcements and the like, is considered fair practice. For the "good" politician, moreover, these deceptions and distortions create moral dilemmas that result in the problem of what Michael Walzer calls "dirty hands."

> Here is the moral politician; it is by his dirty hands that we know him. If he were a moral man and nothing else, his hands would not be dirty; if he were a politician and nothing else, he would pretend that they were clean (1973, p. 68).

To deal with these moral and ethical dilemmas, politically oriented administrators must have a personal and professional philosophy that can justify their actions to themselves and to their publics. This is a difficult task and one for which many professionals are ill-equipped. Without it, however, professionals are prone to retreat from their essential purpose—the application of their knowledge and skills to the practical realities of human affairs—into a "value-free" technicism which is as much a violation of their public trust as is crass power grabbing to promote selfish ends.

Implications for Theory and Practice

The foregoing discussion might leave the reader with the impression that politics is all there is to administrative work. This was not my intention. Administrators must attend to several other concerns besides the political. There are the pragmatic realities of the daily operations of complex organizations and programs; the technical challenges of adapting advances in management science to the operational needs of social agencies; and the professional concerns of designing programs that are informed by what is known about the best ways of providing help to people. Politics has been singled out both because of its critical role in social-agency administration and its growing importance in administrative practices in general.

Traditional theories of public administration make a sharp distinction between policy making (the realm of politics) and policy implementation (the realm of administration). There is evidence, however, that this distinction may no longer be appropriate. In a recent cross-national study of the relationships between bureaucrats and politicians, Joel Aberbach and his colleagues found that

> *both* bureaucrats and politicians engage in policymaking, and *both* are concerned with politics. The real distinction between them is this: Whereas politicians articulate broad, diffuse interests of unorganized individuals, bureaucrats mediate narrow, focused interests of organized clientele (1981, p. 9; emphases in original).

They go on to suggest that future administrative practice may well take the form of a "pure hybrid" between politics and administration:

> In behavioral terms the two roles have been converging—perhaps reflecting . . . a "politicalization" of the bureaucracy and a "bureaucratization" of politics. Carrying this notion to its logical conclusion . . . suggests speculatively that the last quarter of this century is witnessing the virtual disappearance of the . . . distinction between the roles of politician and bureaucrat (p. 16).

Given the growing influence of politics in all forms of administrative work, social administrators are well advised to take pains now to prepare themselves for this change. Part of the work will entail clarifying our thinking about the appropriateness of political behavior in professional practice. The next and more demanding step will be to incorporate these ideas into the ways we select, train, and advance the people who will direct the social agencies and programs of tomorrow.

Note

1. This discussion has benefited greatly from several points raised by Professor Rino Patti in a review of an early version of this chapter.

References

Aberbach, J.D., R.D. Putnam, and B.A. Rockman. *Bureaucrats and Politicians in Western Democracies*. Cambridge, Mass.: Harvard University Press, 1981.

Austin, D.M. "The Flexner Myth and the History of Social Work," *Social Service Review* 57 (1983):357–77.

Brager, G. "Advocacy and Political Behavior," *Social Work* 13 (1968):5–15.

Donnison, D.V. "Observations on University Training for Social Workers in Great Britain and North America," *Social Service Review* 29 (1955):341–50.

Finch, W.A., Jr. "Declining Public Social Service Resources: A Managerial Problem," *Administration in Social Work* 6 (1982):19–28.

Gummer, B. "A Power-Politics Approach to Social Welfare Organization," *Social Service Review* 52 (1978):349–61.

———. "On Helping and Helplessness: The Structure of Discretion in the American Welfare System," *Social Service Review* 53 (1979):214–28.

Hasenfeld, Y. "The Implementation of Change in Human Service Organizations: A Political Economy Perspective," *Social Service Review* 54 (1980):508–20.

Howe, E. "Public Professions and the Private Model of Professionalism," *Social Work* 25 (1980):179–91.

Lasswell, H. *Power and Personality.* New York: Viking, 1962.

Lee, L.J. "The Social Worker in the Political Environment of a School System," *Social Work* 28 (1983):302–7.

Levinson, D., and G. Klerman. "The Clinician-Executive: Some Problematic Issues for the Psychiatrist in Mental Health Organizations," *Administration in Mental Health* 1 (1973):52–67.

Long, N.E. "The Administrative Organization as a Political System." In S. Mailick and E.H. Van Ness, eds. *Concepts and Issues in Administrative Behavior.* Englewood Cliffs, N.J.: Prentice-Hall, 1962.

Martin, P.Y. "Multiple Constituencies, Dominant Societal Values, and the Human Service Administrator: Implications for Service Delivery. *Administration in Social Work* 4 (1980):15–27.

Mott, P.E. *Meeting Human Needs.* Columbus: National Conference on Social Welfare, 1976.

Murdach, A.D. "A Political Perspective on Problem Solving," *Social Work* 27 (1982):417–21.

Neugeboren, B. "Social Policy and Social Welfare Administration," *Journal of Sociology and Social Welfare* 6 (1979):168–97.

Patti, R.J., and C. Maynard. "Qualifying for Managerial Jobs in Public Welfare," *Social Work* 23 (1978):288–94.

Patti, R., et al. "From Direct Service to Administration: A Study of Social Workers' Transitions from Clinical to Management Roles," *Administration in Social Work* 3 (1979):131–51, 265–75.

Patti, R. *Social Welfare Administration.* Englewood Cliffs, N.J.: Prentice-Hall, 1983.

Pawlak, E.J. "Organizational Tinkering," *Social Work* 21 (1976):376–80.

Price, D.K. *The Scientific Estate.* Cambridge, Mass.: The Belknap Press of Harvard University Press, 1965.

Rabinovitz, F., J. Pressman, and M. Rein. "Guidelines: A Plethora of Forms, Authors, and Functions," *Policy Sciences* 7 (1976):399–416.

Randall, R. "Presidential Power and Bureaucratic Intransigence: The Influence of the Nixon Administration on Welfare Policy," *American Political Science Review* 73 (1979):795–810.

Sarri, R.C. "Effective Social Work Intervention in Administrative and Planning Roles: Implications for Education."In *Facing the Challenge: Plenary Session Papers.* New York: Council on Social Work Education, 1973.

Schram, S.P. "Politics, Professionalism, and the Changing Federalism," *Social Service Review* 55 (1981):178–92.

Selznick, P. *Leadership in Administration.* New York: Harper & Row, 1957.

Strauss, A., et al. *Psychiatric Ideologies and Institutions.* New York: The Free Press, 1964.

Terrell, P. "Beyond the Categories: Human Service Managers View the New Federal Aid," *Public Administration Review* 40 (1980):47–54.

Thompson, J.D., and A. Tuden. "Strategies, Structures, and Processes of Organizational Decisions." In J.D. Thompson et al., eds. *Comparative Studies in Administration.* Pittsburgh: University of Pittsburgh Press, 1959.

Walzer, M. "Political Action: The Problem of Dirty Hands," *Philosophy & Public Affairs* 2 (1973):160–80.

Wax, J. "Power Theory and Institutional Change," *Social Service Review* 45 (1971):274–88.

Weber, M. "Politics as a Vocation." In H.H. Gerth and C.W. Mills, eds. *From Max Weber.* New York: Galaxy, 1958.

Zald, M.N. *Organizational Change.* Chicago: University of Chicago Press, 1970.

**Part II
Understanding What:
New Strategies for
Executive Performance**

3 Approaches to Cutback Management

Richard Weatherley

The 1980s pose difficult challenges for managers of human-service organizations. The Reagan administration has made significant progress in rolling back basic welfare-state programs (Palmer and Sawhill 1982). A lagging economy is yielding decreasing public tax revenues even as severe unemployment places additional strains on all kinds of public services. Few human-service organizations have escaped the need to scale down in some way. Retrenchment is the watchword of the day.

A recurrent theme among those assessing the causes and consequences of the economic decline is that citizen demands on government have exceeded government's capacity to deliver. With declining resources, we become a "zero-sum society," wherein competing interests are locked in an increasingly bitter struggle over shares of a shrinking pie (Thurow 1980). Lockean values stressing material self-interest and individualism are firmly imbedded in our political culture, institutions, and traditions (Hartz 1955), yet they do not serve us well at a time of economic decline requiring individual sacrifice, loss, and suffering (Bell 1976, Huntington 1976).

These issues are most relevant for human-service executives who are themselves political actors in the larger arena, contending with others for declining resources. At the same time, the leadership of human-service organizations under stress poses challenges and choices analogous to those confronting the larger political system. The economic values of classical liberalism are insufficient for building the kind of civic ethic necessary for coping with crisis, either in society at large or within organizations. Economic incentives, narrow trade-offs between interests, and cost-benefit considerations can only exacerbate the zero-sum struggle among interests; political values, such as justice, fairness, and concern for the collective good, are necessary for guiding the difficult decisions about how to allocate losses.

This chapter examines two leadership approaches suggested by

I wish to thank William Keaney, Cathie Martin, Sylvia Perlman, and Felice Perlmutter for their valuable comments on an earlier draft.

Selznick (1976) and considers the implications of each for the management of human-service organizations in an era of declining resources. This discussion considers how each type of leader might approach the management of decline; it then presents a range of cutback options and examines the choices one might expect the two types of leaders to select; finally, it suggests approaches the statesman might use in implementing cutback strategies while attending to the interests of clients and staff, and safeguarding, as much as possible, the organization as a social system.

Executive Leadership: Technician and Statesman

Philip Selznick draws a useful distinction between two kinds of organizational leadership. One views the organization as "a technical instrument for mobilizing human energies and directing them toward set aims . . . an *expendable tool,* a rational instrument engineered to do a job." The other approaches it as "an 'institution' . . . more nearly a natural product of social needs and pressures—a responsive, adaptive organism" (1976, p. 564). Technical leadership relates primarily to the formal organization, altering rules and structure and using incentives and sanctions to obtain desired objectives. The institutional leader is also attendant to the needs of the organization itself, as an ongoing social entity with a distinctive culture, tradition, a history and future. He or she articulates the broad goals and protects and promotes institutional values. These contrasting approaches are analytical constructs, representing the extremes in leadership styles; yet they suggest different paths that may be taken by human-service executives, providing new ideas and innovations, securing external support and legitimacy, advocating on behalf of clients, and, most important, attending to the socioeconomic needs of organizational participants. The scope of leadership functions and the relative emphasis given to each necessarily varies according to the capability, personality, training, and experience of the executive, the needs of the organization, and the demands and constraints of the external environment.

In reality, executives typically combine both styles in varying degrees, perhaps emphasizing one or the other at different times. The two styles may be compared with respect to the ends they serve or values they seek to advance; the means used to secure these ends; the time perspective for considering the impact of decisions; and the criteria for assessing organizational effectiveness (table 3–1).

Table 3–1
Executive Leadership: Technician and Statesman

Technician	Statesman
Ends	
Economic values: efficiency, cost-effectiveness	Political values: justice and fairness
Organizational maintenance	Safeguarding institutional values
Accountability to funding sources	Accountability to clients
Maintaining market share	Maximizing collective good; fostering a civic ethic
Means	
Instrumental-rational	Idealistic-emotional
Generic management techniques	Substantive expertise
Top-down; command and control	Bottom-up; backward mapping
Authoritarian management style	Democratic management style
Time Perspective	
Short term	Long term
Precipitous, to head off opposition	Deliberate, to build support
Criteria of Success	
Quantitative measures	Qualitative measures
Cost-effectiveness	Quality and scope of service
Output and outcomes measures	Impact on clients
Size, budget, and market share	Quality, distribution, and impact of services

Ends

The technician operates with a predominantly economic paradigm. He or she seeks to maximize the efficiency of the organization and further its continued maintenance while being accountable to and satisfying external funding sources. The technician strives for growth or at least for maintenance of relative market share. He realizes that an organization perceived as declining may be written off by funding sources as less deserving.

The statesman is concerned about the organization as a social entity meeting certain needs of its participants and embodying values that emphasize service, however that may be defined. As a political actor, the statesman strives for fairness in adjudicating the conflicting demands of constituent interests, clients, and staff and seeks outcomes that are just. He stresses quality of service not only for the benefit of clients, but to engender a sense of pride in staff. While seeking not to alienate staff or clients, the technician looks primarily outward, seeking recognition and approval from other administrators, funding sources, politicians, influential elites, taxpayers, and general public. The statesman, while also looking outward to these groups, remains primarily accountable to clients.

Means

The technician operates in the scientific management tradition of Frederick Winslow Taylor. The organization and its staff are viewed instrumentally, as a means to an end. Performance measures stress standards expressed quantitatively: numbers of operations completed, clients served, contact hours, forms filled out. There are work-load standards to assess and regulate productivity, and a variety of management controls to regulate the work flow and limit the discretion of front-line staff. While not necessarily operating in an overtly authoritarian fashion, the technician relies on a top-down, command and control system based on the formal chain of command. Written directives and formal sanctions are used to direct and motivate staff.

The statesman is much more attentive to the informal structure, particularly at the lower levels of the organizational hierarchy. The statesman recognizes that those at the front line are themselves policy-makers, in the sense that their individual actions in dealing with clients, taken in the aggregate, are what the organization actually does. The official rules and policies determine front-line behavior, but only up to a point. Front-line staff, or street-level bureaucrats, as they have been called, are subject to a number of additional influences and constraints. What they do is also determined by their work situation, the work load, the behavior and mix of clients, the physical setting, their training, professional ideology and values, and the actions of other agencies. Front-line workers do not simply execute policy or carry out rules; they cope with a complex and frequently stressful work situation, and the coping mechanisms they employ yield outcomes that are, individually and in the aggregate, often at odds with "official" policy (Lipsky 1980, Prottas 1979, Weatherley 1979).

The statesman appreciates that human-service organizations are "blunt instruments" (Allison 1971) and therefore does not put excessive confidence in the efficacy of instrumental administrative mechanisms. While not at all abandoning the formal organization, he or she takes a "backward mapping" approach to management (Elmore 1979–80). Following this approach, one seeks to understand the pressures and constraints on the front line and realistically takes them into account when designing policies and procedures. One begins with the desired outcome and works backward, conceptually, to create the conditions necessary to bring about the desired result. For example, one state human-service agency, seeking to reduce the error rates in AFDC and food stamps programs, imposed statewide "corrective actions" based on the central headquarters analysis of errors. However, since the type of error and its causes differed from place to place, the statewide corrective actions worked in only some local offices and probably con-tributed to increased error rates in others where staff was diverted into unnecessary and time-consuming activities yielding few results. A back-ward mapping approach, in this instance initiated by local office man-agers, sought to develop data pinpointing the kinds of errors most prevalent in each office. A staff task force in each local office then developed its own corrective action plan more directly tailored to local sources of errors.

The statesman, like the technician, is attendant to the internal politics of the organization; however, he or she is more likely to adopt a democratic approach. The statesman seeks to protect the interests of weaker parties, lower-level staff, and clients against the domination of stronger interests. This is accomplished through delegation, through mechanisms for securing front-line review of prospective policies and procedures, and by efforts to secure, wherever possible, consensus on vital issues affecting the organization.

Pay, benefits, and working conditions are not simply regarded as costs to be kept as low as possible, but as essential determinants of the organization's continued viability. Staff morale is a central concern of the statesman. Even though the trauma of decline may engender a sense of despair among staff, the statesman projects an attitude of caring and an affirmative striving toward improvement. Instead of taking a defensive posture toward deteriorating conditions, problems are openly and frankly acknowledged. When it becomes necessary to terminate staff and discontinue certain operations, the statesman openly acknowl-edges these traumatic losses to the collectivity through appropriate ceremonial gatherings as well as written announcement.

Time Perspective

One theory frequently advanced to explain the relative decline of U.S. industries in that today's managers have been trained and rewarded for maximizing short-term profits over long-term growth. Critics like to point to the Japanese model, which they say encourages managers to take the long view. According to this thesis, Japanese industry is better prepared to take advantage of capital-intensive but ultimately cost-saving technology; immediate profit is sacrificed to secure a long-range competitive advantage. While this view ignores a host of political, cul-tural, and economic factors that make such comparisons perilous, none-theless it does call attention to an important dimension of executive leadership.

Many human-service organizations today operate in a context of continual crisis; much time and energy is necessarily devoted to putting out fires. This is true for statesman and technician alike. At the same time, the technician is more concerned about short-term objectives and more likely to give greater weight to immediate tactical issues over long-term strategic considerations. For the technician, the most relevant temporal demarcations are the annual budget cycle and, in the public sector, the electoral cycle. The statesman cannot ignore these realities, yet a concern for the organizational mission requires a sense of history and a vision of the future. Day-to-day decisions are assessed for their long-range implications. Organizational decision making usually proceeds incrementally, with marginal adjustments being made to current policy (Lindblom 1959), yet these small, gradual changes can produce major cumulative shifts over the period of just a few years. The executive who fails to anticipate and be guided by long-range considerations risks default in an essential leadership task, that of setting the course.

Political scientists have recognized that items left *off* the public-policy agenda—"nondecisions" as they have been called—may be just as significant as those matters receiving official attention (Bachrach and Baratz 1963). Because there is no strong left opposition party in the United States, for example, issues concerning income distribution generally are not explicitly addressed. Organizational leaders too, in setting the managerial decision agenda, are necessarily selective in what they choose to take on. The statesman is a proactive leader, seeking to set a long-term agenda insofar as possible while recognizing that political and economic events and the usual day-to-day crises will dictate much of what has to be done.

The technician and statesman also differ with respect to the time allotted for implementing policies. The technician's no-nonsense command-and-control styles avoid many of the additional time-consuming steps taken by the more democratic statesman. The statesman moves more slowly in order to bring all interests along, involve the affected parties, seek their advice and support, and foster consensus. The technician keeps involvement to a minimum and moves more precipitously, not only for the sake of efficiency, but also to foreclose potential opposition.

While the differences in temporal perspectives and their relation to organizational planning, agenda setting, and decision making are subtle, the consequences may be substantial. To state the contrast most starkly, an organization led by the pragmatic technician concerned primarily with short-term survival may inadvertently and incrementally adopt policies that undermine its long-term viability and subvert its mission. The statesman must also muddle through current crises, but he sees today's choices in the context of a broader vision. That vision seeks to protect and promote organizational values; it assesses policy options according to their long-range implications for organizational goals as well as their immediate practicality. In other words, the statesman seeks to guide the organization toward a better future, defined and constantly redefined in a complex interplay of organizational goals, and external and internal forces and constraints.

Criteria for Measuring Relative "Success"

The technician, cognizant that the operation will be judged according to its relative size and budget, constantly strives to enlarge the scope of responsibilities and resources, particularly in relation to competing organizations. Most of today's managers were trained in an era where growth was considered an absolute good. The statesman is certainly not above playing this kind of game, but relative size is assessed with respect to the nature of the organization's mission and the tasks to be performed.

Technicians and statesmen also favor different criteria for measuring organizational performance. In general, the technician uses quantitative measures of aggregate inputs and outputs. However, statistics do not necessarily tell you much about what is happening to individuals or why. The statesman supplements quantitative tools with qualitative measures to assess the work process and organization-client interactions. He or she also seeks to assess the *impact* of service on clients. This is an important distinction. Management technology is rather good at providing measures of what organizations do in terms of the categories of service and numbers served. The differences these services make to individuals and groups, their impact, is much more difficult to determine. The statesman supplements formal output measures with process surveys, evaluations of organizational performance, and client assessments of services. For example, the former secretary of health, education, and welfare in the Carter administration, Joseph Califano, used informal staff task forces to conduct his own assessments of how certain programs were going. This had the advantage of being much faster and cheaper than outside evaluations. Being done by insiders, it was also relevant to internal implementation choices and strategies.

The statesman recognizes that cost-effectiveness is only one of a number of possible measures of organizational performance; it is not always the best. In the human services, costs are more easily measured than benefits. Cost-benefit analysis is biased toward least-cost alternatives. For example, in Washington State, hospitalization of involuntary mental patients cost about $70 per day in the state-operated hospitals, but as much as $250 to $270 per day in community hospitals, leading some to advocate increased utilization of the state hospitals. Part of the difference is reflected in the accounting for space costs, but a major share of the difference reflects the much richer staffing and better treatment program in the community hospitals. A cost-effective approach might indeed favor putting more persons into the state hospital and reducing community treatment; but cheapest is not always best.

Cutback Strategies

Three general kinds of cutback strategies will be discussed here: administrative and labor efficiencies; service reductions; and, finally, cost-sharing and merger. Of interest is their utilization by the technician or statesman.

Administrative and Labor Efficiencies

Reduction of Support Services. Initial attempts to manage with less resources often involve the elimination of organizational slack and the reduction of less essential support functions, a variety of expedients that fall under the heading of "lightbulb snatching." Such things as trying to reduce energy cost, cutting back on duplicating and materials expenses, and reducing or eliminating educational leaves or training costs are natural choices, for they can be effected without necessarily reducing program staff or restricting services, except in a very marginal way. It should be noted, however, that some relatively low-cost items—educational leave, travel reimbursement, or photocopying privileges, for example—may have great significance for staff. In one mental health agency, educational leave was eliminated for social workers but not doctors. The social workers felt demeaned and devalued. Incipient rivalry between the two groups was transformed into a kind of class warfare, morale suffered, and the teamwork necessary for the smooth functioning of the agency was undermined in a significant way. Seemingly small matters may have great symbolic value.

Increase Work Load. More significant for human-services managers are labor efficiencies. The human services are especially labor intensive, and it is difficult if not impossible to reduce costs without looking to the work force. In a period of inflation, wages can be lowered by failing to grant wage and benefit increases commensurate with a rising cost of living. As times get worse, we are more likely to see more outright pay and benefit cuts, such as those now occurring in the private sector.

Though rarely pursued as an explicit policy, managers can also seek to get professional workers to increase their hours of work by simply increasing the work load. The Motorola Corporation recently requested its white-collar employees to increase their hours from forty to forty-eight per week on a "voluntary" basis. Human-service managers can accomplish the same objective by scheduling meetings outside regular working hours or by scheduling working hours so tightly that paperwork and preparation must be done at home.

Professional employees are socialized to expect to have to do some work away from the workplace. They are also constrained by their sense of responsibility to clients to continue providing services even when this means working beyond official requirements. An example is the implementation of the Federal Education for All Handicapped Children Act. The requirements that each handicapped child be evaluated by an interdisciplinary team vastly increased the work load of teachers, psychologists, social workers, and other specialists. In most instances, the professional staff completed at least some of the mountainous paperwork requirements outside normal working hours. The local implementation of this federally mandated procedure was made possible in large part because of this hidden subsidy provided by these conscientious workers (Weatherley 1979).

Contracting. Another cost-saving approach is that of contracting out, either for individual professional services or for more general functions. Mental health and family-service agencies, for example, often retain part-time contract therapists who work on a fee-for-service basis. The agency pays them only for the contact hours, offers no benefits, and incurs only minimal overhead costs. With high unemployment in the human services, there is no dearth of workers willing to accept this kind of episodic, low-paid work. Another way agencies can cut costs is by contracting out certain functions at a fixed price, thereby delegating to the contractors the responsiblity for effecting economies through service reductions or pay cuts. Home Health Aides in Massachusetts, working for a proprietary agency under contract with the state, recently went on strike demanding the minimum wage. They were currently being paid at the minimum wage but only for the actual time spent with clients. They received no pay for the often considerable travel time spent going from one household to the next. In this instance, the private contractor had been able to offer a subminimal wage which the state would have been unable, politically, to do had it operated the service directly.

Deprofessionalization and the Subdivision of Tasks. During the more affluent 1960s many of the human services were expanded and enriched through the recruitment of paraprofessional or "nonprofessional" workers (teacher aides, community workers, and child-care assistants). As budgets have tightened, we are witnessing an opposite trend. Professional positions are being eliminated or downgraded to be performed by individuals with less education and training, and consequently at lower pay. Wherever possible, the work is subdivided and routinized so it requires minimal skills or training. Yet declassification, the elimination of professional training and experience as a prerequisite of administrative or service-delivery jobs, is but a recent example of what some deem the inevitable and inexorable deprofessionalization and proletarianization of the work force (Braverman 1974, Zimbalist 1979).

Executive Performance. In some respects, the technician enjoys an advantage over the statesman in effecting administrative and labor efficiencies. The technician's approach is to move fast to head off potential opposition and to go for the big-ticket items. He or she may also opt for strategies that obscure the nature of the cuts, for example, by failing to grant pay increases commensurate with inflation or by permitting work loads to rise without increasing staff. Such wage cuts and speedups may be presented as inevitable responses to forces emanating from outside and therefore presumably beyond the control of the executive. A soft labor market and shrinking resources offer the technician opportunities for getting rid of "deadwood" and restructuring the work so that tasks may be performed by less skilled and less costly staff. The technician is more likely to prefer merit to seniority systems for implementing reductions in force as these offer greater managerial discretion and enhance executive authority.

The statesman is indeed more constrained in some respects. He may choose to forego potential cost-saving measures as having severe long-range implications or as being bad for staff morale. The statesman recognizes staff concerns about job security as legitimate. Rather than attacking seniority (and directly threatening those with the longest tenure), the statesman seeks other means to reconcile concerns for job security with the need to reduce expenditures. The statesman seeks to avoid staff layoffs by carrying out reductions in force through planned attrition. This means offering incentives for early retirement, exploring job sharing, leaves, and furloughs, expanding part-time work opportunities, and spreading out the reductions over a multiyear period to take advantage of natural attrition through voluntary departures and retirements. Recognizing their significance for staff morale, he or she is also likely to fight for those prerogatives and benefits that are of such importance in securing staff commitment to the mission of the organization.

The statesman has additional options not likely to be employed by the technician. A number of efforts have been undertaken to enlarge and enrich jobs, involve workers in finding ways to improve productivity, and generally enhance the quality of work life. These kinds of efforts, under the general heading of human resource development (Mills 1975), have attained considerable legitimacy in the private sector. Ironically, they have been avoided by most human-service managers, who feel obliged to maintain an image of no frills, cost-conscious administrative orthodoxy.

Service Reductions

There are essentially three ways to reduce services: cut them out, ration access, or dilute them.

Eliminating Programs or Services. Perhaps the most straightforward reduction is to eliminate specific functions or programs, presumably starting with those deemed least essential and/or most costly. However, life is rarely that simple. A proposal for the outright elimination of programs may serve to mobilize opposition from various vested interests, including staff, clients, and oversight bodies. It may also raise equity issues, for some units may be more vulnerable or more essential than others (Levine 1978, p. 322).

Rationing Access. There are several ways of rationing services, including the shutting down of branch offices, limiting hours of service, changing eligibility standards, maintaining queues and waiting lists, or erecting various barriers to access—delays, more complex and time-consuming application procedures, rude reception personnel, limited telephone access. All of these measures, invoked in the administration of public-assistance programs from time to time, are becoming more widespread in the 1980s. The shutting of offices has a dual cost-saving impact. The office overhead is saved, and at the same time, services are rationed, for clients must travel to less convenient locations. The other rationing techniques have the advantage of appearing to be an act of fate rather than a deliberate policy decision, and are less likely to attract focused opposition.

There are costs to these strategies that should be considered. When demand exceeds capacity, workers will use their own informal rationing devices, and they will inevitably act in ways that depart from official rules. Access to services may become a question of the survival of the fittest, the most articulate, or the most persistent. The most needy may be denied services. For example, new, more restrictive rules and complex procedures for school lunch programs have discouraged the poor from participating. Three million children were eliminated, and 1,500 schools have dropped out of the program altogether (Chira 1982). Finally, as demands for services increase in relation to resources and access, the atmosphere in human-service offices can become increasingly tense. It has become commonplace to have guards in public-assistance and hospital emergency room waiting areas to maintain order. People may become more desperate as benefits and services become harder to obtain.

Diluting Services. This differs from rationing in that access is not limited, but the quantity and/or quality of service is reduced. This may be done affirmatively as a matter of policy, as when the number of visits or duration of service is limited. Brief therapies and groups, for example, may be promoted over more costly, longer-term individual therapy. Dilution may also be accomplished more covertly by reducing staff and letting workers cope as best they can. A reduction in monitoring and oversight capability, internal as well as external, may also provide a tacit acceptance for the dilution of services.

Executive Response. The technician and statesman approach the reduction or elimination of services in somewhat different ways. The technician might favor across-the-board cuts, which have the appearance of fairness and are therefore the most palatable politically. The statesman is cautious about carrying percentage cuts too far for fear of generally weakening the organization and unfairly burdening lower-level staff with the responsibility for implementing cuts without explicit policy guidance about how to do it. The statesman recognizes staff burnout as an organizational rather than individual problem. By developing clear decision guidelines, he seeks to insulate staff from those wrenching lifeboat situations where one must choose whom to help among the needy. While the technicians may deliberately choose to deemphasize or even obscure the effects of service reductions, the statesman endeavors to identify *all* the consequences of alternative options, making explicit the costs and who will bear them.

Cost Sharing and Mergers

Cost Sharing. Many competing metropolitan newspapers have dealt with rising costs by joint publication ventures whereby certain overhead and production expenses are shared, while management and editorial functions remain separate. Some human-service agencies have adopted similar strategies, sharing office space or developing joint arrangements for such things as lobbying, public information, staff training, book-keeping, or janitorial services and insurance coverage.

Certain kinds of joint or collaborative service arrangements have become institutionalized, including information and referral services, centralized recruitment of volunteers, or the development of consolidated crisis "hot lines." Just about any function that would benefit from an economy of scale is a potential candidate for joint arrangements. Those requiring a large capital investment and skilled staff—word processing, mechanized accounting, and/or client-information systems, for example—are particularly good possibilities. Such arrangements are perhaps easier to work out with the assistance of some outside group, a mental health board or United Way budget committee, for example.

Faced with declining enrollments, most school districts in the country now have surplus school property to contend with. Outright sale or long-term lease for private use are attractive alternatives for hard-pressed districts facing a loss of revenues along with the loss of students. Human-service agencies can make a good case for the publicly subsidized use of surplus school space. Joint use, where school programs coexist with social agencies in the school facility, permits a school district to keep open schools even with a small enrollment; leasing surplus school property to social agencies keeps the property in the public domain while allocating it to a public purpose. Current demographic projections suggest that a delayed echo from the baby boom will again require expanded school facilities available for continued public use. Social-agency executives can argue that it is less costly to offer school facilities without a rental charge than to board them up. Vacant properties become targets for vandalism and can deteriorate quickly (Weatherley, Narver, and Elmore 1982).

Merger. Merger, increasingly common in the business world, is a far more radical step that may fundamentally alter the program and organization. One function of the small but significant voluntary agency sector has been to innovate with new programs and services that are then adopted, enlarged, and institutionalized by public agencies. Recent examples include rape crisis centers, shelters for battered women, the hospice movement, and some home health programs. Public agencies are not looking for additional responsibilities, and such takeovers frequently bring a bureaucratization deplored by the innovators. A further disincentive is that the newly constituted programs are generally operated with a new, more formally credentialed staff, and the founders find themselves out of a job.

Yet merger need not necessarily mean going out of business or getting swallowed up by larger, established, or establishment agencies. Difficult as it may be, bargains can be struck to guarantee staff security and program integrity while taking advantage of the efficiencies that can result from consolidated operations. Vertical integration seeks to combine under a single administrative umbrella functions that are sequentially related and interdependent. Just as the major oil companies have acquired the means to explore for, transport, refine, and market the oil, women's groups have pieced together coalitions and collaboratives that provide case finding, shelter, counseling, legal, and financial assistance for battered women. Horizontal integration refers to the grouping of like functions or services. One tire manufacturer may acquire a competitor to reduce competition, expand the market share, gain additional assets, and enjoy economies of scale. In like fashion, human-service organizations serving a particular clientele (women, children, the elderly, tenants) or offering a particular kind of service (counseling, meals, shelter) may also be merged.

Mergers represent one extreme on what may be viewed as a continuum of joint or collaborative effort. Mergers may involve a loss of agency identity and the relinquishing of some managerial prerogatives, but all such collaborative efforts do to some extent. We normally think of the "strong" executive as one who fights hard for the agency, not one who willingly gives it away, in whole or in part. Interagency collaboration puts statesmanship to the test by requiring some sacrifice of organizational autonomy and managerial control in exchange for benefits to clients and staff. However, the most successful organizations are those with the capacity to change in anticipation of and in response to a changing environment. The statesman facilitates and nurtures the adaptability of the organization.

The ultimate cost-saving measure is termination. While most executives would see this as failure, there comes a time when other cost-cutting or fund-generating options would so compromise the program and organization that termination becomes the right thing to do.

Is Statesmanship Possible for Cutback Management?

The technician enjoys a considerable advantage over the statesman in selecting and implementing cutback strategies. He need only be concerned with the relative feasibility and cost-effectiveness of the various options. The big-ticket items, including the various labor efficiencies and program and staff reductions, may be most appealing, along with efforts to generate additional income through fees and fund raising. Where there is likely to be opposition from entrenched interests, the technician may opt for fast, decisive action, perhaps in response to some immediate crisis; alternatively, he or she may elect the less visible strategies, diluting and rationing services or deferring maintenance, for example.

The statesman is much more constrained. For the statesman, cost-effectiveness and political expediency do not suffice as criteria for carrying out cutback strategies. Equally important are ethical and professional considerations, assessments of how the various options will affect clients, staff, and the organization itself. At the same time, a finite number of choices is available, and the executive, technician, or statesman has to do something, even if it means selecting the least bad of the available options.

So what is the executive to do? The key to statesmanship is contingency planning and forecasting. Contingency planning and forecasting serve several functions. The most obvious is providing alternative plans that can be implemented quickly as circumstances change. Planning permits the conceptual weighing of alternative scenarios as an adjunct to rational decision making. But there are other benefits as well. The planning process itself can be a means of involving those most likely to be affected in doing something tangible and affirmative in a situation of stress and uncertainty. The development of alternative plans can provide intelligence on likely sources of opposition and support, but most important, it can prepare people individually and collectively for impending adversity. The promulgation of multiple realities can be reassuring psychologically and can prepare the organization and individuals for difficult changes likely to occur (Edelman 1977). People may mentally rehearse alternative scenarios to get ready for what is to come, and be prepared for the worst.

One of the ironies of cutback management is that many of the tools for a technical-rational approach to planning are least available when most needed. Policy analysis, evaluation, and information systems are less important in times of growth when mistakes do not threaten the organization's survival. When the organization's survival is at stake, such planning resources are rarely available because of cutbacks (Levine

1978, p. 317). The involvement of staff and clients, while possibly engendering conflict in the short run, brings new resources to bear at a time when they are sorely needed. It can serve to build support for measures that will ultimately have to be taken. But it also taps an essential source of organizational intelligence to compensate for the myopic stratagems that too frequently result from top-down, command-and-control approaches. And as suggested earlier, the involvement of those likely to be affected also facilitates and legitimizes anticipatory grieving for the losses that will ultimately come.

There are many ways of involving clients and staff, including the use of surveys, hearings, task forces, committees and the like, as well as formal delegation. It is essential that the executive be clear about the limits of participation and how and why decisions will ultimately be made. Staff or clients who sense that their participation is intended to be co-optive may become more resentful than if they had not been consulted at all. There are inherent conflicts between management, labor, and clients, and this should be acknowledged openly at the outset.

Conclusion

The management of declining organizations severely tests the political and technical skills of the executive. Strategies and techniques that worked well enough in an era of growth no longer suffice. Shrinking resources create a zero-sum situation pitting clients, staff, organizational subunits, and competing human-service interests against one another. At stake are careers, services to the needy and dependent, and organizational survival. While much in vogue, management models stressing economic values, rational-choice techniques, and formal hierarchical controls are ill suited to these calamitous times.

There is another approach. In times of adversity, we look to our national leaders for statesmanlike behavior. We expect them to articulate some vision of a future good for the collectivity, to acknowledge and grieve for those suffering the most, and to steer a course of action based on some conception of fairness and justice. When such conditions are met, we are more inclined to endure the sacrifices that may be required. So too with executive leadership in organizations. The statesman is both idealist and pragmatist. He uses what technical implements are available, but considers immediate actions in their long-term context. He or she is decisive, but broadens the scope of deliberation to include all affected interests, weak and strong. The statesman is intelligent, systematic, and rational, but relates to the organization as a whole and to its constituent parts with feeling and emotion, sharing and acknowledging the grief that accompanies loss. With some measure of statesmanship, the human-service executive can steer a course that finds opportunity in adversity, reaffirms the organizational mission, acknowledges the worth of staff and clients, and builds a stronger, though perhaps leaner, program.

References

Allison, Graham T. *Essence of Decision*. Boston: Little, Brown, 1971.

Bachrach, Peter, and Morton S. Baratz. "Decisions and Nondecisions: An Analytical Framework," *American Political Science Review* 57 (1963):632–42.

Bell, Daniel. *The Cultural Contradictions of Capitalism*. New York: Basic Books, 1976.

Braverman, Harry. *Labor and Monopoly Capital: The Degradation of Work in the Twentieth Century*. New York: Monthly Review Press, 1974.

Chira, Susan. "New School Lunch Rules Stir Debate," *New York Times*, 29 November 1982, p. B2.

Downs, Anthony. "Up and Down with Ecology—the 'Issue-Attention Cycle'," *The Public Interest* 28 (1973):38–50.

Edelman, Murray. *Political Language: Words that Succeed and Policies that Fail*. New York: Academic Press, 1977.

Elmore, Richard. "Backward Mapping: Using Implementation Analysis to Structure Policy Decisions," *Political Science Quarterly* 84 (1979-80):601–16.

Hartz, Louis. *The Liberal Tradition in America*. New York: Harcourt Brace Jovanovich, 1955.

Huntington, Samuel P. "The Democratic Distemper," *The Public Interest* 41 (Fall 1975):9–38.

Levine, Charles. "Organizational Decline and Cutback Management," *Public Administration Review* 38 (1978):316–25.

Lindblom, Charles E. "The Science of Muddling Through," *Public Administration Review* 19 (1959):79–88.

Lipsky, Michael. *Street-Level Bureaucracy: Dilemmas of the Individual in Public Services*. New York: Russell Sage Foundation, 1980.

Miller, S.M. "The Political Economy of Social Problems," *Social Problems* 24 (1976):638–51.

Mills, Ted. "Human Resources—Why the New Concern?" *Harvard Business Review* 53 (1975):120–34.

Palmer, John, and Elizabeth Sawhill, eds. *The Reagan Experiment.* Washington, D.C.: Urban Institute, 1982.

Prottas, Jeffrey. *People-Processing.* Lexington, Mass.: Lexington Books, 1979.

Salmans, Sandra. "The Debate Over the Electronic Office," *New York Times Magazine,* 14 November 1982, 132–57.

Selznick, Philip. "Leadership in Administration," In Robert T. Golembiewski et al., eds. *Public Administration.* Chicago: Rand McNally, 1976, 563–75.

Sugarman, Barry. "The Nonprofit Manager as a Guerilla Leader," *Sharing.* July-August 1982, 1–4.

Taylor, Robert E. "New Laws are Raising Prison Population at Fastest Rate in 56 Years, Statistics Show." *Wall Street Journal,* 8 November 1982, p. 12.

Thurow, Lester. *The Zero-Sum Society.* New York: Basic Books, 1980.

Weatherley, Richard. *Reforming Special Education: Policy Implementation from State-Level to Street-Level.* Cambridge, Mass.: MIT Press, 1979.

Weatherley, R., B.J. Narver, and R. Elmore. "Managing the Politics of Decline: School Closures in Seattle." *Peabody Journal of Education* 60 (winter 1983):10–24.

Wolin, Sheldon. "The New Public Philosophy," *Democracy* 1, no. 4 (1981):43.

Zimbalist, Andrew, ed. *Case Studies on the Labor Process.* New York: Monthly Review Press, 1979.

4

The Voluntary Sector Can Remain Alive—and Well

Ernest M. Kahn

This chapter focuses on the impact of changes initiated by the federal government under President Reagan on one segment of the American social-welfare community: its voluntary agencies. It seeks to examine issues and concerns that have arisen for these agencies as a result of the developments described elsewhere in this volume. In doing so, it focuses particularly on the resulting problems that confront executives of these agencies and the alternative strategies available for coping with these concerns. In the course of this examination, an effort will also be made to highlight those alternatives dependent on cooperation between the public and voluntary sectors of the social-welfare community.

Voluntary organizations to address a variety of social concerns have existed in this country since the early days of the Republic. Most were initially based on religious denominations and, to the extent that they were initially an integral part of religious institutions, they functioned even during the Colonial period. From that time on, voluntary organizations conducted their efforts in addressing a variety of social problems parallel to the efforts of public institutions of whatever unit of government.

At no time in American history was there ever a formal division of responsibilities between the public and voluntary sectors of social welfare. However, from early New England origins, functional divisions developed, continued, and expanded. In simple terms, the legal responsibility for the "dependent, defective and delinquent," for the most basic provision of food and shelter, for the care of the mentally ill and mentally retarded, and for the control of criminal offenders was in the hands of public bodies. Practically, during most of our history voluntary agencies carried parallel responsibilities—except for corrections—and also provided supplementary programs. They also focused their attention on concerns outside the purview of the public agencies (Leiby 1978, pp. 3, 35–36, 86). These concerns varied in different periods of our history but frequently represented innovation both in the concerns addressed and the approaches employed. Many of these approaches were eventually integrated, particularly during the twentieth century, into the expanding scope of the public agencies. In the development of innovative programs, voluntary agencies frequently dealt with concerns prior to the development of a consensus about public responsibility for the particular program or population group.

A system of service delivery developed in which almost all voluntary agencies in the social-welfare arena were closely linked with the public agencies. This linkage made many voluntary social agencies vulnerable to the social policies of the Reagan administration. While the effects of these changes were most evident in the funding of programs, they also extended to the types of programs to be supported and the manner of service delivery (Doherty 1972). Above all, they challenged the previously established consensus on public responsibility for social problems.

The impact will be examined with regard to three areas of social agency operation: agency mission and strategic planning; political agenda; and the boards of directors. In each of these areas, an effort will be made to review the changing context and to suggest new directions and executive strategies to deal with it. Finally, the changes in all three areas will be discussed with regard to the implications for executive leadership in voluntary social-welfare agencies.

In these considerations the term *voluntary agency* will be used in preference to the frequently used term *private agency*. The voluntary agency is, essentially, one in the not-for-profit sector and not a unit of government. The private agency is one in the profit-making sector. The distinction takes on added significance because federal policies and those of some states, while ostensibly treating both types of agencies similarly, have begun to create different environments for these two types of agencies. This is especially true where changes in regulations are concerned. The distinction may assume added significance in coming years as nonprofit agencies consider entry into profit-making activities.

Agency Mission and Strategic Planning

In the face of outside pressures, agencies and their executives can seek to resist change or to accommodate to it. In either instance, the expectation is still that the executive will endeavor to keep the institution, in this case the agency he heads, continuing to function as a viable entity. This is not to suggest that this is always the best response to change. Rather, it is the expectation held by the members of the agency's board of directors, the staff, the clients, and various members of the communal service network. Perhaps most important, it is the expectation held by the executive. The fact that all of these expectations have more than a tinge of self-interest does not make them any less valid. It does, however, complicate the resolution of the problem. The response of an institution to major changes in its environment needs to include the consideration of all options. By definition, these include the termination of the agency, major changes in objectives and programs, various forms of affiliation with other institutions, as well as less drastic changes in service delivery. The executive will want to assure that the self-interests of various stakeholders are one factor in the decision—not the sole or even the predominant one (Finch 1982).

Amidst major change and the desire for institutional and personal self-preservation, the first responsibility of the executive is crisis management. The analogy of the military under fire comes to mind, as do the instructions given to commanding officers of ships, aircraft, and certain industrial plants, where prompt response to emergencies is deemed imperative in order to save life and property. In all of these instances, continued maintenance of control over the internal situation and "keeping a cool head" are vital. The social-agency executive under crisis circumstances will be expected to function in a similar manner. A few agency executives may actually have had such experience in working on civilian disasters, such as floods and tornados. Most have not previously encountered such circumstances.

The triage function is not, however, unfamiliar to many agency executives. Simply put, it involves rapid decision as to courses of action based on limited available data and under pressured circumstances. In its ultimate form, it involves medical decisions as to who will live or die. While the decisions of the social-agency executive will be less immediately dramatic, they may have similar consequences for segments of the agency program. The concepts to be applied include those of damage control, emergency repairs, and, above all, the buying of time for orderly retreat and regrouping of the agency's forces.

In turn, the opportunity for retreat and regrouping is most likely to depend on securing early and reasonably accurate information about impending changes. In the case of changes in government policy, it may therefore require closer monitoring of governmental plans than was the case when executives and their assistants simply reviewed the *Federal Register,* RFPs, newsletters and similar materials for new funding opportunities. Acquisition of such information is closely linked with legislative lobbying, discussed later in this chapter. It requires attention by institutional representatives, on the national, state, and sometimes county level, to the administrative agencies as well as the legislative bodies. Agency executives who review their own functioning may find models in their own similar activities at the city level. Agencies with strong interests in governmental activities, whether for funding or policy reasons, will want to utilize lay leaders as well as professionals for such contacts and will seek the optimum number of opportunities to interact with government. Recent experience suggests that executives need to separate their feelings concerning government policy changes from operations management while infusing the agency's advocacy efforts with them.

Orderly retreat and regrouping for the maintenance of the agency are not primarily mental health activities, although they should have a salutory effect on staff morale. Rather, they are intended to make time and space to enable the agency to deal with change.

Tregoe and Zimmerman (1981) sum it up by focusing on an organizational fact of life: "All organizations are confronted with change. How well an organization negotiates the hurdles, is key to its survival and success" (1981). The authors pay attention both to internal and external change and emphasize that "both require strategic questions first, before any action is taken."

The same authors define strategy "as a framework to guide those choices that determine the nature and direction of an organization." For the social agency, the statement of agency mission often serves the same purpose. If significant change in the environment requires the rethinking of the strategic framework of an organization, the same applies to the mission of a social agency. This is not to suggest that the previously stated mission is no longer valid. If anything, all assumptions must be subject to thorough review and scrutiny. Such a review is always an intensive and frequently lengthy process. Some specialists in organizational operations use the term *strategic planning* to differentiate the process from *operational planning,* while others emphasize that development of a strategic framework differs from planning. Regardless of terminology, the agency executive must be aware that a strategic planning process demands time, energy, intellect, and resources. In anything but a small agency, it cannot be conducted while the executive devotes full attention to the day-by-day operations of the agency. Moreover, involving as it does fundamental decision making, the process cannot logically be conducted without the active involvement of the key executive(s).

The scope of such a strategic-planning process must be wide-ranging and requires exploration beyond that feasible within the scope of this chapter (United Way of America 1983). Suffice it to say that it needs to include all aspects of the agency's operations and particularly such elements as agency purpose, client needs, priorities of programs, and the allocation of resources.

Although strategic planning may speak of "the allocation of resources," the reality of the 1980s is an increasing scarcity of resources for social-service programs. Having recognized both the instinct and expectation for organizational maintenance, executives must avoid the threat of "goal displacement," the substitution of organizational-maintenance goals for service-effectiveness goals.

The current existence of an institution with all of its subunits is not in itself justification for its continuation. In most instances, services being delivered, client needs, effectiveness of programs, and similar factors justify continuity. The changes in governmental funding streams and policies concerning eligibility for service create the need for many agencies to consider their future directions. Since the needs being addressed by these agencies are not readily subject to change by mandate, most agencies will find reason, if not resources, for continuation. Parenthetically, a decision not to continue with current services need not mean the automatic termination of an agency. Manufacturers have switched to different product lines, and among nonprofit agencies, the experience of the March of Dimes, which focused on birth defects after it helped conquer polio, is well known. Emphasis on service delivery needs to be the bedrock of the social agency's strategic planning. If such is not the case, even the most finely attuned process can produce erroneous results, just as the most advanced surgical instruments can be the cause of death when improperly utilized.

Recent publications by both Miringoff (1980) and Woocher (1982) suggest several key questions that ought to be posed in order to avoid goal displacement. The first question concerns which areas of service most directly express the agency's basic values, what it stands for institutionally and communally. A second question would ask about the areas of program or service in which the agency possesses the best staff and technological capabilities. Third, the process should determine the likelihood of future growth. In doing so, it should obviously consider various reasons for such growth. Finally, it is both proper and necessary to ask about the areas of service for which the agency is most likely to be able to generate resources.

One comment concerning the development of resources: in the era now ended, resource development for social agencies seemed to move in two directions. On the one hand, there was the often noted honing of skills in grantmanship, proposal writing, and related activities. On the other hand, there was some awareness of the need for cost containment. This needs to be continued and intensified. However, skills in fund raising on the part of most social agencies have not been developed or practiced while it was easier to obtain significant sums of money through the grant and proposal development routes. Similarly, creativity in such fund raising seems in recent years to have been limited to large numbers of people running, biking, skating, walking, or otherwise propelling themselves about their communities while motivated by the contributions of others.

It is already clear that foundations and business enterprises to whom social agencies and other nonprofit organizations have recently directed their proposals will not be able to substitute their funds for those of government to any meaningful extent. Social agencies will need to develop creative new efforts while reapplying sound knowledge of fund raising. Perhaps even more important, in order to produce income, social agencies will need to consider in their planning the marketing of the resources in both skilled staff and technical capacity which they have available. In some instances, this may mean the delivery of social services in a different manner. Witness the contractual arrangements for employee-assistance programs already developed between some major corporations and social agencies. Some voluntary agencies have begun to explore new opportunities for human services which may exist in suggestions that traditional public services (sanitation, libraries, and others) be performed on a contractual basis by private industry. Precedents for this already exist in the human services. In other instances, the development of additional income may take the social agency rather far afield from its basic mission. Here the precedents set by academic institutions and recent efforts of health-care agencies may offer valuable examples. Voluntary agencies could, for example, expand income-producing services focused on populations other than their traditional clients. Such income could help offset costs of service to regular clients and, in some instances, expand universality of service. Participation in the service delivery of mandated entitlement programs may offer another option for income enhancement. New opportunities may develop from new public policies, such as recent recommendations for achievement standards in public schools and the resultant need to assist students and families in coping with these expectations.

Finally, even where institutional maintenance is a consideration, the continuity of the agency in its present form may not always be best suited either for service delivery or institutional interests. Mergers of social agencies are not a new phenomenon and may, in certain circumstances, provide continuity of service and forward agency goals. The variations on mergers developed in the business community, in part as a response to some of the same economic circumstances presently confronting social agencies, warrant careful review by these agencies. Conglomerates may be only one means to provide both continuity of service and agency mission. Similarly, there are significant unexplored areas of potential relationships between voluntary, not-for-profit social agencies and the newer private, profit-making social-service organizations (Kamerman 1983). Still further, new structural and contractual arrangements between social agencies of the voluntary and public sectors should be studied. The suggestion by O'Connell (1976) that we think of three kinds of social agencies—government, quasi-governmental, and independent—has never been fully explored. Similarly, the concepts advanced by Berger and Neuhaus (1977) in their discussion of "mediating institutions" seem particularly suited to the ideology of the current era and could apparently meet significant needs of government, social-agency clients, and the voluntary agencies themselves.

Van Til (1982) has recently suggested a further refinement for interagency linkages through the idea of "co-production." Similarly, the levels of interagency collaboration developed over the years appear to be far less than what is feasible and warranted under current circumstances. Recent work by Lippitt and Van Til, Gamm and others (1981) strongly suggests that agency executives need to factor such considerations much more prominently into their future strategic thinking.

Political Agenda

Significant as these issues are, a major concern for the executive will still be the agency's relationship with the body politic. The single biggest consideration on an agency's political agenda is still government funding for voluntary social agencies. The issue will undoubtedly be debated for a number of years. It will loom large in the strategic thinking and mission formulation of voluntary agencies. The complexity of the issues does not allow for their full consideration in this discussion, but Weaver has posed the dilemma well in a recent article:

> Dependence on government funds also curbs the freedom of voluntary agencies to change and innovate, one of their supposed advantages over government. Heavier government support of the services voluntary agencies provide can lock these agencies into those clients and programs for which the government is willing to pay. The government thus may, in effect, "buy up" the autonomy of a private agency. . . .
>
> By the same token, as government agencies rely more on the private sector to deliver services, the government's ability to change priorities and the emphasis of programs is diminished. In effect, the government agency loses the discretion to plan or set priorities if these depart from its current pattern of resource allocation. Politically, it is difficult, if not impossible, to discontinue a contract or service if doing so would damage a voluntary agency.
>
> Thus, the greater the dependence on purchase agreements or contracts, the greater the overlap of roles, the greater the competition

between government and the voluntary sector, and the stronger the
forces against changes in both sectors (1982).[1]

Both short- and long-range objectives need to be considered by
agency executives when dealing with issues of political activity. In the
short range, the agency presumably will want to try to maintain those
governmental resources that it was receiving prior to the advent of
Reaganomics and the rise of similar philosophies in many state houses.
Significant differences have already developed among the states in their
reaction to federal cuts in human-services funding. Some states, such
as New York, have sought to utilize their own resources as substitutes;
others, such as Pennsylvania, have made further cuts. Moreover, the
formulas applied to some legislation, based on census data and similar
factors, may actually make additional resources available in some areas.
Since significant amounts of federal and state monies continue to be
allocated for social-service purposes, this is a reasonable and understandable goal for voluntary agencies. However, the availability of funds
and possible continued funding of programs of voluntary agencies should
not be viewed by the executive as a rationale for the avoidance of basic
strategic thinking. Entirely aside from whether the funds available are
adequate for the task at hand, neither the continuity of their availability
nor the desirability of continued funding should be assumed.

Those voluntary agencies that until recently confined their transactions with government to the submission, negotiation, and implementation of proposals now must devote attention to activities
traditionally labeled "lobbying." However, as such lobbying must focus
on both the legislative and administrative agencies of the federal and
state governments, except for the largest voluntary agencies, it should
be carried out collaboratively for the sake of economy of effort and
cost as well as for political effectiveness.

A number of voluntary agencies have already recognized the shift
in the "action" from the federal to the state level and have, accordingly,
either increased or newly initiated lobbying efforts in their state capitals.
For example, in recent years associations of Jewish Federations have
established representation in eight state capitals. Such efforts must be
in addition to continued attention to the Washington scene and therefore do represent additional costs at a time when discretionary funds
are in short supply. Also, while the basic principles of lobbying are
identical regardless of the level of government being approached, there
is need to recognize differences in style and procedures as practiced on
the state level. In a number of states, voluntary agencies have also
begun to pay further attention to the county level, since some block-

grant funds funnel through these units of government. Executives will also want to review options to shift support for a particular program from one government funding stream to another, such as from Title XX to a state's child welfare program.

Regardless of level of government, lobbying efforts by social agencies should be collaborative efforts wherever feasible. The demands for governmental funds, especially in a time of economic recession, are such that government is hard pressed to respond even if it is philosophically committed to the purposes for which the funds are being requested. Competition between social agencies in the public arena is therefore likely to be detrimental to all agencies involved, since it increases opportunities for government to avoid their requests. Coalitions between the social-service community and other nonprofit organizations or groups should also be established where possible.

Two notable omissions appear in the arguments by social agencies and their executives for continued funding of voluntary agencies. Entirely inadequate emphasis has been placed on the fact that the programs and services of voluntary agencies which have been funded by government represent, in most instances, the most essential services of these agencies. Government has not been funding supplementary activities or "frills." Therefore, if such governmental resources are not available, the voluntary funds may well have to be shifted to the continuation of these programs, creating problems both from the inadequate amount of such voluntary dollars available and from the elimination of programs previously supported with voluntary funds. An important consideration with regard to the latter is that significant numbers of voluntary agencies function under sectarian auspices and have used their own funds for the support of precisely those sectarian programs that are both at the heart of their mission and ineligible for government support. For them, a failure of governmental funding will present an unenviable choice between services most needed by clients and those deemed most essential for the continuity of the sponsoring group. Moreover, substituting voluntary dollars for withdrawn governmental funding will probably impact most on the "near poor," those with resources enough to make them ineligible for public support but not enough to function without help. In day-care programs, for example, such a shift in funding in some instances has caused a drain on voluntary funds. With child day care unavailable for "near poor" single parents, some mothers must leave gainful employment and return to the welfare rolls.

Inadequate attention has also been given to the conditions created by the continuing deregulation of a large number of social-service programs. While the initial focus on funding is most understandable, it is to be hoped that agency executives will recognize that over the long run, the maintenance of proper standards of care for many population groups will be at least as important as the amount of funding available in any one year. Those familiar with concepts of social change will recognize that appropriation bills are frequently more easily adapted to changing conditions than standard-setting legislation or even regulations.

Advocacy for the continuation of fundamentally sound standards of care, even where they represent some additional cost for the service provider, must be on the political agenda of social agencies. While this concept has merit in its own right, it also serves to illustrate a further principle of political intervention by voluntary agencies. As the agencies review and possibly reformulate their future mission, they should give attention to addressing social-service issues in a number of ways. Direct service delivery may well be the most necessary response to social problems, but it is only one level of response. Advocacy in the halls of government can represent another form of agency response to social-service needs. As such, it will warrant consideration as an agency activity even by those voluntary agencies that opt to forego further governmental funding. Participation in social-policy development is an essential part of the voluntary agency's mission.

In political intervention, as in institutional maintenance, self-interest is a valid and legitimate motive. A number of years ago, a Maryland legislator, after expressing great discomfort with social workers who came to lobby on behalf of various populations in need, went on to suggest, "When you come to get social work licensing for yourself, that's something I can understand, and I'll vote for it." In that vein, the political agenda of social agencies should include the advocacy of expanding incentives for charitable contributions and strong opposition to any efforts to restrict nonpartisan, issue-oriented advocacy by non-profit organizations. These are recurring concerns that should be on the long-range political agenda for social agencies.

The same holds true for the development of coalitions beyond the social-agency network under whatever auspices. In an era where self-determination has become the theme of the federal administration, citizen organizations concerned with consumer issues, the environment, and the urban condition represent logical allies. Neither the business community nor the labor movement should be assumed to be protagonists or antagonists. In recent history, the social-welfare community has generally disagreed with organized labor on immigration legislation and substantially agreed with big business on changes in social security legislation. Significantly, at the same time representative of social-welfare institutions were in coalition with labor on a number of issues while opposing the business community on a number of others. In a still more dramatic example, social-welfare agencies in several states engaged in coalitions with private nursing home operators to achieve more realistic reimbursement rates while, at the same time engaged in disputes on several matters with the same operators.

Social-agency executives—indeed all social workers—would do well to recall that coalitions are built one issue at a time. They should also remember an old truism: in politics, there are no permanent allies and no permanent enemies. The social-welfare community has not been very effective in its coalition efforts, and many social welfare issues have little public appeal in the early 1980s. However, agency executives would do well to monitor constantly the moralistic tenor that continues to infuse much of our advocacy efforts. Except in very rare instances, such as child abuse, such approaches are counterproductive.

Political pragmatism is not synonymous with unethical behavior. Professionals who endeavor to be nonjudgemental about clients as a basic tenet of their practice should consistently apply the same concept to their political allies. There is also need to come to grips with our emphasis on process and the involvement of all interested parties. The time frame of the political process, particularly near the end of sessions or during final votes on major issues, frequently does not allow for maximum participation. Accordingly, executives need to develop structures for rapid communication and decision making by small numbers of key people; delegation of wide discretion to one or two individuals on the scene; and the involvement of wider groups in the determination of basic goals and objectives rather than detailed positions. Educating board members, clients, and staff that politics is "the art of the possible" is an important executive function.

Executives also must provide leadership to their boards and policy-making bodies on another vexing issue in the political arena. It is true that advocates of a particular course of action need not themselves propose solutions for the dilemmas facing legislators and/or administrators. However, there is need for the leaders of social agencies to think through what possible solutions for legislative issues are acceptable to them. To mention the most obvious: Will voluntary social agencies and their lay leadership be willing to support tax increases if they provide for more funding for social services?

Boards of Directors

Under the changed circumstances in which voluntary social agencies now function, their board of directors undoubtedly will assume a greater importance. On the one hand, they will no longer be faced with many of the federal or state regulations that, in effect, assumed many of their policy-making responsibilities. On the other hand, the same boards will be confronted with policy development on many of the issues previously discussed. Little in the experience of most board members individually or collectively will offer guidance in this work. The staff support and assistance provided the board by the agency executive therefore can be expected to assume increasing importance. Such an expanding role for the agency board is predicated not only on the need for increased decision making but also on the responsibilities of the board and its members in the vital areas of financial support, political action, and interagency negotiations. The assumption is also grounded in the continuing validity of lay governance of voluntary agencies.

This expanded role of the board is not without concern for the agency executive. It has been suggested that the power of the executive of a social agency is often in direct proportion to the power exercised by the agency board. In a time when negotiations between professionals of service-delivery systems and funding bodies resulted in the necessary resource procurement, the agency executive held considerable power. With the cessation of many of these resource channels, the development of alternatives will have to be pursued on many fronts. It may be expected that in dealing with legislators and lay leaders of central funding bodies, and in fund raising with the community at large, the agency board will play a significantly larger role. Agency executives will have to resolve their concerns about this change in their power in order to function effectively in this new environment.

To enable agencies to take advantage of the new environment, changes in the composition of board membership probably will take place. Whereas in recent years major emphasis was placed on citizen participation, it is now likely that board recruitment efforts will focus on "community influentials." There will probably be numerous demands for the participation of those community leaders who have exhibited an interest in social-service issues and are known to have influence with people with means, political power, and/or access to private resources. To the extent that direct fund raising by an agency is contemplated, the inclusion of board members who themselves have significant means is a logical first step. None of these steps inherently preclude continued citizen and/or client participation on the agency board. However, it is likely that this will be of lesser concern, and efforts must be made to maintain such participation or develop alternatives, such as advisory groups and board committees including non-board members, to utilize the important input the agency can derive from it.

A uniquely difficult situation will be faced by those voluntary agencies and citizen organizations that are geographically based and often represent single ethnic constituencies. The same may be true for some single-issue groups. These groups will be confronted with the need to recruit influential board members from outside their communities and possibly outside their interest group as well in order to assure themselves access to established power. Executives and other staff working with such organizations face the prospect of helping local leadership to give up a degree of local control over their own organizations. The change may be so wrenching that it may not be feasible for some groups and possibly should not even be considered even though funding and effectiveness may be seriously curtailed.

Agency executives used to dealing with board members who were primarily citizen or client representatives may have to reorient the manner in which they function with their boards. The board members who may be recruited as best able to help the agency will come with both different life experiences and different expectations from the executive (Weinberger 1974). They will probably require much less help in understanding the role and function of a board member, will be more concerned about the financial and business operations rather than the specifics of the services being provided, and may well have different expectations concerning the attention given to their suggestions as well as their individual needs than citizen representatives on the board. Efficient management will be a fundamental expectation of all board members (Turem and Born 1983). Most important, they will probably expect to function much more independently on behalf of the agency in the general community. New channels for communication, relationships, and consultation between these board members and the agency executive will need to be developed. Education about the roles of board members will be an increasingly important executive function.

On the other hand, the agency executive should be aware that these board members will provide the agency, and the executive particularly, with a much wider range of information than did the citizens of the local community or clients of agency services. This information includes the professional and personal knowledge and contacts of board members, their understanding of other community developments, and their general knowledge of legal requirements, business conditions, financial options, and similar issues.

In those agencies where there has been ongoing participation from influential members of the general community, there has been some concern in recent years about a "new breed" of board members. Essentially, these are young professional or business executives, highly trained in the most advanced methods of management, communications, and financial operations, who tend to focus on the results and effectiveness of programs rather than on process or byproducts. Since their orientation frequently differs drastically from that of the traditional training of social-agency executives, a number of these executives have not been able to cope successfully, and some have lost their position as a result. Social-agency executives of the future can anticipate the need for a new level of integration of social values and managerial effectiveness. Some executives will want to consider additional training in administration.

This is not to suggest that this new breed of board members has no commitments to social values or agency goals. Those who agree with the social philosophy of the Reagan administration may well be willing to act on their convictions by aiding voluntary agencies in various roles. Still further, new roles and styles of board members do not mean that traditional board functions should be eliminated nor that all board members should be drawn from such backgrounds. Difficult as this new breed of younger community leaders may be for agency executives, their early identification and recruitment to agency boards will be a distinct advantage for the agency that locates, involves, and thereby utilizes the skills and energies of the next generation of community leaders.

Conclusion

It has been said that the influence of the British Empire lasted as long as it did because it did not seek to solve problems but rather to live with them. That perspective can be of considerable value to executives of voluntary agencies, provided they recognize that it contains much truth and an important fallacy. The much vaunted British habit of "muddling through" will not be an acceptable style for agency executives in the 1980s. Neither will "business as usual" be acceptable. The consequences of a reduction in resources must be faced and dealt with. For the short term this may mean reorganization through retrenchment of personnel and reductions in service. For the longer range, it will mean involvement in strategic planning and reorientation of the agency based on the decisions that result from such planning. The executive who wishes to bring his agency through the 1980s can avoid neither the short- nor the long-term approach.

At the same time, the British imperial policy of waiting for the dust to settle offers an important insight. Some fears about possible actions by the Reagan administration have already proven exaggerated. Congress, the courts, and some state governments have already rejected some proposals of the current federal administration. Political pressures and unavoidable needs have combined to delay or cancel other plans of the administration. Ideology has not proven all pervasive; witness the shift from the administration's advocacy of child care by parents to its more recent stance encouraging development of day-care centers by business and industry with federal tax write-offs and other inducements. For the short range, reductions in resources and services for people in need appear unavoidable. For the longer range, a continuation of current administration policies could actually prove a stimulus for nonprofit voluntary agencies in our social structure.

To take advantage of opportunities, it is important for voluntary agency executives to understand that the advent of the Reagan administration produced two major changes in the social-service structure of the United States. The more immediate—and therefore the better recognized—change is curtailment of federal funds available for social-welfare programs. For the long range the philosophic stance of the Reagan administration, which questions government's responsibility to address many of the social problems of this country, is a far more fundamental issue than that of the level of funding for any one program. The executives of voluntary agencies will need to be social statesmen who address this issue in almost every aspect of their professional activities even while they deal with the more immediate financial concerns. If social services are to devolve from the federal level, so must the social policy on which these programs are based. A denial of governmental responsibilities for various populations in need of help need not itself be a denial of public responsibility. Still further, responsibility to help need not in itself mean the delivery of direct services. The alternative, usually termed "nonservice approaches," can be of help, if not of direct service. Lay and professional leaders of voluntary agencies should engage in the development of such approaches and utilize their results.

A growing conservatism, if it continues in this country, need not represent the rejection of a helping hand for people in need. Rather, it would endeavor to substitute other hands for those of government. In these emerging trends there are important opportunities for voluntary social agencies. They are very well positioned, by experience, personnel, auspices, and many other factors, to serve as the alternative helping hands as those of government are withdrawn. Moreover, the more marked the withdrawal of government, the more will the voluntary agencies have legitimate claims for support by the general public through financial contributions, gifts in kind, and volunteer service.

The potential difficulty in such an appeal for increased support is that an increasingly conservative society is likely to be more judgmental with regard to the "worthiness" of the people to whom it will extend help. It is therefore possible, if not likely, that agencies in the voluntary sector will position themselves to provide services for population groups that are more appealing to the general public and raise fewer doubts about meriting support. While the general public is, on the one hand, likely to encourage innovations to provide services with increasing cost effectiveness, it will in all likelihood not be willing to support populations groups or activities that deviate widely from accepted social norms. The stimulation of understanding for such groups and their legitimate needs, if not their legal rights, will challenge social-agency executives and their staffs both in their professional roles and personal values. Some examples of refusal of service to nonpaying clients by agencies have already emerged. Human considerations aside, such policies, if generally applied, are likely to be counterproductive for these agencies.

A drastically different situation is likely to prevail as far as financial resources are concerned. Even if there had been no change in the philosophic stance of the federal administration, we would still be confronting reductions in financial resources for human-service programs. The impact of the recent recession and the major transition in which American industry is currently engaged are too well known to require discussion here. Suffice it to say that for the 1980s economic conditions are likely to be such that we will not again see the extensive resources that were available in the last few decades. Long-range economic forecasts give some hope that different circumstances will prevail in the 1990s and may therefore offer additional encouragement for social-agency executives. While an administration motivated by a different social philosophy might have made its reductions in resources in a different manner, reductions would have occurred all the same.

As suggested earlier, the need to make choices and to set priorities is unavoidable. It has been suggested that in spite of extended discussions over a period of many years, few good instruments for the objective measurement of program effectiveness have been developed. While there is validity to this claim, agency executives need to be very clear that such priority decisions need to be made and will be made—with or without their cooperation. The role of the executive should be to give direction and focus to such determinations, bringing into consideration all of the relevant factors and such objective data as can be marshalled. In simplest terms, the setting of priorities involves the decision that one particular activity, service, person, or neighborhood is more important than another. The executive will be managing not only a data-collection process but one in which much individual and collective pain may have to be assuaged. The literature of evaluation research offers criteria that can be helpful in the setting of priorities.

Particular caution is in order with regard to the costs of services. In an era of declining resources, it is always tempting to focus on those services that produce at least partial reimbursement if not an actual profit. Voluntary-agency executives will need to recall that the mission of most of their agencies includes service to those unable to pay; they must develop responses that continue to allow such service. This is likely to involve efforts in board education and interpretation to financial supporters of the agency as well as to the clients themselves. It will probably also mean an increasing role for coordinating agencies such as the United Way, federations, and social-service planning councils, who may be called upon to coordinate the sharing of the burden represented by clients whose needs cannot be addressed by any one agency. A similar coordinating role may also evolve for the same bodies in dealing with that clientele least likely to elicit public understanding and support. The executives of voluntary social agencies will go through the 1980s on a narrow path strewn with obstacles and pitfalls. What makes the journey worthwhile is the recognition that their agencies and services assume an increasing importance to many people in need as government reduces its role in the funding, sponsorship, and regulation of social services.

Any assumption that the concept of a welfare state can be abolished or even reversed as we approach the end of the twentieth century is highly unrealistic. Rather, before the end of the current decade it is likely that the United States will be judged in the international arena precisely on the extent to which it can be a successful welfare state. A country contending around the world for the political allegiance of millions of people in dozens of countries is in no position to claim that the well-being of the citizen is not a matter of governmental concern. Moreover, the world will look at this country as "one nation indivisible" rather than as fifty or more varying units. Therefore, to the extent that the United States government takes the position that the provision of social services is not an appropriate role for the national government, there will be new opportunities and needs for the voluntary sector to continue and expand its traditional functions. In doing so, it may actually assume a role in deciding whether the American political system still represents "the last best hope of mankind."

Note

1. Reprinted with the permission of the American Public Welfare Association from the *Washington Report,* Vol. 17, No. 5. Copyright 1982 by the American Public Welfare Association.

References

Berger, Peter L., and Richard John Neuhaus. *To Empower People: The Role of Mediating Structures in Public Policy.* Washington, D.C.: American Enterprise Institute for Public Policy Research, 1977.

Doherty, Robert B. "Getting Flexibility with Purchases of Service," *Human Needs* 1, nos. 4–5 (October–November 1972):5–7.

Finch, Wilbur A., Jr. "Declining Public Social Service Resources: A Manager's Problem," *Administration in Social Work* 6, no. 1 (Spring 1982):19–28.

Kamerman, Sheila B. "The New Mixed Economy of Welfare: Public and Private. *Social Work* 28, no. 1 (January–February 1983):5–10.

Leiby, James. *A History of Social Welfare and Social Work in the United States.* New York: Columbia University Press, 1978.

Lippitt, Ronald, and Larry Gamm, eds. *Journal of Voluntary Action Research.* Special Issue Interagency Collaboration 10, nos. 3–4 (July–December 1981).

Miringoff, Marc L. *Management in Human Service Organizations.* New York: Macmillan Co., 1980.

O'Connell, Brian. "Voluntary Agencies: What Price Independence?" *Channels* (Communication Forum), May 1977.

Tregoe, Benjamin B., and John W. Zimmerman. "How to Recognize and Implement Your Corporate Driving Force," *Enterprise* (30, no. 6 (May–June 1981):2–5. Reprinted by permission.

Turem, Jerry S., and Catherine E. Born. "Doing More With Less," *Social Work* 28, no. 3 (May–June 1983):206–10.

United Way of America. *What Lies Ahead: A New Look.* Alexandria, Va.: United Way of America, 1983.

Van Til, John. *"Toward Co-Production in the Human Services."* Unpublished ms. Annual Meeting, Association of Voluntary Action Scholars, August 1982.

Weaver, Edward T. "Blurred Roles Plague Public, Private Agencies," *American Public Welfare Association Washington Report* 17, no. 5 (June 1982):1, 4, 7.

Weinberger, Paul E. "Executive Inertia and the Absence of Program Modification," In Paul E. Weinberger, ed. *Perspectives on Social Welfare.* New York: Macmillan Co., 1974.

Woocher, Jonathan S. "The Politics of Scarcity: Jewish Communal Service in an Era of Resource Pressure." *Journal of Jewish Communal Service* 58, no. 3 (Spring 1982):189–95.

5 State Politics Is the Name of the Game

Joseph J. Bevilacqua

Introduction

According to Justice Louis D. Brandeis,

> "It's one of the happy incidents of the federal system, that a single courageous state may, if its citizens choose, serve as a laboratory, and try novel social and economic experiments without risk to the rest of the country" (Jehl 1983).
>
> State government is where many political newcomers get their start. They are often full of enthusiasm and they haven't made a lot of deals. (Remember, most state campaigns cost a fraction of what it takes to get to Washington.) Some state offices are obscure enough to enable good people to slip in unnoticed by the interest groups.
>
> Then, too, while there is a shortage of lobbyists crawling around Sacramento, Albany, and even Helena, Montana, the special interest logjam can be a bit looser in the states than in gridlocked Washington, D.C. On top of this, needs at the state level frequently are more defined, and solutions can be more practical and concrete. It's one thing to frame a housing program for Iowa City and Des Moines. Then toss in Anchorage, Miami, Detroit, and the South Bronx, plus a bevy of congressmen from well off suburbs who need to bring home some bacon of their own, and you begin to have real problems (Jehl 1983).

It is unfortunate that the great attention paid to state government during the 1980s has the makings of a fad. Many of us, particularly professionals in the human services, seem astonished that state government is alive and well. I say unfortunate, because as a fad, it will assume a transitional posture for many professionals, and the substance of state government as a significant arena of action will not be well understood.

I believe there is a negative bias in many professionals' view of state government. There is an acknowledgement of the important functions of running prisons, mental hospitals, and helping the poor. There also is the stereotypical perception of patronage, inefficiency, and bureaucratism at its worse. The general sense is that state government performs important functions but that it does not look for excellence in its medical care or competence in its social-services intervention. This is admittedly a harsh view, but not too far off the mark of how state government has been traditionally perceived.

There clearly have been changes in the management of state government. The caliber of those involved in both elective and administrative roles is more sophisticated. Services in health and welfare have become more professional, and these programs have gained greater visibility through the actions of the courts and advocacy groups (Bradley and Conroy 1983). If, then, the role of state government has been legitimized and is an important focal point of government, and indeed is more than a passing fad of a national administration (as I believe it is), how can human-service interests share in this development?

A first important question is: What primary value is attached to the political systems in the states? Lynn has suggested that "economy and efficiency are salient issues in the states and nothing is likely to alter that picture" (1980). Of course, the human services, particularly health care, the mental disabilities, and social services, are neither efficient nor economical. The federal government has, since the mid-thirties, provided major impetus to upgrading these services; state participation has been at best ambivalent. Higher standards and regulatory pressure have come from Washington. Interestingly, the one area where the states have always provided the major share of the resources has been mental health, but until relatively recently they were considered hardly effective (Bevilacqua 1982). The issue of efficiency and economy—even more prevalent today, with the New Federalism—makes it more difficult for human services affecting the poor, the mentally disabled, and the prison population to compete with other services such as "business interests, liquor, highways, racetracks," and the like (Lynn 1980, p. 19).

Against this specific value set of the state political system, an approach to accessing must identify a framework in which an analysis can take place. It is not an elegant theoretical framework. It is rather a set of practical assumptions that I have derived from my state experience, assumptions that make sense to me. These are preceded by a number of trends that describe the contemporary scene in state government as it relates to human-service activities.

The Rapprochement between the State System and Human Service—Five Trends

First, the traditional state agency organization has focused on a particular physical or mental disability or on a particular service orientation. A "department of mental health" or "department of social services," for example, may need to give way to a more general designation.

Task forces, blue-ribbon commissions, and the like have been the usual avenue to moving beyond the agency boundary. Sometimes locating a function within the governor's office gives it more clout, but it is of limited duration. Service integration into larger domains of secretariats have had mixed success. Structures that retain flexibility, identity, and the ability to respond relatively quickly, while maintaining the capacity for innovation, are the ideal. Thinking through these dimensions will become more and more important in the years ahead.

Second, the type of budget development that reflects agency boundaries must give way to one that articulates a clearer relationship between client need, cost, and organization. The organization and management of these services must be driven by client need and cost; too often it is the reverse. Residential services, for example, are required by many clients whose needs cut across agency lines. Proper integration of this kind of program is ignored when each agency-focused budget dominates.

This, of course, is the operational side to the first general point made above. The political dimensions of efficiency and economy have been identified. We have not devised budgets that can address problems that go beyond agency boundaries. State legislators and executive offices will increasingly look more closely at budgets for crosscutting potential; the domain of health or social services may be in a housing or rehabilitation program. Budgets will be forced to have that kind of flexibility.

Efforts in previous years to develop program budgeting have not fared well because neither the relationship between agencies nor the impact on programs has been addressed. Primary budgetary attention has been given to the agency and not to the program. All the formal and informal attributes of organizational life place an emphasis on agency sustenance rather than on program or service effectiveness.

Consider the strength of bureaucracies, organized labor, and the guild orientation of professions. You can see how formidable the agency becomes and how difficult it is to change its direction.

Third, constituency development must be more broadly based and defined, especially as it pertains to state and local groups.

A movement has developed to temper the special-interest dominance at both state and national levels. Special-interest groups in human services are, at best, uneven and, at the worst, in disarray. The success of major breakthroughs in the field of mental retardation can be largely attributed to an effective and aggressive constituency. It is apparent, however, that single interests will be less effective as government at the state level becomes increasingly political. The increased competition for resources will require a reexamination of how human-service constituencies mount their efforts.

How major issues develop and acquire sufficient consensus is a complex process that is not well understood. How they are sustained is equally unclear. We do know, however, that a favored place in the political sun is not permanent. There is a rhythm to issues that dominate the political field. Poverty dominated the 1960s; environmental issues, the 1970s; and in the 1980s, education is emerging as a favorite topic of attention.

Behind these patterns, of course, are the various interest groups. The "band wagon" effect is not unusual. More important is staying power. This is the factor that the broader-based constituencies must address. The problems of mental illness, poverty, child abuse, and the like are not dealt with by a reformist strategy alone. The remarkable success of improving the life of mentally retarded persons in this country has come about through a persistent and consistent approach, which has included:

1. national, state, and local organizations with consistent policy objectives
2. clear ideology: mental retardation is not a disease
3. active engagement of families of the mentally retarded
4. multipronged program approaches including education, habilitation, and residential care as a core part of the needed actions
5. major legislation dealing with programs and funding as well as standards
6. use of the courts to challenge state government to do better
7. acceptance of the reality of the disability while realizing that its impact can be managed.

These activities cut across professional disciplines, political parties, and social clases. In a real sense they form a prototype of success in forging a broad-based constituency.

Fourth, technical issues, professional services, and the administration of these enterprises are essentially political activities. Their control and operation do not exist at single points in the state or local government, nor are they the sole province of professional disciplines.

The relationships betwen management technology and professionalism will be under greater scrutiny as competition for access to the state system intensifies. The traditional guild mentality will be dysfunctional. Increasingly, staffs of important legislative committees are individuals trained and educated in public and business administration, law, and economics. The basic human-service disciplines, such as social work, medicine, and psychology, are seen as neither relevant nor germane to state government human-service management. Failure to understand this seriously hinders our competitive capacity. Lynn points out:

> Though state human services organizations seem large to state legislators, they are small relative to federal bureaucracies. Because of this, government at the state level seems inherently more penetrable—though not, of course, always penetrated—by elected officials. Except where governors and legislatures are ineffective, or where an agency facility such as a state hospital plays a large role in a legislative district, "iron triangles" (unbreakable alliances among state agency officials, interest groups, and key legislators) are less common in state government, at least in human services (1980, p. 18).

Professional disciplines too rarely see the necessity of giving equal weight to the political requirements of "economy and efficiency" and the provision of services to those people defined as being in need. There are no easy answers to this dilemma. It appears to me that ritualism is sometimes pursued at the expense of efficiency and economy. Incredibly lengthy analyses, delayed decision making, and hiding behind professional culture often obstruct implementation. We seem to find ideology where none exists.

An interesting example from our social work makes the point. The settlement: house movement has been rediscovered and touted as a new program for the chronic patient in the community. Unfortunately, social work has abandoned this approach in their education for practice, and others have been left to sing its virtues. Professional education must remain relevant to practice needs. Too much distancing from the needs causes a credibility problem for a given profession. In state government, this is sensed very quickly.

There is no single resolution to the question of states' responsibilities and human values as they relate to human services. Each state must evaluate this question. The diminishing federal presence and the absence of categorical mechanisms will make the value choices more immediate. This may be the ultimate political question. As Lynn has pointed out:

> The impression is inescapable that state officials would mix and match human services resources in different ways if not for Federal categorical restraints. Professional human service agencies, and their associated interest groups, in general, do not have the same standing

with governors, legislators, and county commissioners as they do in Congress (1980, p. 18).

Fifth, the judiciary and the media have played important roles as instruments for promoting advocacy. The judiciary is, of course, the third branch of government. The media is commonly referred to as the "fourth estate."

The full impact of the court as an agent of social change has yet to be fully evaluated (Herr, Arons, and Wallace 1983). A number of class-action suits, particularly those affecting the mentally disabled, have gained national attention and have brought focus to issues such as adequate staffing, right to treatment, and right to refuse medication, among others. Currently there appears to be a slowing down of litigation and some reexamination of other methods that might be less costly and more conducive to cooperation between the state and certain advocacy organizations.

Involuntary commitment statutes are being reexamined in many states, and a somewhat less libertarian view is emerging. This is in contrast to the late 1960s and early 1970s, when involuntary admissions statutes were made restrictive. This shift has been due in part to increased activity on the part of the families of the mentally ill. Those families now have a national organization as well as a number of state chapters under the rubric of the National Alliance for Mentally Ill.[1]

The media is a less predictable instrument for advocacy. It performs an overseeing function through the increased use of investigative journalism but is unpredictable in its application. Media needs are not necessarily consistent with client or public needs. None the less, the presence and power of the media, particularly television, is a reality and a force that is poorly understood by human-service managers.

At the state level, the government has been generally wary of advocacy. At the federal level, there has been a reduction in support for programs such as Legal Aid and the protection and advocacy aspects of the developmental disabilities program. The trend of a less activist court and unpredictable media attention spells an uncertain future for advocacy.

A Set of Assumptions

Managers and administrators, in the last analysis, rely on their own judgment and vision to make decisions. The context for judgment and vision will vary, of course. In government, the degrees of freedom in decision making are markedly different from those in private industry. Significant differences exist even between levels of government.

There are, however, certain assumptions that taken together form a framework against which one can review management behavior and possibly distinguish between success and failure. The framework provides at least some degree of probability toward realizing successful outcomes or, just as important, avoiding serious failure. I consider the following subjects important:

professional values

political ideology

dual aspects of the management role

leadership and turnover

placement of actor and patterns of action

elective and appointive relationships

staff and level of influence

budget

constituencies

Professional Values

A given professional discipline will have certain inherent values that may be inconsistent with the normative trends of the setting in which the discipline operates. Traditional mental health practitioners, for example, who assume administrative roles as commissioners of state agencies often reflect this inconsistency more directly than professionals trained in public administration or the law. Clearly, understanding these inconsistencies is important. The value of efficiency and economy inherent in state government is a case in point. The arbitrariness of political decisions affecting resource allocation, priorities, and legitimacy is not usually part of the practitioner's process of judgment and practice. By emulating the private-practice model of medicine, other professions, such as social work, psychology, and nursing, have increasingly "creamed" the "ability to pay" client and have left those unable to pay to be served by the public sector.

Classic values such as self-determination and freedom of choice become issues of compromise in settings where the clients are poor, chronically disabled, or where their behavior is sufficiently deviant to disturb community norms. Commitment laws and hospital accreditation standards are examples of processes that institutionalize norms whose ends may be inconsistent with certain professional values.

An illustration of this dilemma can be seen in the struggle of the Joint Commission on Accreditation of Hospitals to develop standards that will satisfy public and private hospital needs, and attend to the professional mores of medicine as well as those of a host of other disciplines. The trouble, of course, is that psychiatric hospitals and general medical hospitals have different requirements, and public and private psychiatric hospitals have very different capacities and capabilities. Attempting to draw together a set of standards that will apply to all these elements is difficult. The most vulnerable units will be the public mental hospitals. If they are put in the position of being unable to meet these standards, a further polarization of mental-health care occurs, affecting practice and constraining the role of the state as it attempts to accommodate to this problem.

The professional who attempts to manage this issue, in his role as state administrator, will be caught between a number of conflicting demands, many of which will be value issues. It should be obvious that the resolution of the standards question I have identified will become a political issue. Exactly how, at this moment, is unclear. The process that I have described, however, is essentially a value issue. Often it is not seen as one, but whatever the resolution, you can be sure it will challenge a number of values. Double standards of care, professional credentials, financing mechanisms, and professional education are the more obvious ones.

It is at the state level of government where many of these issues are most visible and where their solutions rest within the political process. The policies that are developed, changed, and redesigned challenge a set of values that are diverse and often contradictory. Successful governmental managers must recognize and understand this process.

Political Ideology

"It is not an attempt to legislate morality," the Governor said when asked about his previous support for a uniform, 21 year old drinking age. "It's nothing I feel visceral about" (Richmond *Times Dispatch*, 1983).

This quote signifies a representative attitude of the pragmatism of most state governors. Ideological issues are not confronted unless they command a very broad mandate. And if such a mandate exists, confrontation has little utility, other than for rhetorical or ceremonial purpose.

Advocates for given idological positions do exist but not usually in the workaday government. The human-service agencies, transportation, commerce, and regulation, all involve degrees of ideology. However, the managers of these enterprises are very cautious in promoting any specific point of view. A kind of homogenization takes place.

And yet, issues such as the rights of the mentally disabled, necessary and appropriate care, mandated services, and the like are present and made visible through accrediting standards, certification procedures, evaluation, and, occasionally, either through the courts oversight activities or the legislature. Dealing with ideology directly is usually avoided. Interest groups and constituencies do move toward ideological positions, but even here they are usually narrowly drawn, unless coalitions are developed. The lives of coalitions, on the other hand, are short and do not have the sustaining power that ideology requires.

Does this suggest a flat and purely pragmatic arrangement? Is the government manager a neutral robot? No. The manager is neither strictly pragmatic nor indifferent to "visionary theorizing" (Webster's definition). The manager acknowledges numerous positions within the government. He also acknowledges that his particular area of interest in human services does not have a high priority base. Consequently, accessing the system requires deliberative behavior; it requires building into his organization technical competence, a good sense of values, and as broad a participatory engagement of outside forces as he can develop. And he maintains a focus on the purpose of the agency. That purpose requires more than ideology. Too often the professional in government assumes that having an ideology is sufficient. It is only a part of a larger process.

The Dual Aspects of the Management Role

The balance of the administrative role and its relationship to professional or technical skill is often misunderstood in political government settings. The administrator looks for feasibility in the action being contemplated. The professional desires freedom to perform his skill with minimal interference. One attempts to broaden the mandate as much as possible, while the other moves to narrow and isolate his application of skill. Both want to minimize interference, but for different ends.

This inherent conflict between the different roles has no prescribed course or simple formula. In the end, it reflects leadership quality and management style. Certain constants such as conflict, risk, uncertainty, vagueness, and crisis are always or nearly always part of the milieus of state government management. The use of self both as a leader and professional goes beyond the role inherent in the prescribed position. Factors such as timing, anticipating the blend of events, distinguishing between initiative and aggressiveness, and reading power scenarios of superiors, peers, and subordinates—all reflect an environment that can be molded to some extent but ultimately requires the action of the person. I am not suggesting a "who do you know" mentality; rather, I am asking how well the actor can gauge himself and what will be required of him as he examines the environment in which he must operate.

The National Association of State Mental Health Program Directors reports that it is not unusual for the tenure of commissioners in the United States to run on the average about eighteen months. Each year some nineteen states replace those in commissioner positions. Such a high turnover rate does not necessarily reflect incompetence. As a matter of fact, the screening of those positions is thorough and comprehensive. The professional credentials are usually scrutinized by peers at the request of the executive branch. Until fairly recently, little attention has been paid to such skills as working with legislators and constituency groups. No questions were asked about the commisioners' ability to articulate policy or to communicate information to audiences with, at best, mixed levels of understanding and interest. In the final analysis, the single most important attribute is the ability to convey the dual responsibilities of professional and administrator.

Leadership and Turnover?

The term of office for governor varies across the country. There is a one-term limitation for some, and for others a governor can succeed him- or herself without limitation. In any event, the position is never viewed as permanent and there is, consequently, a climate of urgency that pervades the accomplishments of the incumbent against the rhythm of the election cycle. Commissioners similarly have a lack of permanency, though the process of their assuming office is by appointment.

The turnover of leadership at the state level does impart a sense of style to state government. This can have consequences for the operation of the permanent state civil service. The system's ability to change, assume risks, and manage itself flexibly are, in important ways, reflective of the leadership it receives.

Placement of the Actor and Patterns of the Action

The state governmental system, of course, has the executive, legislative, and judicial branches. The management activity being addressed in this paper takes place primarily in the executive branch, with important linkages to the legislative branch. This system includes:

1. the organizational arrangements that a governor places in his office
2. the relationship of his immediate staff to the established agencies and their heads
3. the layers of hierarchical organizational activity between the governor and the agencies
4. the location of the budget office within the executive branch
5. the linkages between the three branches of government by identified individuals and their designated roles, or some combination of influence through role and person
6. key legislators and key committees and the dominant political party
7. significant actors not in the government who relate in some way to the decision-making activity of the governor

Governors are politicians. They have sought their office consciously and worked hard to attain it. They are ambitious and energetic. They are usually honest and care a great deal about doing a good job. They are not necessarily intellectual, but they are intelligent. Few governors are reformers or locked into ideological positions. They tend to be centrists and cautious in their actions. They are not usually risk-takers, and they assume positions on issues only after extensive consultation with many people. This brief sketch, though not applicable to any one governor, does focus on a generic goal of most governors: to achieve consensus with a stamp of personal identity. The implementation of action, given this paradoxical quality, rests ultimately with the staff he selects and how he organizes and utilizes that staff.

Understanding this pattern is not easy. We probably know more about the president of the United States and his White House operations than we know about governors and their staff activities. This is partially due to extensive media coverage of the national office and the usually superficial attention paid to state capitols. Analytic coverage of a governor's administration is generally thin, with more attention paid to the ceremonial than to the substantive. Notwithstanding this lack of in-depth visibility, it is important for state-government managers to understand, as much as possible, the arrangements and makeup of the governor's office. The style of governing will emerge from these activities.

The governor, as the chief executive officer of the state, more often than not will have appointed or reappointed the major agency heads in health, welfare, mental health, and the like. The status of these positions is not the same as the staff the governor brings with him when he assumes office or the group that will work directly out of his office.

These usually include a chief-of-staff, press secretary, and a host of young assistants usually inexperienced in government but enthusiastic, aggressive, and alert in their behavior. Many have been active in the governor's election campaign, and they know and understand the governor intimately. Actually, this staff knows the governor better than most other members of the administration. They serve as important gatekeepers to his office. Letters of complaint on a myriad of subjects go through their hands, and many of these letters obviously concern agency operations and services. Familiarity with this staff is important to assure the governor's awareness of agency activities and to provide necessary corrective information if a situation turns into a flap. Good working relationships are developed through prompt and efficient response to letters of inquiry and complaints. Positive agency support of the governor whenever possible (and preferably through agency initiative) is imperative.

States will vary on the organizational structures and layers of the executive branch. The important point is the type of access available to the agency. Usually the human services are not viewed as a high priority; as a result, routine mechanisms of access are insufficient. Considerable thought should be given to "getting the word" to the governor. Care must be taken that this process does not become manipulative; rather, he should receive the information he needs in order to know more about a particular subject or issue. This requires creative energy, confidence in the worth of the agency effort, and a strong desire to have the governor identify and involve himself with the agency in some way. This approach can include ceremonial activities, but more than ceremony is needed. Getting mental health or mental retardation on the governor's agenda and having him speak to the issues publicly help to broaden the access base of support from the executive office.

Constituencies and legislators also are important, for they communicate agency interest and efforts to the governor. Their access is different but no less important in providing information and knowledge. The agency must keep this in mind and generate information through these conduits, as well as through formal state bureaucratic structures.

An important office within the executive branch is the agency that develops the state budget. It is a critical link, and its director, because of his large responsibility, usually has high status in the governor's office. Often budget directors are seen as the "informal" governor, and because of their extensive involvement with all agencies, they assume a unique familiarity with the system. Consequently, their relationship with the governor himself is also unique. He sees them as a validating checkpoint. They become the repositories of institutional memory and a broker between the reality of the fisc and the many demands made upon state resources. The responsibility for revenue projections and expenditures makes this office an important data base for the governor. He uses it for planning as well as for successful implementation of his agenda. It can validate his promises to the electorate. The budget agency, sometimes called the Office of Management and Budget, or simply Administration, is "first among equals."

The agency head must have a fiscal staff who can negotiate and deal with its counterpart in the governor's office. The agency cannot, however, simply replicate the budget function. There must be a balance between the numbers and the programs. Too often budget offices within agencies are allowed to speak for the agency and to dominate staff actions at the expense of service responsibilities. The agency head must manage this tension between programs and budget staffs to assure that agency mandates are met.

Once the budget process within the executive branch is completed, it is presented to the state legislature, and a whole new set of relationships is played out. The money committees of both houses and their staffs begin the work of reviewing and building the budget to reflect the sentiments of the legislature. For some states the authority of the governor is paramount, and therefore the budget activities of the legislature are routine and uncontroversial. In a number of states, the legislature is a powerful and dominant force in building the budget. Factions, party rivalries, and the play of interest groups become important parts of this process.

Increasingly, state legislatures have developed their own budget staffs to do the work. Interestingly, concurrent work by the appropriation staff, the governor, the budget office, and the agencies is more and more common. This pattern of interactions has obviously complicated the process by making the issues involved more visible, lengthening time involvement, and modifying the roles of the different levels represented. A complex process becomes even more complex.

This system requires increased sophistication on the part of the agency in articulating its needs and developing strategies. It also brings more clearly into focus the political process and administrative-professional relationships. As can be seen, this process engages in varying degrees the other assumptions I have identified. It is when they are together that we see the full play of successful access.

Elective-Appointive Relationships

The degree of insulation that state agencies have from the ordinary political and elective process is important. The more obvious example is patronage, but equally important are the questions of how far down into the established beauracracies the appointments go, and how frequently the appointments are made.

I believe it fair to say that patronage is a vanishing personnel practice. Better educated personnel and the increased complexity of government have resulted in a more technically proficient work force. This development has depoliticized to some extent the relationship of elected officials to permanent state employees. Ironically, it has highlighted the closer relationship between the legislative and executive branches, for technical staffs now exist on both sides.

This suggests the greater importance of leadership at the agency level and the flexibility of personnel policies. Commissioners serve at the pleasure of the governor. The policy is less clear at the next level. Assistant commissioners and institutional directors, if permanent, can provide their own resistance to change. Too little attention has been given to this middle level of management.

Staff and Level of Influence

The focus here is on what staff or staffs. For example, the staff to the appropriation committees and the staff to the budget office and the governor's own staff form different relationships over different issues. Each relates differently to the state agencies. A power configuration can emerge, or degrees of influence can be identified, by the behavior patterns of these different staffs. The kinds of people who sit in these staff positions, their education degrees and experience, can be important in developing strategies and tactics both in the legislature as well as the executive branch.

Human-service agencies have paid too little attention to these patterns. Rarely is an attempt made to relate issues to staff configurations, yet these staffs are critical in moving the process of state government. Not simply a budget or a given policy but the basic purpose of the agency needs to be seen in relation to the character of these different staffs. In this way, better information systems are established, goals are more clearly drawn, and points of consensus are developed earlier and more easily. It is not the selling of the agency; rather, it is the recognition that, at the state level, linkages for support, promotion, and achieving economies of scale become management tools. They provide more options and create a greater variety of implementation approaches to meeting the purpose of the agency as well as complementing the intent of other state functions. Beyond the simple maintenance function, successful accommodation of agency purpose is clearly enhanced by this broader view as a regular mode of operation and not simply as a required application at certain times of the year.

Budget

Budget activities have a mystique all their own. In the general structure of budget preparations, there tends to be a kind of adversarial climate. Each agency is obviously promoting its interests, and the state budget office attempts to negotiate for the larger interests of efficiency, economy, and equity. The state budget office also serves as the direct staff to the governor, thereby managing his priorities.

When negotiations and revisions are completed, the governor formally presents the budget, which is now the administration budget, to the state legislature. This second phase is crucial and probably contains the most uncertainities. This phase is open to public hearings, and debate can be intense. The actors will be state officials, including the agency representatives as well as the interest groups and general citizens.

There are a number of phases involved:

1. Internal agency deliberations, which involve input from other agencies as well as from the field. These usually include the constituencies and interest vendors.
2. The agency presentation to the state budget office, where it becomes their document for negotiation.
3. Finalization of the governor's budget and presentation to the legislature.
4. The legislative money committees, where a final budget is processed and returned to the governor for his signature. It usually ends here, but if serious disagreement exists, the budget can be vetoed and returned for further negotiation.

Inherent in these phase sare numerous behind-the-scenes deliberations, both ceremonial and substantive. Exchange and trade, sometimes open and sometimes covert, take place. It is a complicated dance of partisan politics, technical information, and vested interests. The full play of values, ideology, and professional interests and skills takes place. In an important sense, this process represents success or failure of the agency, the budget administration, the governor, and the legislature. It is not necessarily a winner-take-all scenario, but the ritual does determine the focus of power and influence in a state.

Constituencies

Constituencies represent consumers of service, providers, advocates, and professional associations, to mention only the more obvious members. They are important. The direction and sustaining power of influence are also significant considerations. An agency without constituencies cannot compete for attention, resources, or legitimation. Constituencies are the bridge between the political, professional, and consumer interests. The constant tension over the competition for support requires consensus across interest groups. It is the achieving of consensus that is the main work of constituencies.

Conclusion

> Management means that attention should also be given to essential roles for governments, program design, linkages with agency strategy, developing linkages and reducing the insularity of human services. When their concerns are addressed, managerial performance can be improved (Agranoff 1983, p. 20).

This chapter has attempted to provide a primer on looking at one level of government—the state. It identified a selected contemporary trend and described a number of assumptions useful in examining and describing state government. A constant theme that underlies these assumptions is the ability of human services to enter into the governmental political system and compete for its share of resources and support. There is the recognition that human services, for a number of reasons, are hard pressed to overcome certain obstacles. I firmly believe that many of these obstacles can be addressed. This chapter offers a basic map to assist the practitioner in making his way through state government.

Note

1. National Alliance for Mentally Ill, 1200 15th Street, N.W., Room 400, Washington, D.C. 20005.

References

Agranoff, Robert, "The Public Management Challenge," *The New England Journal of Human Services* 3, no. 2 (1983):20.

Bevilacqua, J.J., ed. *Changing Government Policies for the Mentally Disabled.* Cambridge, Mass.: Ballinger Press, 1982.

Bradley, V., and J.W. Conroy. *Third Year Comprehensive Report of the Pennhurst Longitudinal Study.* Philadelphia: Temple University, 1983.

Herr, Stanley S., Stephen Arons, and Richard E. Wallace, Jr. *Legal Rights and Mental Health Care.* Lexington, Mass.: Lexington Books, 1983.

Jehl, D. "Stars of the States," *The Washington Monthly,* August, 1983, p. 48.

Lynn, L.E., Jr. *The State and Human Services.* Boston: MIT Press, 1980.

Richmond Times-Dispatch, Richmond, Virginia, 28 July 1983.

6

Resource Development as Executive Leadership

Roger A. Lohmann

Contemporary Challenges

The stark realities of Reaganomics have offered an unprecedented challenge to executive leaders in social services to develop new resources. During the past two decades, the discretionary grant has become the primary fiscal device for allocations decision making in the United States. At the same time, the implicit premise of discretionary grants, the "budget increment"—that annual, predictable and dependable increase in funding which allows evolutionary "growth" and gradual innovations—has become a standard assumption of executives everywhere (Wildavsky 1974).

If, however, gradual growth of the service state in this manner cannot be assumed, as in the years since 1980, the entire relationship between executive leaders and the future is altered. Under the condition of a "steady-state" future of incremental growth, the executive role in resource development is narrowly political: organizing and participating in pressure groups and coalitions directed at increased appropriations and "new program" development. (Mahaffey and Hanks 1982). Broader political or "planning" questions of defining the range and scope of service-delivery systems are effectively translated into narrow technical issues of resource availability and assigned to grant writers. At the same time, a sense of the future as a coherent whole is effectively lost through conversion into a series of annual increments.

Even a brief disturbance in the pattern of annual increase, however, tends to present a serious challenge to the public economy of discretionary social-service grants.

The years since 1980 have been a time for despair among personal-service leaders. Just about the noblest scenario that anyone held forth during this period was inherently regressive and timid: Concerted political action by sympathetic interest groups and newly formed coalitions *might* be powerful enough to stave off additional budget cuts and hold the line until 1984, when the election of a political liberal would restore normal funding to existing grant-in-aid programs and enact a program of national health insurance.

The widespread sense of despair and limits in the early 1980s has come about because personal service leaders are sufficiently realistic to realize that some very fundamental shifts have occurred in the political fabric of the "welfare state—American style," making further dramatic increases in the service state unfeasible or impossible. However, the ideology of the service state is so deeply ingrained in the thinking of most personal-care leaders that alternative futures, in which gradual and continuous expansion of public-service bureaucracies does not serve as the primary model of social change, appear equally impossible.

This chapter examines one possible alternative future for the "personal-care services" and the profession of social work (Morris 1979, Kamerman and Kahn 1976): the emergence of a "welfare society" in which personal-care services are delivered primarily by small-scale commercial enterprises, and social workers evolve from their present roles as public bureaucrats into autonomous professional entrepreneurs and "shopkeepers." Such a development is consistent with the classic argument of Wilensky and Lebeaux, who wrote: "Under continued industrialization all institutions will be oriented toward and evaluated in terms of social welfare aims. The 'welfare state' will become the 'welfare society' and both will be more reality than epithet" (1965, p. 147).

The underlying rationale for this development is twofold: There is a very large and growing need for personal-care services. Indeed, if current estimates are to be believed, the actual number of aged, disabled, dependent, neglected, abused, retarded, chronically and mentally ill, and others in need of personal-care services may exceed 30 million—more than 10 percent of the entire population. Even under the most optimistic of resource assumptions, restoration of annual increments (sustained growth of the public services budget *and* increased voluntary contributions), it is difficult to imagine future public resources adequate for this total need. Under present circumstances, where there are large and important disagreements over how to deal with these problems (e.g., the debates over institutionalization and community-based services) and a seemingly strong political momentum behind "negative budget growth," envisioning adequate levels of funding for personal-care services in the future becomes nearly impossible.

Except for the most ideologically blind, therefore, the need to discover new patterns of more effective resource develoment to supplement or even replace the present discretionary-grant system is obvious. The view presented here is that small-scale commercial enterprise, together with suitable public regulation, offers a reasonable alternative resource base for a major portion of existing personal-care service needs.

Personal Care and Personal Services

Personal-care services are the most recently emergent segment of a large, complex, and diverse personal-services industry in the United States. Personal services together are a large, but largely unmeasured factor in the American economy even today, and their prospects for growth are substantial. In the conventional social-work view, the goals of personal-care services make them necessarily products of public or voluntary enterprise. As we shall see, however, their similarities to other forms of personal service that are already fully commercialized suggests this issue may not be as open and shut as we have believed.

Personal-care services refers to that portion of the human services currently of greatest interest to social work, including foster care for children and adults, day care, home health programs, hospice services, family services, most types of counseling and therapy, services for the elderly, disabled, mentally ill, handicapped and abused, shelters, group homes, and similar support and maintenance arrangements. Purposely excluded from this conception are explicit medical services as well as elementary, secondary, vocational, and higher education, housing, and income-maintenance programs.

By virtue of their role in assisting in the tasks of everyday living, these personal-care services are related to other major segments of the personal-services industry in the United States, including "commercial" personal-service establishments such as pharmacies, barber shops and beauty parlors, grocery stores, dry cleaners and commercial laundries, and a class of independent service entrepreneurs, both paid and unpaid, including domestic workers, gardeners, housewives, babysitters, and live-in tutors.

Anyone who doubts the connections between personal-care services and these commercial personal services should examine closely the daily activities (not the practice philosophies) of, for example, Title XX service providers. These diverse services share marked tendencies toward small-scale service establishments (a "shop" mode of organization); no major significant recent advances in productivity such as those found in assembly-line manufacture (a craft orientation); the desirability of close personal (or, at least quasi-personal) relations between provider and consumer of the service, who must work together to "co-produce" the service; and marked problems in the measurement and control of service quality. Indeed, the problems of determining standards of a high-quality haircut, housecleaning job, or therapy session all share similar problems of subjectivity, taste, and expectation affecting the evaluative process. As a result, large-scale vertical integration is seldom an economic necessity in personal services, and there are few marked tendencies toward monopolistic control of personal care, despite seventy years of strictures by well-intended funding sources to avoid "duplication of effort" in public and voluntary personal-care services. Lubove cites a funding requirement by the Cleveland Chamber of Commerce in 1910, for example, "to cooperate with other charitable institutions in promoting efficiency and economy of administration in the charities of the city as a whole, and in preventing duplication of effort" (1969, p. 250). This sounds like it might have been written last week.

Traditionally, personal-care services, unlike the other personal services, have been organized as "voluntary" or "public" agencies. However, this is more a matter of political commitments than of economic necessity. The most critical economic factor here is "market failure" (Hansman 1980, 1981). As we shall see, this applies only to a small percentage of total personal-care service needs. The expectation has always been that voluntary or public funding could adequately finance personal-care services. No one has ever seriously argued that public and voluntary funding were already meeting needs, only that sustained future growth would eventually reach that point. Reaganomics has seriously dampened such optimism. If present trends continue, pressures may increase dramatically for the evolution of personal-care services away from the "service state" pattern of public support and toward diverse forms of "business" organization. In the process, personal-care services may come increasingly to resemble other sectors of the personal-service industry.

The most critical factor in this shift will be the need to generate resources (or "capital") adequate to the tasks at hand. As awareness of the need for personal-care service spreads, the need for capitalizing them may become so great and the recognition so widespread that it will overcome the traditional resistance of human-service providers to commercial ("for profit") activity. Three types of capital are most critical to personal-care services: Investment in plant, equipment, and other tangible assets; operating funds, necessary for the continued operation of services; and "venture capital" to allow initiative and innovative activity by individual service-producing units. While discretionary grants are concentrated primarily upon operating capital, the discretionary-grant system is notoriously weak in providing investment capital (seed money) or venture capital, most demonstration projects funding notwithstanding. Current government policies that allow third-party payment to both nonprofit and commercial establishments are doing much to facilitate this evolution—as in the case of nursing homes—by demonstrating the viability of commercial enterprise in human services.

In some ultimate sense, all of the resources (or capital) of personal-care services are vested in people; their intelligence, experience, patience, skill, and dedication represent the only real assets of most existing or foreseeable personal-care services. With the emergence of paid employment and professional careers as primary vehicles of service deliver, however, development of these resources has become overwhelmingly a question of raising money to purchase the necessary personnel times. Thus, as a practical matter, resource development in personal-care services today is primarily an issue of fund raising, or "capitalization." Donations and solicited contributions are the traditional fund-raising approach of the voluntary sector, while in the public sector there is typically a multistep process of tax collection, legislative allocations, and agency distribution of funds. In recent decades, the discretionary grant has been the foremost distribution arrangement in public and voluntary personal-care services. Personal-care services based on fees most closely approximate the commercial situation in the present personal-care services, and fee-based service delivery would almost certainly be a major element in any future commercialization of personal-care services. It is essential that we understand, therefore, why fee-based services are proving superior to other forms of resource generation, as well as what the limits of fee-based services may be.

The conventional approach to the problem of capitalizing personal-care services has been to assume that *all* types of personal care are inherently nonmarket in nature and that sale of such services inherently prostitutes the nature of the service relationship. From this point of view, therefore, personal-care services must be public enterprises, supported by taxes or donations. Strong ideologies grounded in American progressivism and British Fabianism have for decades supported this conclusion (Addams 1910, Crunden 1982, Mackenzie and MacKenzie 1977).

In *Breaking Even*, I reviewed the particular strengths and weaknesses of each of these resource development strategies as well as their historical context. (Lohmann 1980, pp. 59–79). I wish now to show how changes in the post-World War II era have made fee-based funding (and, consequently commercial services) increasingly possible, without solving the traditional limitations on public and voluntary funding.

Two problems have traditionally limited the effectiveness of voluntary fund raising for the support of personal-care services. First is the weakness or absence of reciprocity between personal-care service clients and givers, and second is the effect of the law of diminishing returns on consolidated fund raising.

"Giving" is a trait of most human cultures, although it takes many diverse forms (Mauss 1966, Titmuss 1970). A common theme in research is that the seemingly altruistic and self-denying act of giving a gift is, in reality, an interactive, reciprocal act defining the relationship between self and other, an affirmation of social bonds highly gratifying to the giver. Thus, a Pacific Coast native who gives away all his belongings in the traditional potlatch does so secure in the expectation of like return by his neighbors.

This "norm of reciprocity" appears to form the outer limit of voluntary contributions, with large contributions where it is present and small (or no) contributions where it is absent. In most instances today, religious, communal, familial, and other social bonds that might assure such reciprocity between voluntary donors, service staff, and clients of personal-care services are, from all appearances, either very weak or nonexistent, with the result that such contributions are extremely small in proportion to the total wealth of the society. Until such time as strong and real bonds can be established between givers and clients, the likelihood is that voluntary contributions will continue to be similarly limited. The perspective taken here is that for a family with a $40,000 income to give less than $200 to a charitable service is neither a particularly noteworthy gift nor a voluntary solution to the resource problems of personal-care service agencies.

In addition, it would appear that voluntary fund raising also has to contend with an effect of diminishing returns. The theoretical assumption in consolidated funding campaigns is that if agencies consolidate their efforts, equal amounts of funds can be raised at lower fund-raising cost. In many instances, however, it would appear that consolidation may also reduce disproportionately the size of contributions, thus becoming self-defeating.

Major weaknesses in the system of discretionary grants have limited the effectiveness of public sources for the support of personal-care services. The foremost problem has been that the dependence of personal-care services on the annual federal budget cycle necessarily structures instability into the system of organizing and delivering care, instability that has no direct relationship to the circumstances of either service provider or client. Such structured instability—sometimes mistakenly termed "social change"—creates artificial and irrational fluctuations in the availability and levels of service completely unrelated to need or demand. Although most such fluctuations since 1980 have been "downers," the entire history of public personal-care services features such "artificial" fluctuations.

Other factors built into the present discetionary-grant system work against stable, adequately funded services. The system of funding by grants, for example, together with express prohibition of agencies from keeping surplus funds, acts to guarantee levels of imprudent expenditure and increased cost. Further, in the present annualized system, no grant-funded agency has assurance of continued support beyond the present fiscal year and, thus, no real incentive to plan. In addition, the system of "competitive" funding awards means that agencies often invest much effort in fund raising with little real promise of return. A recent DHHS announcement, for example, indicated that in the previous fiscal year 5620 requests for grants were received, while 167 awards were made (Office of Health and Human Services 1982, p. 55112). This is a success rate of less than 3 percent!

In the final analysis, however, the greatest problem with discretionary grant funding is the political limit of the federal income tax. It is sobering to remember that the "golden age of social services" (roughly 1968 to 1980) was accentuated at *both* ends by tax cuts. Public revenues can be a sufficient source of capital for personal-care services only when two conditions are met: there must be strong, widespread public support for personal-care services, and that support must be translated directly into widespread public willingness to accept higher rates of taxation to support those same services. Tax revenues can never be sufficient to underwrite the staggeringly large cost of the needed personal-care services in any society where abhorrence of high taxes and big government is as great as it is in the United States. The democratic service state will fail in this country because the American people are unwilling to meet its necessary conditions. The political issue of greatest significance for social work, therefore, is whether to attempt to impose such spending upon an unwilling and reluctant public.

This brings us, then, to the advantages of fees and, through them, to the possibility of commercialization. There have traditionally been two primary objections to fees in personal care. On the one hand, it is often objected that it is morally wrong to assess persons a fee for helping them. If such moral objections are valid, of course, they rule out the moral acceptability of paid careers in organized services as well, for precisely the same arguments would hold that paid employment in helping is also immoral.

The second objection is partly moral and partly pragmatic. If clients must pay for services, it is often suggested, the most needy are excluded by definition. How can one assess fees to clients too poor to pay for them?

The pragmatic part of this issue might be termed, following Hansman (1980, 1981), "market failure" and relates directly to the traditional case for public and voluntary funding: If there is insufficient private demand for a good or service, because of the poverty of prospective clients, and yet overriding arguments for the provision of such goods or services, that provision must be publicly or voluntarily funded. To this extent, personal-care services must live within the "poverty of the public sector," which Galbraith so accurately predicted three decades ago (1958). However, if market failure due to poverty is extended as an argument to cover public support for all types of personal care, an already threadbare public purse would be completely exhausted. To this extent, public funding of all personal-care services is improbable at best.

The moral part of this issue also follows directly from presumed market failure: Is it not a moral outrage to attempt to sell needed services to those too poor to afford them? (Just as it would be outrageous to attempt to sell water to a poor person dying of thirst?)

Together these moral and practical objections are sound and must be considered. However, they do not extend to the nonpoor, nor have they been notably successful as arguments in support of increased public or voluntary service funding to needed levels.

This leaves social work, then, with a dilemma of major proportions: If the commercialization option is rejected on moral grounds, or on behalf of the poor, two prospects exist: One is for a future in which large personal-care service needs go unmet, and the other is for non-social-work occupations and interests to develop the available commercial markets, as they are already doing in long-term care.

If, on the other hand, social work attempts to meet a larger portion of existing needs through commercialization, the prospect is almost certain that the tendencies toward a dual service-delivery system will be extended and enhanced: one system (for those who could afford to pay) would be fee-based, and another (presumably financed by existing public and voluntary funds) would be for those too poor to purchase their own services. One way out of this dilemma is to redesign the "technology" of personal-care service and improve productivity to the point where even the poor can afford the needed services and to supplement the incomes of the very poor to enable them also to purchase needed services.

Ultimately, then, we are left with the issue of price. *The key question for the future development of personal-care services along commercial lines is whether adequate service packages can be organized and delivered at prices that clients are able and willing to pay.* While it may at first appear insurmountable, this problem could yield to a variety of schemes for long-term financing, insurance, and other financing arrangements of contemporary consumer society.

Social Policy or Subsidy?

A commercialization strategy would require a dramatic reconceptualization of the role of government—particularly the federal government—in personal-care service provision. Under the discretionary-grant system, the issue has become decidedly confused as the federal role has evolved increasingly beyond the fiscal and into substantive issues of social policy. The formal design of programs such as Title XX sets federal "goals" which, it is suggested, are "implemented" through networks of purchase of service contracts and intergovernmental transfer payments. This design structures ambivalence into the existing system, for nonprofit and commercial corporations—autonomous and self-governing under state law—become vehicles for the implementation of federal policy. However, law and tradition preclude effective federal control over this system. A wiser course would be to limit the federal role in personal-care services to providing initial capitalization through subsidies and tax policies, and to subsidizing support for the very poor. Personal-care services might then be developed as a free-standing industry, not an uncontrollable appendage of federal social policy.

At the same time, the federal government could be taken entirely out of the sphere of quality control. It simply lacks the constitutional, political, and legal basis for effective action in this area, as nearly two decades of ineffective efforts to introduce cost-controls in health care amply demonstrate. Under the American constitutional system, the police powers of state government offer a more reasonable base for such regulation.

Redefining the problem of funding personal-care services as a problem of capitalizing new service industries in an emerging welfare society does not, by itself, resolve any of the major issues involved. In fact, it merely sharpens the increasingly poignant dilemma already well understood by many social-welfare leaders: If, on the one hand, personal-care services continue to insist on the necessity of public and nonprofit enterprise, the future can be expected to be a direct continuation of the past, with chronic resource shortages infrequently interrupted by short bursts of new funding and periodic outbursts of public indignation at highly publicized improprieties which serve to further undermine the weak credibility of such services. If, on the other hand, these same services were to opt for commercialization, there is at least a possibility that the problem of capitalization could be solved, but at the cost of raising a host of quality-control and consumer-protection issues.

The critical question for personal-care leaders raised on the progressive ideology is whether high-quality services can be delivered "for a profit" by commercial organizations? If so, what circumstances would support such quality service delivery? The question is reasonable and deserves further consideration.

Some of the commercial possibilities can be hinted at merely by noting how many of our present activities of daily living are supported by commercial services: grocery stores, repair shops, cleaners, restaurants, taxis, pharmacies, news information and entertainment services, barber and beautician shops. The principal difference between these services and personal care may be less a matter of the inherently non-market character of the latter than it is of the necessity to "socialize" the risk involved in defining markets and standardizing service technologies for such personal services. Once standardized, many current forms of personal care could become commercially viable. To take a simple example, it would have been unthinkable to offer widespread counseling services through a private practice in most American cities thirty years ago. Today, however, such services are becoming commonplace. Why? In part, because accreditation, licensure, market pressures, and other factors have introduced a modicum of standards which allow the informed consumer a basis for risking the expenditure against the chance of receiving help. It is not difficult to think of many other services in which a comparable progression makes sense: senior activity centers, retirement counseling, adult day care, information and referral, and so forth. In each case, the issue remains the same: whether our resistance to the idea of such services being offered commercially exceeds our discomfort with the alternative, large numbers of potential clients going unserved.

A Privatization Strategy

What actions would be necessary for commercialization of personal-care services to succeed, not only in making a profit, but also in providing effective services? At least six major problems areas can be identified.

First, it will be necessary to make room in general and specific personal-care ideologies for realistic and legitimate views of markets, competition, profit, and private business activity. (Social work might look to other "shopkeeper" professions like dentistry or pharmacy for specific guidance here.) There are two broad ways in which such an ideological transition might occur. To the extent that there is a degree of historical necessity and inevitability to the need for personal-care services, it is entirely possible that we may see tendencies toward a kind of Paretoan "circulation of elites" in which leadership in personal-care industries passes gradually from die-hard progressives and public social-welfare types to those more sympathetic to private and commercial outlooks. To some degree, such a process has already partially occurred, as businessmen have come to replace old-line progressive elites on boards of directors and funding agencies, and as MBA and MPA degree-holders have entered the ranks of agency administration in larger numbers.

A distinct alternative, of course, would be conscious reformulation of the practice ideologies of social work and related disciplines, in effect rethinking the relationship between service and profit. Very few people today would seriously argue that a career in personal-care service is the altruistic, self-denying activity portrayed in the ideals of the progressives (Addams 1910, chapter 1; Crunden 1982). Recent work in organization theory has considerably muddied the dividing line between public and private action, particularly on these crucial questions of self-interest and private gain (Downs 1969). It is simply untenable to suggest, for example, that your local barber is a robber baron and your local fire chief a saint.

For the "intelligentsia" of personal-care services—those leaders in universities, government agencies, and others involved in opinion formation and knowledge transmission—such a transition may be particularly difficult, since it involves challenging some intrenched truisms dating back to Sinclair Lewis, Thorsten Veblen, Karl Marx, and beyond. However, for many agency practitioners, who are less steeped in the alienation of modernism and whose daily life involves significant contact with businessmen active in the sale of personal services, such a transition may be considerably easier and less heretical. If such a transition in ideologies occurs in social work, therefore, it is less likely to come from the universities than from the administrative offices of agencies.

Second, for a transition to commercial services to prove viable, an effective system of public (state-level) regulation is essential. Concerted efforts are needed, for example, to discover what types of service are inherently nonmarket in character (such as prisons and public welfare) and what types might be commercially possible. Further, as noted, effort is necessary to standardize service technologies, articulate clear and recognizable outputs of service, and develop clear and explicit quality standards for public regulation.

Three steps will be necessary for the emergence of adequate systems of regulation. First, there is a need for expert consensus among researchers and practitioners about what is important and critical in the case of various types of personal care. Lack of such consensus is a major impediment to control of service quality today and should be a high priority whether or not commercialization occurs. If services are commercialized, such consensus is imperative.

Second, there is the need for widespread public education programs to create informed consumers for various service industries. Recent experiences in educating health consumers on the importance of prenatal care and on the necessity for regular cancer, heart, and other screenings leave limited room for optimism here.

Third, full commercialization of the personal-care services will almost certainly require the development of a range of new financial and fiduciary institutions falling roughly under the heading of what Titmuss called "occupational and fiscal welfare." In many cases, the objections to fee-based services turn out to be a less a matter of exceeding the overall ability of a client to purchase such services as they are a matter of appropriately spreading the cost over a sufficient period of time and/ or pooling risks over a sufficiently large pool of insured persons. The former strategy in the immediate postwar years made homeowners out of millions who were, on the surface, "too poor" to afford housing, and the latter protects all of us from such risks, for example, as automobile accident, fire, or theft.

In some cases, such possibilities are almost common sense. All employers in large urban areas could routinely insure their employees against such threats as mugging, divorce, or rape, for example, with adequate counseling service provided as needed. The case for rape-victim-counseling insurance seems at least as strong as the argument that such services are a public responsibility.

The general need for insurance coverages and employee fringe benefits is already widely recognized and understood. It remains only to extend them to personal-care settings (a task likely to be considerably easier than securing adequate, sound public funding for similar services). It is curious indeed that so many Americans have adequate protections against rare tropical diseases and poisonous spider bites, while they have no protection at all against the financial or personal implications of being abused, depressed, divorced, having to care for a senile parent, spouse, or retarded child, coping with the impending death of oneself or a significant other, and other commonplace events toward which personal-care services are addressed.

Fourth, it is important to recognize the attractiveness of the relationship between scale and effectiveness in personal-care services. Large-scale, corporate service delivery is, in most instances, not noticeably more humane or reasonable than public bureaucratic handling of the same services. Much contemporary criticism of modern business—credit cards, banks, insurance companies—is directed at service enterprises. Generally speaking, most of us prefer some level of intimacy and personal attention in personal services, whether from a butcher, insurance agency, or therapist. While some service enterprises today are vertically integrated into gargantuan national and international conglomerates, the economic necessity of such integration is anything but clear cut, and personal services are probably most effectively handled as small-scale operations. In particular, for those service enterprises where tangible goods are not a critical factor of production and centralized purchasing may be advantageous, it seems likely that "small is beautiful" as well as efficient and effective. In such cases, small-scale "shop" forms of organization, such as those found in the printing, barber-beautician, dental, and many other personal-service industries, may be the most effective form of organization for personal care. Enforcing small-scale operations should therefore be a central concern of state regulatory activity.

Fifth, an additional critical area of concern for the potential commercialization of personal-care services would be a period of experimentation with various forms of economic organization. Perhaps "franchising" may be a legitimate form of integration in cases where standardized service packages can be organized and protected. Despite the prominent role of multinational corporations in national life, the American economy actually encompasses a wondrously complex array of economic organizations beyond the business corporation, nonprofit agency, and government bureau. Many social workers engaged in private practice are already familiar with forms of professional incorporation, partnerships, family corporations, and publicly held corporations. In recent years, other possible forms of organization, including employee stock option plans (ESOP) and community-employee owned firms (CEOF), have been undertaken in industrial communities and might be extended to service firms. Hansman has suggested that the cooperative, long a stable form of enterprise in agricultural service industries, may offer a viable alternative to nonprofit organizations (Hansman 1980, 1981). Social-service agencies in Pennsylvania and West Virginia (and presumably elsewhere), have already begun to experiment with profit-making subsidiaries as a basis for creating self-financing service enterprises. Commercial food-service vendors, already predominant providers on many college campuses, are also experimenting in West Virginia with provision of meal service to older people. Limited-profit contracts, management fees, and similar financial arrangements also may be relevant to the personal-care service setting. Without some experimentation, however, we will never discover whether such arrangements are feasible.

Finally, it is important to examine the manpower implications of the commercialization of personal-care services very carefully. In an age of chronically high unemployment, it is conceivable that opening up new personal-care service markets could be a major new source of employment, especially for women, minorities, and unskilled labor. Even today, social work is predominantly a small island of graduate-level professional practitioners within a much larger sea of paraprofessional and nonprofessional service deliverers. However, the anathema of the nonprofession label has proven a weak sanction for controlling entry into social service positions. A more defensible role for the profession would be in defining and standardizing service routines for less skilled and highly trained workers, who have proven amazingly adept at outreach, some types of group work, information and referral, intake, and many other personal-care service tasks. The sheer size of the populations in need of personal-care services makes employment in this area a potential economic force of major proportions, perhaps on a par with other major American industries. In particular, the labor-intensive character of personal-care services may make them a major element in future manpower-planning considerations.

It is important to note that this is not a neoconservative manifesto, but rather a pragmatic effort to assess a reasonable alternative to weaknesses and failure of the service state. There are two points at which a commercialization approach is particularly vulnerable: the provision of services to the poor, and the issue of adequate regulation.

Commercialization, by itself, leaves completely unsettled the problem of poverty. Poor people who cannot presently purchase services from nonprofit and public vendors will be no more able to purchase them from commercial vendors. However, it is easy to overstate this issue in the case of personal-care services. To a far greater degree than in the past, personal-care problems are not restricted to low-income persons; retardation, abuse, cancer, stroke, and other personal-care problems are distributed across the population. Nevertheless, for that portion of the population who are poor, the only adequate solution rests with adequate income maintenance.

Commercialization will also predictably exacerbate the problems of quality control and regulation which already plague the personal-care services. The nursing-home industry offers an enlightening—and sobering—case study. It is altogether too easy, however, to conclude that private ownership and the profit motive are at fault here. Such a conclusion vastly oversimplifies a complex regulatory situation and completely ignores the comparable problems of abuse, neglect, violence, exploitation, dehumanization, and poor service quality in public and voluntary institutions for the mentally retarded, mentally ill, and dependent children.

It would be shortsighted to reject the alternative of commercialization of personal-care services solely on the basis of these two objections. Far wiser would be to consider them necessities of any adequate solution. Increases in income-maintenance support for the poor to reflect a "basic need" for certain types of personal care would, for example, almost certainly be less expensive than any program to provide publicly supported personal-care services to all who are in need, regardless of income. Similarly, regulation of personal-care services should be no more controversial than public regulation of weights and measures or the purity of dairy products have proven to be even in the present conservative era. For even partisans of the New Right to claim that alleged rights of free enterprise and profit extend to licensing abuse or violation of actual individuals would expose them to the accusation that profit is then set up as a higher good than even freedom.

Conclusion

In conclusion, the welfare state clearly has proven an inadequate vehicle for adequate funding of needed personal-care services. Further, as long as key American publics continue to favor low rates of taxation and limited government, adequate financing of personal-care services is inconceivable. It is, therefore, both necessary and desirable that social-welfare leaders concerned about personal care begin seriously to consider alternative forms of support for such services. Reliance upon voluntary fund raising, however popular, will only be acceptable if new and more effective ways of overcoming its limitations can be discovered.

For many personal-care services, commercialization on a small-scale basis may prove a realistic basis for financing needed services. For commercial services to be effective, however, a range of new and supportive financial and regulatory institutions must be developed. The proposals set forth in this chapter should not be read as a blueprint for action, but rather as an agenda for much needed discussion.

References

Addams, Jane. *My Twenty Years at Hull House.* New York: Macmillan, 1910.

Crunden, Robert M. *Ministers of Reform: The Progressives' Achievements In American Civilization, 1889–1920.* New York: Basic Books, 1982.

Downs, Anthony. *Inside Bureaucracy.* Santa Monica: Rand Corporation, 1969.

Galbraith, John. *The Affluent Society.* Boston: Houghton Mifflin, 1958.

Hansman, Henry. "Reforming Non-Profit Corporation Law," *Pennsylvania Law Review* 129, no. 3 (January 1981):497–623.

———. "The Role of Non-profit Enterprises," *Yale Law Journal* 89, no. 5 (April 1980): 835–902.

Kamerman, Shiela, and Alfred Kahn. *Social Services in the United States.* Philadelphia: Temple University Press, 1976.

Lohmann, Roger A. *Breaking Even: Financial Management in Human Services*. Philadelphia: Temple University Press, 1980.

Lubove, Roy. *The Professional Altruist*. Atheneum: New York, 1969.

Mackenzie, Norman, and Jeanne MacKenzie. *The Fabians*. New York: Simon and Schuster, 1977.

Mahaffey, Mary Ann, and John W. Hanks, eds. *Practical Politics*. New York: NASW, 1982.

Mauss, Michael. *The Gift*. London: Cohen and West, 1966.

Morris, Robert. *Social Policy in the American Welfare State*. Englewood Cliffs: Prentice-Hall, 1979.

Office of Health and Human Services. Program Announcement #HDS-83-1. *Federal Register,* 47, 235 (7 December 1982), p. 5512.

Titmuss, Richard. *The Gift Relationship: From Human Blood to Social Policy*. New York: Vintage, 1970.

Wildavsky, Aaron. *The Politics of the Budgetary Process*. Boston: Little, Brown, 1974.

Wilensky, Harold, and Charles Lebeaux. *Industrial Society and Social Welfare*. New York: Free Press, 1965.

7

The Demonstration
Project: Politics Amid
Professionalism

William W. Vosburgh and
Felice Davidson Perlmutter

Demonstration projects are a relatively recent phenomenon, having an upsurge in the 1960s, when the federal government became actively and directly involved in the planning and funding of human-service programs. Two circumstances support the argument that demonstration projects in fact served political rather than professional ends. First, there has been little use of the actual results obtained from the projects, and most of the findings are lost in the files of the various governmental agencies. The lack of utilization of findings from government-sponsored studies and projects, demonstration and otherwise, is notorious. Not too long ago, the federal government was encouraging the development of the field of "research utilization" as a partial antidote. Second, the programmatic intent of the projects has constantly shifted to reflect the dominant interests of the party in power. Thus, the support for community mental health and retardation, the poverty program, and services integration waxed and waned with each changing administration; current emphases on voluntary and local activities are a case in point. The effect of this reality on social administration is to accentuate the need for political behavior and sensitivity on the part of the administrator.

This chapter will first examine the relationship of demonstration projects to the micro and macro systems within its purview; it will then present a theoretical model that posits three stages of development for demonstration projects. The focus of the discussion is the implications for the political aspects of the executive role.

Characteristics of Demonstrations

Demonstration projects are usually undertaken, as their name suggests, to provide practical experience with new programs or routines under conditions which, while still under some sort of control, approximate the complexity of those encountered under actual operating conditions. In the recent past, demonstrations have been used to subserve a number of other purposes as well: as a vehicle for moving large-scale funding into particular areas; as a means of inducing change; and as a way of defusing controversy by acting out a given course of action, thus disarming its advocates. While demonstrations may serve as a test of programs or procedures, it is a mistake to regard them as experiments. Although they almost always have evaluative components that aim at documenting the experience, the circumstances under which they take place seldom, if ever, provide the control conditions necessary for an experiment. Demonstrations are really large-scale field tests under restricted conditions, and generally conducted with added resources. The question at the root of the average demonstration is really whether or not the technique, organization, or whatever is effective in ameliorating the problem under realistic, but optimal, conditions.

That demonstrations are time-limited places heavy burdens on the project to gear up rapidly and to be initiated with a great deal of momentum. Time simply is not available to deal with many key problems. Rapid answers to facilitate or back up large-scale planning are needed and tend to place rigid time limitations on these projects. Consequently, the executive of a demonstration project must simultaneously deal with a diverse set of imperatives: to organize a program that will reflect credit on the judgment of several different sets of sponsors; to provide a vehicle for testing the ideas subject to trial or demonstration; to ensure that the demonstration, as a program raising problems of change, will be minimally disruptive to the rest of the service system; to ensure that the demonstration will prove compatible enough with the bureaucratic superstructure from which it must draw resources so that those resources are assured; and to provide a working environment within which individuals, relating often to a number of different interest groups, can function effectively.

Assumptions

The demonstration project is viewed here as a *political system* because it involves reconciling the diverse and occasionally conflicting interests of a range of many persons and groups with different stakes in the situation. Consequently, a demonstration project is assumed to represent a coherent political entity with distinct interests, sponsors, allies and enemies, ready to bargain with other organizational units for the resources it needs to carry out its activities.

Large amounts of significant behavior in human-service organizations are often written off as "bureaucratic infighting," "guarding one's turf," and "empire building." As these pejoratives indicate, the activities described are seen as aberrant, counter to the smooth functioning of the organization, and generally deleterious. Inquiries into why such things go on often end up in the identification of a pathological tendency, oft identified as "introversion," "technicism," or "ritualism." This discussion assumes that behavior identified as aberrant may appear more normal if viewed as a system-induced response of individuals with a commitment to the objectives and broader goals of their own sector of the organization. Thus, many jurisdictional disputes are routine interior-boundary maintenance activity, and much empire building is an attempt to insure that the bureau or unit has the resources necessary to do its job. These activities involve initiatives, negotiation, bartering, exchange of favors, alliance, and all the processes characteristic of politics.

This discussion takes the position that this behavior represents appropriate responses to the imperatives of the situation, better seen as instances of political behavior, in Gummer's sense, than as pathological states. As is any social unit, a project is subject to institutionalization: it becomes a focus of sentiments on the part of those involved with it. Commitment involves the acceptance of the goals and well-being of the project as a determinant of action. Consequently, it is also assumed that individual actors in the project have feelings, commitments, and convictions about the project which are vital to its existence.

Finally, it is assumed that the demonstration project is a microcosm of programs developed on a permanent basis and that it has the virtue of forcing attention on processes that might go unnoticed in a slower-moving situation.

Politics Amid Professionalism: Executive Roles

This section examines the relationship of the demonstration project to the micro and macro systems within its purview, with special attention to administrative roles. In this discussion the macrosystem is defined as the broader political level, outside of the demonstration project's purview, which serves to initiate, support, or sanction the demonstration project. Thus, for example, the federal government defined the objectives of community mental health centers in the Mental Retardation and Community Mental Health Construction Act of 1963, while the implementation took place at the local level (Perlmutter 1972, 1973, 1978). Similarly, the services integration discussion took place at the federal level, and HEW, through the 1115 demonstration grants, initiated, supported, and sanctioned several projects including the United Services Agency in Luzerne-Wyoming Counties, Pennsylvania (Perlmutter, Richan, and Weirich 1979).

The microsystem is defined as the internal and external aspects of the specific social program (Perlmutter 1969). The external dimension involves those organizational relationships that take place at the local level and are essential for the work of the agency (Warren 1963). The internal dimension focuses on all of the aspects of the agency operations, such as staff services.

The Macrosystem

A demonstration project requires that the executive become actively involved in the macropolitical realm, in spite of the probability that his capacity to operate on the larger political scene is ambiguous and most of his political expertise most probably resides at the microsystem level.

Demonstrations usually arise as a result of an external circumstance, be it a new public policy, a newly identified social need, or a crisis, disaster, or catastrophe. Frequently, the initiatives required to start a demonstration project mean that a group of persons in the macrosystem have become committed to the problem and have assumed a position of *sponsorship*. Early dependence on sponsorship continues into the life of the project, and the identification of early protagonists persists. The project may be informally known as "Mr. X's project," often indicating someone who has little, if any, formal connection with the program but who is still understood to be its sponsor. While this kind of relationship can provide a strong base, it is inherently fragile because it is personalized and the role of sponsor cannot easily be assumed by other persons. (For example, a senator or congressman can be the sponsor, formally or informally, of a project.) Acquiring sponsorship may involve acquiring the political liabilities of the sponsor, and the project can find itself vulnerable to being used as a means of oblique attack on that individual. Consequently, the administrator must continuously be aware of this reality and broaden the spheres of influence and the stakes in the project both at the macrosystem and microsystem level.

The macrosystem serves a second critical function for demonstrations: closely linked to the sponsorship issue is availability of resources. To establish and facilitate the demonstration, large amounts of extra resources are required. Extra funding, often on a large scale, makes carrying out such an enterprise attractive to administrators, for not only will the agency meet its professional mandate to respond to social need, but it will be politically visible and have a broader fiscal base from which to operate. The executive must be aware of the costs involved and not just opt for the benefits, for the funding stream will carry its own set of constraints, with the potential danger of distorting the original agency program.

A second critical problem related to resources is the time-limited nature of the funding. The consequences of returning to the "normal state" once the project's special resources are terminated are often not planned for. This all too frequent behavior at the executive level is an abdication of responsible leadership.

The macrosystem provides other incentives for demonstrations. A very powerful one is the favored status of the project, for which restrictive rules and policies are often waived. These waivers allow the project to operate in a favored position, a circumstance which, while seemingly advantageous, often provokes hostile reaction in the microsystem. Waivers upset routines and derange priorities, affecting both the internal bureaucracy as well as the external agency relationship at the local level, where other programs must continue their routine operations. (The necessity for the administration to deal with this politically will be discussed in the next section.)

Before leaving a discussion of the macrosystem, attention must be paid to the complexity inherent in the relationship between politicians and social-service institutions. The very word *welfare* is a virtual pejorative, and many politicians run against the "welfare mess"; once they are in office, the tables are turned and some appearance of doing something about it must be maintained. A demonstration offers interesting opportunities to the politician. First, it gives an appearance of knowing where to find the answers. Second, it is likely to inject a large amount of extra funding into the politician's local community. Third, it involves little commitment on the part of the politician except voting for funding. Finally, it will draw favorable attention, both locally and nationally. What makes this different from many normal political situations is that all the preceding advantages essentially involve communication to some constituency other than the direct beneficiaries—an assurance to the larger community that at last something effective is being done about a long-standing problem.

The executive can be more effective if s/he understands that the stakes of politicians in social programming are many and vary with the type of activity, the characteristics of the persons programmed for, and a host of other circumstances. Consequently, the politicians may desire high visibility for their efforts to correct aggravating social problems or to assist worthy recipients. What the politician seeks from the administrator in general is an assurance that the object of the program is under control, that persons are being helped and problems being solved in an efficient manner; once a problem has been dealt with it should be seen to have been laid to rest. While it might seem that a demonstration, being partly experimental, could get away with being less than a solution, such is often not the case. The pressures on a demonstration to "succeed" are heavy, not only because a heavy commitment of resources is often involved but also because a large number of people stand in a sponsorship or professional relationship to it. Further, there is the political reality that the project represents an attempt to apply the best available solution to a difficult social problem, and failure raises the unwelcome possibility that the problem may be insoluble.

Finally, it must be noted that the macropolitical structure, as the arena within which societal turbulence is met and dealt with, exhibits a certain mutability in terms of personnel and policies. An election of an opposition party can lead to the withdrawal of macropolitical sponsorship for various offices and programs. Worse yet, from the point of view of the project administrator, the reelection of a ruling party can still lead to a shuffling of programs to meet campaign promises or simply to provide visible evidence of progress. Any change in federal office is, to some extent, a new beginning, and elected officials prefer to develop new programs that can be identified with them. Supplanting existing programs with alternatives of their own design is a way for top-level officials to make their mark rapidly on the course of events, while sustaining existing programs has little attraction. Even "sacred cows" (i.e. untouchable programs) are supported grudgingly or in a perfunctory manner in many cases. Moves of this kind are essentially macropolitical, although they do have their micropolitical counterparts.

The Microsystem

The political skill of the executive may be most tested in the areas closest to home, within the microsystem, both within the organization and with the external agencies in the local community.

The Agency Bureaucracy. The bureaucratic superstructure extending upward from the local agency level is neither monolithic nor continuous. It is divided into several distinct vertical levels, identified for purposes of this discussion as the policy level, the middle-management level, and the front-line level.

The policy and decision-making level consists of the upper levels of major departments and includes both that sector of the upper echelon subject to macropolitical removal and replacement and the higher administrative personnel in the permanent cadre who are subject to the rules of civil service. The policy and decision-making level has initiating innovation as a formal part of its mission. This level, typically staffed with research and development offices and other paraphernalia of rational decision making, must also define and react to changes in the larger environment, handling major adaptive change as well.

Middle-level administration specializes in the reliable execution of the multiplicity of routines necessary to the functioning of the system as a whole. It provides stability by paying attention to rules and precedent and making sure that others do so. Middle management, which translates the broad decisions of the upper level into the specifics of regulations, is in a position to either assure or block the flow of resources within the system. That persons at this level tend toward conservatism and inflexibility is not remarkable and has often been noted. The exacerbation of this situation through processes of institutionalization has also been the subject of comment. It deserves underscoring, however, for the conviction of the rightness of existing rules and routines—their sanctification—often comes as a shock to other actors in the system. Reactions are sometimes unanticipated because the intensity of these commitments is underplayed or ignored.

The front-line level, the cutting edge of the organization, actually carries out activities and deals with the public by applying resources and normative directives from level two to carry out the policies and decisions of level one. It is here that program specifications and rules are adjusted to reality, and personnel at this level must accomplish this task. The process of interpretation makes them a center of innovation as well, although this innovation tends to be fragmentary and somewhat ad hoc. The challenge at this level is to achieve both formal and substantive rationality, to solve the problems of clients while satisfying the rules that govern the situation.

Political Requisites. For middle-level personnel, a demonstration has a number of frightening aspects. Almost always it can only be incorporated into their realm by a process of *exception*. It is very seldom that a demonstration project seeks to demonstrate that the paperwork it generates on the local level will flow smoothly through the system and prove acceptable to persons not directly involved in the project itself, much less be capable of integration into existing routines. What is under discussion here is not the processing of occasional memoranda; it involves the lifeblood of any project. Requisitions for supplies, contracts with providers of services, hiring of major personnel, conformance to routine reporting requirements, processing of payouts, including travel vouchers, and many other actions not ordinarily thought of as part of a demonstration become part of one in a public program that articulates into a bureaucracy. This simple fact is the source of the mysterious delays tracked down by Pressman and Wildavsky (1973).

The average bureaucracy, even if it defines paperwork from certain sources as an exception, may achieve toleration but seldom affection for these alternate routines. There is always the nagging feeling that something is "wrong" and that project people are "getting away with something."

The response is difficult to deal with, for it generally involves some form of *passive aggression*. Lengthy delays, procedural clarifications, refusal to process paper that is not in standard form—all these devices can be used to show disapproval while leaving their users cloaked in anonymity. If the project shows any sign of weakness—approaching the end of its duration, loss of an important bureaucratic sponsor—resort to this kind of behavior tends to increase.

These stratagems are an indication of *recuperation,* the process by which the structure reasserts itself. Pressures in this direction are always present and can become very heavy. One reinforcement is provided by the tendency of the middle levels to endow their routines with sentiment. The restoration of the system thus becomes a kind of morality play in which the system, by reasserting itself, justifies middle management's faith in its fundamental correctness. Persons at this level will go to some lengths to distance themselves from the demonstration project, saying over and over again that they do not understand what the project is all about, although it has been explained to them a number of times and its documentation is readily available. From the project administrator's point of view, this sort of situation can become a nightmare, for a good deal of time must be reserved for responding to the difficulties raised by this set of circumstances. When a project is having difficulties, this activity tends to increase, and the executive often feels that it is robbing the project of time and effort needed to meet its other problems, thus setting up a vicious cycle. The executive must recognize that attention to this internal arena must be a number-one priority, or the entire demonstration can be at risk. Delegation of authority for internal processes will, of course, be necessary, but the executive must recognize that from time to time direct communication and contact with the project staff is essential.

Processes at the front-line level also generate political events that require executive attention. *Introversion* is a common process found in those units of larger organizations which are deployed as the demonstration program: the project is viewed as a complete unit in and of itself and as disjunctive with the structures surrounding it. It develops special ways of doing things and a pride in its competences and accomplishments. It does not view itself as the lower end of a hierarchy but rather as a unit of accomplishment that receives necessary support from distant sources. When trouble develops, it is "us and them." Introversion is, of course, closely related to morale, unit pride, and other positive conditions. As a process, it only becomes destructive when it so insulates the local unit from its environment that legitimate demands and threats are neither perceived nor reacted to appropriately. It takes little imagination to understand how such a process may give coloration to middle-level complaints about empire building and refusal to follow necessary routines. The problem for the executive in this situation is to endow the program with a necessary sense of reality without destroying its morale. If he is perceived as an apologist for "them," his effectiveness will be diminished.

External Local Relationships

Relationships with the local service network, within which the program operates, constitute a micropolitical world of their own. Public-voluntary relationships are crucial and require much patient work. Public agencies tend to form working relationships more easily with other public agencies than they do with the voluntary sector and quite often are so preoccupied with internal affairs that they simply do not have the time or energy to cultivate relationships beyond those that come most easily. And yet attention must be paid to the nuances in both sectors with which the focal agency or program must interact more or less continuously for various purposes, such as evaluative feedback, clientele (in the form of referrals, purchased-service cases, newly identified or defined service populations), alliances, sponsorship and patronage, advocacy and legitimacy. During the early stages of the demonstration, when the program itself is uncertain of its mission and its organization, it is especially difficult to arrive at the firm understandings that must undergird relationships within an agency network. Compounding this difficulty is the question of the duration of the demonstration in time, which makes other agencies hesitant to become involved with it. The relationships with the local sector is vital, however, in providing the program with legitimacy in the local arena, and this means that the executive must be alert to it and ready to commit time and resources to its cultivation.

These considerations have at least indicated the range of other actors in the micropolitical arena and sketched some of the perils and opportunities that lie within each sort of relationship. The bureaucratic structure has been stressed because it is from this source that the program must negotiate the resources it needs. Other relationships tend to arrange themselves around this central grouping.

Dilemmas of Tasks and Timing:
A Natural History of Demonstrations

The role of the administrator cannot be fully appreciated unless it is understood that the program's political content shifts and evolves across time. Not only must the administrator decide what to go after and whom to work with (or against) to obtain it, he must decide *when* to make these moves. There will be times when he will be concerned almost entirely with internal agency processes, and other times when his energy is devoted almost exclusively to negotiations with outside entities. Barring emergencies, at any given time large arenas of organizational concern, both internal and external, may be placed on "hold." Lower administrators may wait for weeks for decisions; boards and public bodies connected with the program may feel neglected; other agencies with related programs may wonder what the focal program intends—and all because the executive's attention is necessarily directed elsewhere.

A theoretical framework of systematic change and development is a powerful tool for the administrator (Selznick 1957). While it may seem that there is no reason to anticipate shifts of attention from internal to external affairs on any but a random basis, there is, in fact, a periodicity which can be predicted to some extent. Much of the current literature on this kind of developmental change is based on a life-cycle metaphor (Perlmutter 1969, Weick 1979, Kimberley and Miles 1980).

Demonstration projects lend themselves most readily to a developmental analysis, since their course is foreshortened and exaggerated, their stability brief, and their decline assured. There is a momentum to initiating such a project, and there is also a momentum to phasing them out as event reinforces event. This reversal of momentum can take an administrator by surprise. Consequently, the executive must set priorities in regard to his/her role. An analytic tool, such as a model of project development, can be useful in this regard.

A Three-Stage Developmental Model

Three major stages are identified in the life cycle of a demonstration: Preprogram, program, and postprogram. All three stages require both micro and macro political activity, but the emphasis will vary according to the major requirements of each stage (table 7–1). The availability of a theoretical model for demonstration projects becomes important, for these projects must simultaneously initiate change, react to external change, and assure stability and predictability by maintaining and ex-

Table 7–1

A Developmental Model for Demonstration Projects

	Preprogram Stage		Program Stage		Postprogram Stage	
	Sponsorship	Planning	Initiation	Institutionalization	Stabilization	Phase-Out
Macrosystem	X					X
Microsystem						
External/						
Local		X	X		X	
Internal			X	X		

tending rational-legal order. These are, of course, contradictory imperatives, and the tensions among them are major generators of micro and macro political activity. Rather than presenting one major dilemma for the system as a whole, these tensions are experienced as a series of dilemmas within the major parts of the program in which different values are assigned to change and stability. A series of tensions not only within parts, but between parts, results, which requires continuous negotiations, and a demonstration may be both caught up in these transactions and present new problems and conditions for them. The model helps set priorities for this process.

Stage I: Preprogram. During the preprogram stage, the precipitating external event, which can be a new public policy, a new social need, or a crisis, disaster or catastrophe, and which was discussed earlier in the macrosystem section, stimulates the development and formulation of the demonstration program. Two problems must be dealt with during this stage: sponsorship and program planning and design.

The *sponsorship* task has several components: *critical actors* must be obtained who carry sufficient power to help launch the project; the *mission* of the project must be defined; and *community sanction* must be obtained both at the macro and micro levels. The major orientation for the sponsorship task is external, with priorities placed at the macrosystem level.

A number of the characteristics of the demonstration place the executive at a disadvantage in negotiations, chiefly its mortality. The project has a specific life span known to its enemies as well as its friends, and there is a strong preference for outlasting the opposition as a tactic in bureaucracies. The extra resources and exceptions to routines granted the project arouse envy in persons in more routine situations: their common reaction is that they too could accomplish wonders, given these advantages. The necessity for speed and precision in implementation creates pressures irritating to those not committed to the project. Sponsorship is a problematic advantage: it provides the project with impetus as long as it exists, but when it is withdrawn, it signals a state of vulnerability.

Within this context, then, the executive must engage in intensive and continuous micropolitical activity with the other major institutional actors in the system. Specifically, s/he must deal with the program's relationship to the agencies from which it draws resources, an environment of related agencies and programs and service community, and, finally, the micropolitical and macropolitical sponsors of the program.

The *program planning and design* task is an *internally oriented* one which operates primarily at the microsystem level as decisions are being made about the project's structure and lines of activity; there is a heavy emphasis on precision, definition, and agreement. Never again will the project be as clear as it is at this point. Agreement is sometimes achieved by declarations of allegiance to "unanalyzed abstractions": issues are glossed over for fear that close examination would point up intolerable differences (Selznick 1957).

During this stage, the executive must attend to a large amount of detail and pay continual attention to inculcating a uniform view of the project and its activities in personnel as they come aboard. This high level of specification serves also to allow the project to be explained to interested parts of the service network and to assure sponsors that it is going to do what they have intended. The executive's attention is directed heavily inward and focused on specification and socialization of staff.

And while the time-limited reality of the project is not a priority in the preprogram stage, it is essential that it be taken into account with every decision that is made regarding organizational structure, personnel, and clientele. Shifts in the focus of the executive's micropolitical activity must occur on a predictable basis as the demonstration moves from one phase to another.

Stage II: Program Implementation. Two phases of activity can be identified in the program implementation phase: program initiation and institutionalization.

During the initiation phase, getting the project off the ground is the focus. The executive is aided here by a certain amount of momentum and often by the extra resources mentioned above. During this period, the idealized program envisioned in the planning phase of stage I must be realized. The executive now tries to preserve its essentials in the face of the inevitable compromises that execution will bring. The service network, its suspicions fully aroused now that the program is achieving reality, must be reassured, and the benefits that it will bring to particular parts of that network, stressed. Although communications must be established with bureaucratic support systems at this point, these relationships probably will not need concerted attention for some time: the support structures can accept the program as an "exception" for a while at least, and their customary stance toward innovation is, in any event, "wait and see." External sponsors need little attention at this stage, usually being content to know that the program is moving along.

Institutionalization is a crucial aspect of stage II; this is the time that the program becomes invested with sentiments, and a stake in the system develops among the various actors and participants. During this stage, the meshing of the intent of the program with reality—the choices made, the irreducible circumstances encountered, the interpretations of the staff, the needs of the clients, and the myriad circumstances that shape the program—presents the executive with the version of things for which s/he is going to have to settle. A final, intense burst of inward-looking activity becomes a major preoccupation. Reinforcing circumstance is the powerful process of institutionalization as all concerned invest what is going on with sentiments, thereby making a number of things effectively unchangeable for the rest of the program's life. So absorbing is this final attempt to adjust things, to come to an understanding with the people who will bring the program to life in its stabilized form, that the executive will seldom have much time for "foreign relations" during this period.

Stage III: Postprogram. Stage III also has two phases: stabilization and phase-out. The former seeks to ensure the long-term impact of the project, whereas the latter deals with the termination aspects.

In regard to stabilization, when the program has reached a steady state, the executive's attention will usually be determined by exceptional situations, tinkering in effect with working machinery. It is at this point that trouble with bureaucratic support systems can appear. The passage of time brings about recuperative tendencies on the part of the system itself. Waivers and exceptions, which were sufficient to justify departures from procedure during the initiation phase, now manifest themselves as a burden, as the routine processing of paper and the repetitive activating of communication channels give actors deep in the system a chance to register disapproval in various ways. That persons throughout the structure of the demonstration will have established their own relationships within the structure of the support system will help greatly, but trouble can still arise, and a solution is usually sought by bucking it upwards. This means the executive will have extended dealings with administrators and liaison personnel such as project monitors. During these activities the program's sponsors may have to be mobilized to provide leverage. Its friends in a large bureaucracy often have difficulty making the wheels turn when problems arise in line operations. Appeals to outside sponsorship, such as supporters in the political realm, become a tempting option, although subject to the perils noted earlier.

The other focus of attention for the executive is the other agencies and parts of the service network in the program's environment. Both the executive and the environment now have an actual, operating program to deal with rather than an idealized entity of vague and faintly menacing potential. Work can begin on a modus vivendi, and relationships with the rest of the service network can be cemented. The executive has the assurance of a person running a going concern and knows exactly what it can and cannot do. Even though demonstrations have a short life span, there are lessons that have been learned and new approaches to be installed, either within the bureaucracy or within the local community-service system. And this stabilization of the changes wrought by the demonstration project must be a priority of the executive in this third stage.

The final phase of the project is phase-out; during this period, the attention of the entire project is likely to be directed outward. Everyone at one point or another during this time must wonder about their next move, and many are actively seeking other jobs. People depart and are not replaced. Activities constrict as the staff does, and attention turns to such problems as disposing of leases and furniture. It is difficult to convey the spirit of planned demoralization that occurs: nothing really matters very much in day-to-day operations. The executive, during this final stage, will usually see stabilization as a priority and will have developed a focus on the contributions of the project. Thus, s/he will be involved in heightened activity with the sponsors preparing final reports and assessing the lessons learned in an attempt to pass on experience to other agencies. In summary, the internal picture is one of decline and, aside from helping staff members adjust, the executive's attention will be impelled outward.

At this point, a rumor that the program will somehow be carried on beyond the life of the demonstration occasionally emerges as a sustaining fiction. Most staff members realize that it is unlikely and continue to make other arrangements. It does remove some of the apparently increasing futility of day-to-day work, however. Executives and research personnel look toward transfer of lessons learned and technology developed as a similar rationale for sustained effort.

It is imperative that the executive provide adequate support to the staff internally during this final phase and that s/he not be swept away by the external requirements. Since outside responsibilities are more satisfying, as well as more pressing, it is easy to abandon the more demanding internal requirements.

Summary and Conclusions

Demonstration projects serve more than purely professional ends. They are enmeshed in the ongoing web of politics in the macropolitical realm. Just as important for the administrator, however, is the fact that they are also the center of micropolitical activity involving the emerging organization of the demonstration itself, the larger administrative structure from which it must draw its resources, and a set of relationships with the community-service network in which it finds itself. The administrator must be aware of all these lines of activity, but his/her attention must continually shift and refocus as the project moves from stage to stage. These shifts are predictable and can be the object of planning.

By their very nature, demonstrations have unusual characteristics: the experience goes on under a fair amount of control, but is an "experiment" only in the popular sense; in addition to attempts to innovate with the program itself, the conditions under which it takes place are usually changed as well in an attempt to create optimal operational conditions through added resources and such devices as waiving rules and requirements; they are time-limited and must respond fairly immediately to a number of imperatives which may, in fact, conflict, such as the need to deal with outside parties from a stable organizational base while the latter is, in fact, evolving rapidly. The foreshortened time frame also tends to speed up processes that take much longer to work out in ordinary program development.

Demonstrations are surrounded by politics, both internal and external, macro and micro, because a variety of interests are in play, and bargaining for resources is a necessity. Other organizational processes, such as institutionalization, are going on as well, and commitments and motivations of the actors must be seen in this light.

Demonstrations are presented here as fitting into a framework that identifies developmental tasks—securing sponsorship, planning, initiation, institutionalization, stabilization and phase-out—as occurring within sequential time stage: preprogram, program, and postprogram. The tasks appropriate to each stage require a shift in the administrator's attention from the macro to the micro level, from the organization and its organizational support system to the community-service network.

Each of these shifts involves dealing with a different set of actors with different stakes in the situation, with characteristic tactics and reactions, and the capacity to produce different kinds of problems for the focal organization if the tasks are not accomplished or if timing is thrown off. Because of its tight time schedule and explicit structure, the demonstration as a form makes heavy demands on the political skill of the administrator.

A number of conclusions can be drawn from the considerations in this paper:

1. Demonstrations, and indeed all social-service programs, must be viewed as simultaneously involved in several distinct sets of politics going on in essentially different arenas: macropolitics located in policy-making and resource-allocation centers generally beyond the local community level; micropolitics (vertical) involving the superstructure beyond the focal program which provides administrative support, regulation, and resources and which is often jointly accountable with the focal program; and finally, micropolitics (horizontal) taking place in the service network at the operational level in which the focal program must find a place and in the community institutions to which it must relate.

2. Within the macrosystem, politics revolve around sponsorship and accountability. Activity here demands an appreciation of the dynamics of sponsorship in terms of what sponsors stand to gain or lose and accountability in terms of criteria of success or failure.

3. Because of their status as exceptions, their access to sponsorship, extra resources, and, frequently, waivers of policy requirements and regulations, demonstrations can become a focus of resentment and hostility in the middle-management levels beyond the focal program. Politics here poses special difficulties because attacks tend to be indirect and oblique and the motives of personnel difficult to comprehend as well as because this level is athwart the project's lines of administrative support.

4. On the internal program level, administrators should note that front-line personnel have a tendency to become task-absorbed and work groups introverted. These developments work against involvement with reports and paperwork, which are seen as secondary and sometimes illegitimate demands. In view of the extent to which records and documentation are essential to the success of a demonstration, the administrator must exert constant pressure to see that they are accomplished. The neglect of paperwork can also exacerbate trouble with middle management.

5. Demonstrations have a "natural history" composed of stages that can be anticipated and tasks that can be identified in advance. The administrator should see his/her work as involving shifts of attention at predetermined points from one realm to another. These shifts involve

changes in tactics, objectives, and the rules of the game. The need to maintain political harmony in other realms and to provide for emergencies must, of course, be met. These needs are ongoing. Knowing that shifts in the rhythm of work are predictable can be the key to success in demonstrations, an arena that does not provide much time or latitude for trial and error.

References

Gummer, Burton. "The Effects of Inter-Organizational Relations on the Delivery of Social Services," unpublished doctoral dissertation, Bryn Mawr College, 1973.

Kimberley, J.R., and R.H. Miles. *The Organizational Life Cycle*. San Francisco: Jossey-Bass, 1980.

Perlmutter, F.D. "Prevention and Treatment: A Strategy for Survival." *Community Mental Health Journal* 10 (April 1973):276–81.

———. "A Theoretical Model of Agency Development." *Social Casework* 50 (October 1969):467–73.

Perlmutter, F.D., W. Richan, and T. Weirich. "Services Integration and Transferability: Implications of the United Social Services Agency Demonstration Project." *Administration in Social Work* 3 (1979):17–31.

Perlmutter, F.D., and H.A. Silverman. "The Community Mental Health Center: A Structural Anachronism." *Social Work* 17 (March 1972):78–85.

Perlmutter, F.D., and A.M. Vayda. "Barriers to Prevention Programs in Community Mental Health Centers." *Administration in Mental Health* 6 (Fall 1978):140–53.

Pressman, Jeffry, and Aaron Wildavsky. *Implementation*. Berkeley: University of California Press, 1973.

Selznick, Philip. *TVA and the Grass Roots*. New York: Harper Torchbooks, 1966.

Selznick, Philip. *Leadership in Administration*. Evanston: Row Peterson, 1957.

Vosburgh, William W. "Service Integration, Advocacy and the Public-Voluntary Nexus," paper presented at Annual Meeting of the Association of Voluntary Action Scholars, East Lansing, Michigan, 1982.

Warren, R.L. *The Community in America*. Chicago: Rand McNally, 1963.

Wcick, K. *The Social Psychology of Organizing*. Reading, Mass.: Addison-Wcslcy, 1979.

8 Information Management

Murray L. Gruber,
Richard K. Caputo, and
Thomas Meenaghan

As *Time* noted by selecting the computer as its 1982 "Man of the Year," the United States has entered the computer age. Whether we call this age an "information revolution," an "information explosion," or simply "the age of information," the changes taking place in our societary nervous system are the direct result of advances in computer technology, and by all signs, the pace is quickening.

In the human services, the computer-based management information system (MIS) has been relatively inconspicuous, but with the development of the low-cost computer, power once available only on gigantic mainframe computers is now at the fingertips of even the small social-service agency. In all probability, the trajectory for information management in the social-welfare sector is upward and at an accelerating rate, posing a variety of serious policy questions.

In reviewing these issues, this chapter will traverse a broad terrain. First, we will sketch the advent of MISs to the social services. Second, although this chapter is not intended as an information-system primer, we will briefly lay out the contours, functions, and development of MIS. This is designed to lay the groundwork for subsequent discussion of important public-policy and administrative questions. It is also intended to overcome a disturbing schism between the technically narrow and the genre of technology assessment that is socially oriented and critical. Each tends to be rather extreme, for if the former is socially innocent and lauds technology with light-headed puffery, extreme versions of the latter invoke Orwellian images of a technological dystopia overseen by Big Brother. We will move between these two extremes and, after discussion of the more prosaic technical aspects of MISs we will consider a variety of potential problems and social changes that may be in store as a result of information management, as well as some steps that might be taken to deal with them.

The Coming of the MIS

Ever since the 1960s, there has been a steady drumbeat of criticism of human-services management, of the inability to specify outcomes, the lack of a "bottom line," the fuzziness of objectives, and so on. Simultaneously, there had been a long rise in social spending, culminating in the late 1970s in a dramatic turnabout from abundance to dismal scarcity.

Earlier, the "systems approach," with its quasi-formalistic and quantitatively oriented models, had entered promising administrative rationality: "formal designs to systematize decision-making, to use information better, to 'reprogram' human service organizations, to develop better analytic capabilities, and to reveal what is being done with what results and at what costs" (Gruber 1981).

Not surprisingly, the stern logic of scarcity accompanied by highly rationalistic approaches to administration began to produce dramatic changes. By the time of the Nixon administration, federal costs for state social-service programs had risen rapidly, but because of the lack of clear and measurable objectives, accountability was in a mess.

The search for a solution came to rest on a hierarchical structure of specified program goals (MBO) linked to more specific subobjectives (goal oriented social services) and a vertical management information system to report results from the local to federal level. This system would also be linked to the planning and budgeting systems within state departments of public welfare. Although the comptroller's office in HEW noted that the system was such an elaborate structure that the states could not possibly cope with it (Mott 1976), it was a significant step in the coming of the MIS to the human services.

It is, of course, always difficult to trace the social itinerary of new inventions, and one does not want to overplay the developments of the Nixon years. If pressures came from the federal government to develop information systems, that pressure was also related to a semiautonomous trend—the growing influence of management science both within and outside of government.

Social-work administration, especially the growing body of writing, found much that was attractive in management science. And, with characteristic trendiness, it became feverish with the exaggerated promises of "tough-minded" rationalistic models. Indeed, the mainstream theory that was evolving in social-work administration ran parallel to Nixon's MBO, and it became an article of faith that it was essential to have clear and specifiable goals and objectives and that output measures should replace input measures. Only in this way could we evaluate programs and, in turn, advance the cause of accountability. Here was the essence of what some had called a true "management stance" (Turem 1974). Also, with planning and budgeting systems linked and a vertical information system to keep track of it all, it was assumed that it would be possible "to 'reprogram' human-service organizations, to develop better analytic capability, and to reveal what is being done with what results and at what costs" (Gruber 1981). No longer would social-work administration be vulnerable to the charge of soft-mindedness.

The fruits of that so-called management stance have proven elusive, and the Reagan administration has destroyed the idea that tough-minded administration would advance the political cause of the social services. Even so, the promise of such fads as MBO and program planning budgeting systems (PPBS) has been replaced by the promises of MISs. Today, of course, funding bodies are now requiring massive amounts of information in all fields of service and from all sorts of agencies, and more and more, agencies are struggling to implement computer-based information systems. This is not to say such systems do not have enormous potential ability; it is only to observe that the MIS comes to the social services surrounded by hyperbole and puffery and that in actuality much of today's utilization of MIS is for mundane office management. This is a far cry from the sophisticated planning and evaluation functions envisioned for the MIS.

Computer Technology

With or without the computer, all agencies have some type of information network of formal and informal information flow. Data are collected, processed, and disseminated manually, by machine, or in a combination of these two. File cabinets are information systems of a sort. So are budgets and case records, primitive though they may be in contrast to systems designed around the computer. Indeed, the computer emerges as central because systems of the "count and sort" type are inadequate to contemporary demands for timely, accurate, and comprehensive information. What follows is therefore a very short, nontechnical discussion of the computer and the components of an MIS.

The first generation of modern programmed electronic computers began about 1947, and since then, as they have grown immensely more powerful, there has been no change in their "architecture" or basic scheme of operations, that is, the stored program computer in which a central processing unit (CPU)—the brain of the computer—executes its calculations one step at a time, serially storing each result in its memory before moving on to the next calculation. In the 1950s, it was realized that "scaling down" the size of electronic digital computer circuits would improve speed and efficiency, but both the primitive vacuum-tube computers as well as the next generation of transistorized computers worked along the same lines. Even the supercomputers, working at blistering speeds with signals shuttling back and forth through a dense mass of hundreds of thousands of chips, still depend on serial processing.

Although the basic scheme of operations of the computer has not changed, a variety of significant advances have occurred. One of these is the development of the chip, a silicone wafer of fingernail size on which is printed all the computer circuits and components.

Important advances have also occurred in "peripherals," input and output means. For instance, instructions can be entered in the CPU by means of a keyboard console or by tracing them on a video screen with a light pen. The results can be retrieved on the video screen, also called a cathode ray tube (CRT), through word-script and graphing devices. They can also be retrieved via the common line or page printer. Changes have also been occurring in software programs, the list of instructions the computer can understand. Because it is difficult for even programmers to understand and use computer language, programming has been simplified by allowing the user to write a program in a more easily understandable form, which is then translated into a machine language by another program called a compiler. Also, more and more programs are being developed that will be compatible with computers of different designs.

The MIS

Educating oneself about the computer and about the MIS is a task of some magnitude. A major reason for this is that there are too many choices now available in computers, floppy discs, hard discs, software packages, printers, graphic plotters, modems, and so forth. For the prospective buyer, there are by now numerous primers, magazine articles, and journal articles, all dedicated to guiding the information-system neophyte. For our purposes, it is only necessary to concretize the basic elements of a system, the functions of the MIS, and the steps involved in installing the system.

The Components

The basic elements or components of a computerized MIS can be specified in short order. These are: input devices; a central processing unit; memory or storage devices; software (programs), routines or systems for providing instructions; and output devices. The organizational procedures and routines written to guide use of the system (for instance, who has access) are also considered a part of the system system itself.

Likewise, the data to be fed into the system. It is common to differentiate "data" from "information." The latter refers to processed data, data aggregated, manipulated, summarized, or otherwise arranged into a form that is meaningful and usable. If the data put in are trivial or worthless, that is what comes out. This is another way of saying that a fast but dumb machine is no substitute for judgment; the user must decide what is wanted out of the system.

Information-System Functions

There are a variety of classification systems in use that help to define the functions of an MIS. One conventional approach is to cross-hatch organizational functions and information-systems functions. Basically, there are three functional levels of information-system requirements: operations, middle management, and top management. Most data is gathered at the operational level. Here information requirements are concerned with such matters as client identification, service delivery, resource utilization, and payments. Identification and tracking of clients, documentation of service and worker activities, the generation of scheduled reports, and responding to routine inquiries about amount, types, and costs of services delivered are also ways that the system can be used at the operational level.

Information-system functions are also assigned to the middle-management level, and these functions are obviously derived from the presumed responsibilities of middle management. Mostly, these are control functions: monitoring reports of the timeliness of service delivery after clients' initial contact with the agency; compliance with standards; work-load distribution, client dispositions and outcomes; "tracking" to determine where clients are coming from and where they go to; miscellaneous "demand reports."

MIS functions and information requirements are also specified for top management. At this level, information requirements are mostly concerned with organizational goals, planning objectives, legal actions, responses to legislation, new regulations, and other demands on the organization to carry out or modify its functions. This process involves decisions about resources used to attain these goals and about policies to govern the use of resources. Typical information requests of top managers and of funding sources are: number of people served, outcomes, average costs, and likely impact of changes in funding levels (Project Share 1981).

Fiscal management is worth singling out because it is one of the most common uses for the computer and also the area in which an MIS is most often introduced to social-service agencies. The computer, for example, enables the manager to visually scan payroll reports, accounts payable, accounts receivable, and purchases and to even balance the general ledger every day. Once the general ledger is stored, it can be called back in a variety of ways. When a budget has been set up on the computer, the administrator can ask "What if?" questions. For instance, "What if projected income from Title XX is reduced by 25 percent?" The new income figure is entered and at the touch of a few buttons all of the line items are recalculated. The possible questions are almost limitless and are made possible by some notable software components that let the user set up mathematical relationships between numbers. The numbers are entered, in essence, as points on an electronic grid of up to 63 columns and 254 rows. When the value or relationship of any number changes, the program calculates the effect, if any, on other numbers in the grid.

Planning and Designing the MIS

Installing an MIS in an agency involves a number of steps, each of which is keyed to certain kinds of strategic planning and design considerations. These steps have been conceptualized in a variety of ways (Youchah 1981, Paton and D'huyvetter 1980, Schoech et al. 1981), but generally they seem to come down to a number of prescriptions: Determine if a new or modified information system is economically and technically feasible; analyze the existing flow of information; develop the operational requirements for the new or modified system, including a data model and subcomponent options; design a working system, including people, tasks, output, procedures, forms; test the system, "debug" it, and convert the old system to the new one; evaluate to determine if any design phases have to be entered again.

In schematic form, as shown in figure 8–1, the process is a simple one; in actuality, each phase or step includes many detailed substeps and procedures, and in all of them, there are choices to be made. In fact, the steps, procedures, and choices are far too numerous to be covered here, and they are best left to technical primers.

We have, however, chosen to deal with one main question: how to structure the data base. The reason for this is that while the structure of the data base may seem to be a straightforward and narrow technical question, it is in reality a question of reorganization design in a much larger sense than the MIS itself. By and large, there are two basic approaches to restructuring the data base: the "applications" approach and the "data base management system approach" (DBMS). In the

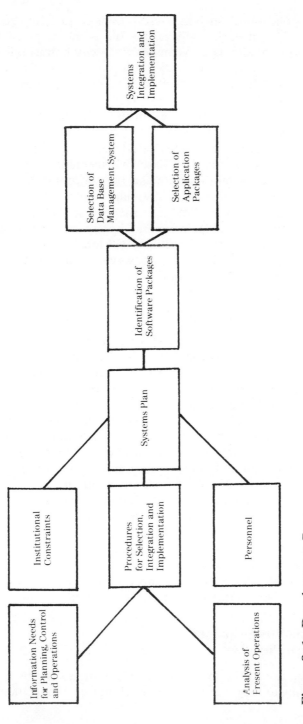

Figure 8–1. Development Process

first, each "application," such as payroll, bookkeeping and client data, is self-contained and each application's file is the responsibility and property of the originating department. In many multiservice organizations, for example, even client data are more likely to be organized by program with little, if any, interface of records kept and used across departments. On the one hand, this arrangement results in data redundancy and inconsistencies while, on the other hand, it contributes to a decentralized agency structure.

With the advent of more sophisticated and less expensive computer hardware and software, the data base management system approach to data processing becomes feasible and the concept of the MIS takes its most contemporary form. Basically, data common to each program are pooled and data files are linked or mapped so that data about any program are easily retrievable, in general, by any user and, in particular, by management. The DBMS approach will tend to move the organization toward greater centralization; however, to modulate this effect, the two approaches can be combined.

MIS and the Techno-logical Viewpoint

Up to this point, the discussion has taken place within a narrow context and, following what is most common in the technical literature, the MIS has been presented in terms of the "techno-logical viewpoint." That is, the components of MISs have been specified and the uses or functions discussed; the development of a system has been sketched, and the functions have been attached to different organizational levels.

This mainly descriptive, technically oriented, and conventional approach is useful, but only to a limited extent. Obviously, the major criteria for the design and implementation of information systems are technical ones in terms of the information system itself. The viewpoint of the system is a narrow one and tends to exclude larger human, organizational, and social considerations. In this sense, it is conservative. And, given the narrowness of the techno-logical viewpoint, MISs tend to be lodged or sited in the organization in ways that reinforce existing organizational structures. In this sense, too, the MIS has a conservative bias. The validity of these propositions is probably not immediately self-evident, so we will examine them in some detail.

Organizational Design and the
Techno-logical Viewpoint

Earlier we discussed the functions of information systems by locating them according to the organizational levels of top management, middle

management, and operations. Obviously, some specialization of information functions must occur, because everybody need not know everything. But which functions must be assigned to which levels is not so
clear-cut as the conventional view would have it. The conventional, or
technological, viewpoint simply takes the organization "as is," as a
"given," in parceling out information-system functions. Never mind
that too many agencies have structural problems and poor communication systems. The techno-logical viewpoint replicates and amplifies
these weaknesses and is, thereby, system-conserving in the worst sense.
The same is true with respect to the design of the data base and whether
to centralize or decentralize it. The technological viewpoint encourages
the design of an information system in accord with the organization as
it currently exists without taking into account the likely need for organizational changes. Thus, for Schoech et al. the recommended *"approach is to design a system that reflects the extent of integration and
centralization of the organization as a whole"* (1981, emphasis added).

There are some obvious problems with this approach. Clearly, it
fails to take account of the fact that the current design of the organization, especially with regard to questions of integration and centralization, may be problematical. Typically, such problems tend to elude the
MIS designer because technical optimality of the MIS is his central
concern, never mind that technical optimality may magnify existing
agency problems. Administrators may like the system maintenance biases
of the MIS, but there are high potential costs attached. Administrators
would do well to be leery of any information-system plan that does not
recommend some changes in existing organizational structure where
the criteria of the changes are in terms of the organization itself, not
technical optimality of the MIS.

The Purposes of MISs

To speak of MIS *functions* is also to speak the language of system
maintenance. This is because functions appear neutral and uncontroversial, while purposes invite questions. In the technological world, charts
and blueprints define a false and antiseptic reality. Power is a word
seldom used in this world. Here, conflicting and competing purposes
are unseen, conflict absent. The language of systems and function seems
clean and clear, neutral and harmonious. But if one steps out of the
frame of technological language and into the frame of political language,
an entirely new and not so clear, not so harmonious reality is created—
the hurly-burly of dissensus, of competing purposes, conflicts, and
interests.

To understand this, consider how, in a somewhat different organizational context than the MIS, technical language masks interest:
agencies with high intake discretion often avoid accepting the most
difficult cases because of the economic principle that says, "Do not
invest resources when there is a low probability of payoff (good outcome)" (Gruber 1980). To mask this, so-called diagnostic (technical)
criteria are invoked so that the client is made to appear "inappropriate"
for the agency. Similarly, when it comes to MIS functions, the language
conceals rather than illuminates *purposes* or intentions. For instance,
the function "client tracking" or "monitoring" reveals little; it tells only
that the MIS puts out information on clients and that this information
is transmitted somewhere. In technical language, the output of the MIS
is input for another part of the system or for a suprasystem. But how
will this information actually be used? "Client tracking," for instance,
might as easily refer to the aim of keeping kids from getting lost in the
foster-care system as it could to Reagan's proposal for a national data
registry to trip up "welfare cheats." Thus, "monitoring" may simply
mean "tracking," or it can suggest "surveillance" or "intelligence."

To the extent that the language of the MIS, especially the language
of functions, creates an exaggerated sense of surface neutrality it aids
in glossing over difficult choices and matters of interest. The administrator talks of "client reporting," but what does it mean to say that
this is a function of the MIS? To a consumer group of parents of
developmentally disabled children, it may mean information regarding
the magnitude of services delivered to the families of these children.
The parent group may also want information on the percentage of funds
allocated to the developmentally disabled or on how many families
were denied services under the guise of referrals to "more appropriate
sources." *Obviously, the same information, the same functions, may
serve entirely different purposes depending upon the actors and their
interests.* To the administrator, "client reporting" may mean nothing
more than compliance with the demands of a suprasystem.

The MIS is a splendid analytic tool that could aid in a variety of
difficult distributional decisions, were those decisions not controversial.
But decisions about program options, preferences, service priorities
and service mixes—in short, who to serve and how to serve them—
are fraught with interests and controversy. Indeed, administrators typically tend to avoid "cutting" these types of decisions. A major avoidant
strategy is the use of a reactive or passive waiting mode of service
delivery. This places the burden on potential agency users to self-identify
themselves. The principle "wait for the client to come in" obviates the
decisions "we intend to target to this group, not that one" or "we
intend to aim services to subgroups in the community in some reason-

able proportion to their incidence of problems." The latter is a proactive planning and targeting mode of service delivery, and it makes visible distributional decisions. Therefore, it opens the way to what administrators dearly love to avoid—controversy. For this reason, the MIS masquerades as an analytic tool when in reality it is used mostly to push paper.

If MIS functions conceal purpose, if they create the illusions of smooth harmony, and if functions seem self-propelled from software entirely absent human agency, then the MIS aids administrators in their system-maintenance, conflict-avoidance tendencies. To "unfreeze" this matter, it is necessary to confront the semantic closure of functions and to ask "Why?" "Toward what end?" and "What is the point?" and to keep asking until purpose is revealed.

User Networks

Human-service administrators tend to be ambivalent about public participation. They are at once schooled and skewed toward open and participative styles, and they tend to eschew conflict because a smooth, frictionless system comes to symbolize administrative effectiveness. System "penetration" by outsiders and their potentially embarassing questions are to be avoided. Not surprisingly, administrators value public participation yet try to tame and control it. Administrators also tend to believe they know best what is good for people (Downs 1967, Almy 1977). These factors also condition and limit the use of the MIS to office-management functions. While the MIS might be a useful analytic tool for a variety of user groups, including clients, consumers, board members and, perhaps, even agencies linked via the MIS, penetrating analyses and questions that "leapfrog" current services and delivery patterns would be a risky proposition in the administrators' quest for stability and security.

Even the term *MIS* biases perception. It says, "This system is for management; management will control it; *they* will receive information about people, programs, events, and problems, and on the basis of this information, *they* will take the action." The system self-validates itself: it *is* a management-information system.

But the more information systems are used to aid decision making, the more important become questions of pluralistic access and public participation. At the moment, MIS use is for fairly mundane and routine purposes, and much of the data collected is sheer junk, hardly usable to either those who mandate it or those who collect it. But we are rapidly moving toward information systems that will contain all sorts of parametric measures of social phenomena. For instance, computerization of hospital patient records and billing procedures will provide as a by-product the basis of a health-information system, and the pooled data of many hospitals could provide a variety of morbidity and illness indicators as well as hospital performance indicators. The point is, we have not come very far *yet*. Just as hand-operated systems generate an overabundance of irrelevant information (Ackoff 1967), so do MISs, but with incredible speed.

Despite all the limitations we have discussed, the foundation for better social management is being laid and with it important questions about public participation. Information power, information used for sensing and responding to all kinds of system states in the organization and in its environment, creates exciting potential for public participation as well as obvious dangers of overconcentration of information power. The most general questions are, how will information power be used, and if the flow of information creates social networks, what will these networks look like, who will be part of them, and what terms will define and regulate the flow of information? In the succeeding discussion, we identify several possible types of networks of information-system users. They are not intended to be exhaustive, nor are the visual representations precise. Rather, they are intended to be suggestive and impressionistic.

The Elitist

This configuration is characterized by high power and low participation. The configuration and its dynamic aspects are dominated by a relatively few MIS experts who are able to impose or at least implant an MIS on "others." The "others" could be few or many in number, but in either case participation is passive or dependent. The probable interest arrangement is a vertical one between management and staff within organizations or between weaker and stronger agencies: a community mental health center, for instance, and its funding body, which mandates and defines the minimum requirements of the MIS. In addition to the intraorganizational and interorganizational dimensions, other important aspects are lay-professional control and consumer-professional control. In the elitist configuration, consumer groups are in a lower power position vis-à-vis information management (figure 8–2). In a literal sense, the information system is a management system.

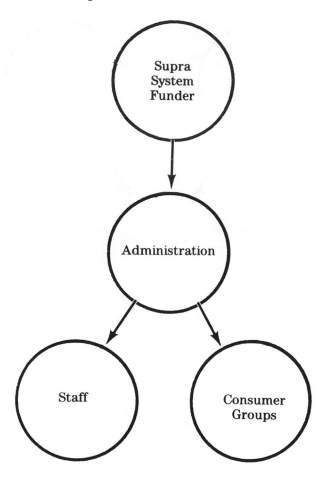

Figure 8–2. Elitist Configuration

The Negotiated

This configuration is characterized by open and negotiated arrangements with a greater, more multiplex flow of communication. In contrast to the elitist configuration, which probably produces a superficial consensus or merely compliance, here it is likely that disagreements erupt in relation to competing demands for data, diverging interpretations, and different preferences (figure 8–3). This format shows many social relations, near equality in size (power) of interests, and the ab-

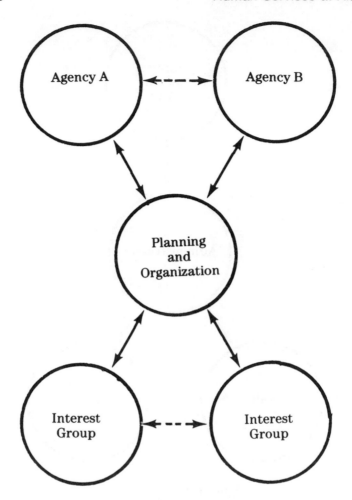

Figure 8–3. The Negotiated Configuration

sence of a compelling center force—in fact, perhaps different center forces varying with the issue or problem. A futuristic view suggests that with "strong data," MISs may become instruments of strategic coalitions, as suggested by the dotted lines. The frame of reference here is one of a win-lose situation in relation to the control of information.

Synergetic MISs

In contrast to the negotiated configuration, the synergetic MISs are characterized by open and egalitarian participation (figure 8–4). Tech-

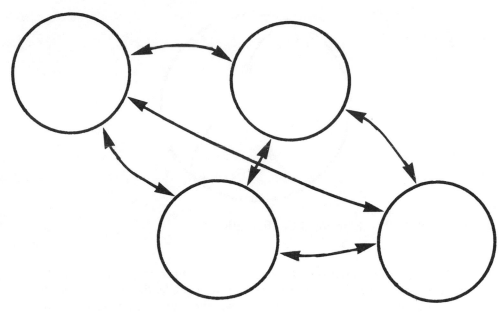

Figure 8–4. The Synergetic Configuration

nical dominance is absent, and in fact, the MIS is used to share information. The alleged power of the MIS is deliberately not pursued by anyone or by any interest group. In fact, the intrinsic value of information may ultimately become the impetus for participation. Not that disagreements or friction will be entirely absent. Rather, a strong commitment to definable ends and purposes will enable the MIS to serve as an electronic-age facilitation device. Here, technical expertise, indeed the information system itself, is the servant of the group or interorganizational system.

Estranged

Estranged or alienated configurations are those in which organizations and MISs become encapsulated (figure 8–5). Social attachments with other interests and organizations are disvalued and the organization defines its interest in self-oriented terms. A high degree of resource independence is one of the preconditions for this configuration. Alternately, declining or stagnant organizations may disengage from what are seen as hostile environments. This type is portrayed by a single system unrelated to any others. The arrows depict self-referential and

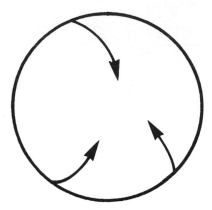

Figure 8–5. The Estranged Configuration

self-serving preoccupations. To disguise self-referential preoccupations, the organization's dedication to service and professional ideals is repeatedly invoked. Meanwhile, of course, the agency gathers information about its clientele and keeps this information to itself, unbeknownst to the clientele.

Regulating Information Systems

Ultimately, if the object of real-time information systems is to regulate and control selected events, the computer and its accompanying complex of communication systems will thrust upon us a new era marked by the urgent need for a public philosophy regulating the use of these systems. Among the general problems a public philosophy must wrestle with are the individual's prerogatives to personal privacy, the traditional relationship between the citizen and government, the questions of public control over a new elite of information-keepers, and the whole problem of democratic consent.

Individual Rights

Information management will compound the dilemma already prevalent in a society committed to widespread reliance on formal record-keeping about individuals. The right to privacy and the right to due process, two major constitutional principles, have long provided a basic legal right and public-policy framework for questions about what personal information should be put into records, with whom it should be shared, and what information individuals were entitled to know and contest about their records when these were used to make judgments affecting their rights and opportunities.

Already, one discerns breaches in the legal protections. The list of agencies that now collect and collate by computer information about people's lives and activities—sometimes derogatory information—is long and frightening. The National Crime Information Center is one. There are also many state criminal justice information systems inter-linked with the national one. Medicaid MISs are chock full of extensive medical information that health-care providers are required to report to federal and state auditors. Insurance companies receive copies of the hospital bill and the patient's medical record before the patient, and millions of personal medical histories regularly pass from doctors to employers and insurance companies. The Medical Information Bureau, a clearinghouse supported by 750 insurance companies, has medical files on 12 million Americans and Canadians. Psychiatric difficulties, "adverse" driving records, attempted suicide, drug abuse, and more are part of those records. The bureau will not show individuals their medical information files, but last year it distributed 20 million reports to insurers. In a large number of states today, any agency *suspecting* child abuse is required to report it to the authorities. Even cable television companies collect and store data about their contacts with sub-scribers—and, on occasion, make that data available to municipal government.

Unfortunately, many of the procedural reforms of the 1970s that protected individual rights have been abandoned by the Reagan admin-istration. With government at all levels possessing bulging storehouses of information on the citizenry, with the dispensation of all kinds of public benefits contingent upon the recipient baring his life, the tech-nology for surveillance is in place. Little imagination is needed to fore-see the potential role of the computer in making it possible for the authorities to watch over us.

Having entered 1984, George Orwell's demonic vision has not yet materialized, but so far have we come that even the time-honored privileged communications betwen a doctor and patient has been cracked open. According to Siegler (1982), medical confidentiality simply no longer exists. In social work, the dangers of privacy invasion are at least as great, if not more so. One reason for this is that in social work the confidentiality protections have had neither the force of law nor of age-old tradition. A second reason is that social work, unlike medicine, emerged as an organizationally based profession. Social workers, even more than physicians, may be prone to accede to the authority of the organization that collects client data and disseminates it.

A Model Code of Ethics

The foregoing highlights the need for a model code of ethics for client-oriented information systems. Such a code should comprehensively define and limit client-oriented information systems. A beginning code would contain five basic protections: the individual would be informed of the existence of a computerized client-information system; the individual would be informed about the use of client information, its dissemination, to whom and in what form (individual data or aggregated data in which individual identity is lost); informed client consent would be required before inclusion in the system, except as otherwise legally required; individuals would be permitted to inspect information about themselves, to correct errors, and to add new information; and individuals would be permitted to expunge their records, except as otherwise legally required.

Information Systems and Social Change

To deal with the social change that information systems will produce and, more specifically, with the issue of democratic pluralism in information management, a bit of intellectual housecleaning is needed to bury the technically self-serving myth that technology is neutral until humans endow it with purpose. Unlike science, technology is action-in-the-world, and not only can action not be neutral, but the potential action flowing from any technology is circumscribed by the technology itself. Simply said, cars do not fly and computers are not kidney machines.

Also, computer-based information systems reinforce a world view, a way of thinking and perceiving, that is decisively antipolitical. The techno-logical viewpoint of information systems, as we have seen, tends to conceal purpose, intentionality, interest, and controversy. And the criteria for technical systems are self-referential; they are technical, not social or political. Technicism, of which information systems are an example as well as an index, implies a world view, a mental environment, in which the vocabulary of agents and intentions has been displaced by a world picture of exaggerated surface composure and order, routine and predictability. This is the world of bureaucratic-managerial elites and technical elites, a world that transforms problems of political interest into purely technical problems. We cannot help but note that the current structure of the MIS and its concomitant world view encourage people to displace their freedom of agency onto experts of all sorts (e.g., information and computer experts) and in so doing to eventuate a loss of human power and dignity.

But these are dangers, not inevitabilities. Clearly, in the years ahead, power will be increasingly based on access to control of information, so there is a substantial political component in information management. The challenge is to make this component clear and obvious so that the groundwork can be laid for a more open process, one that involves collaboration between administrators, planners, politicians, and the public.

The means are at hand for a genuinely participative technology. Indeed, science and technology are part of the cultural inheritance of the people. But alas, that inheritance is being squandered in such "scientific fireworks" and private playthings as home computers for video games, for so-called household financial management, and for retrieval of stock-market data.

In principle, every human-service agency is a real-time information system using feedback and some standards of effectiveness to sense and respond to changes. Today the technology is here for rapidly and efficiently monitoring practically any system state: the availability of community services (day care, homemakers, meals on wheels, etc.), needs-problem indices, program effectiveness, benefit-cost data, the uses of organizational resources (program budgets), and so on. Why should we hold on to this information? Indeed, we can no longer afford to do so, for the growing gulf between the citizenry and the organs of the welfare state poses the threat of even greater erosion of support for the social services, of a politics of resentment and stinginess, not enlightenment.

Obviously, the citizenry needs to know what we the experts know, and we must be willing to hand over the indices, the rules, the models, the information so that the citizenry can evaluate measures of need, choices of programs, and the range of variation in program effects. Imagine the home computer linked to the centralized information system of a planning or funding organization, the United Way for instance, or better still, terminals spotted in community facilities where groups congregate, such as settlement houses. After all, information should belong to the people and to all of them, not just an elite. The technology is at hand; what remains is for us to "give away" our know-how. That our technology is still limited to a technical-managerial elite is not a testimony to the impossibility of sharing; it says only that no genuine attempt has yet been made to do it.

References

Ackoff, Russell L. "Management Misinformation Systems," *Management Science* 14 (December 1967):59–68.

Almy, Timothy. "City Managers, Public Avoidance and Revenue Sharing," *Public Administration Review* 37 (1977):1927.

Downs, Anthony. *Inside Bureaucracy*. Boston: Little, Brown & Co., 1967.

Gruber, Murray L. "Inequality in the Social Services," *Social Service Review* 54 (March 1980):59–75.

Gruber, Murray L., ed. *Management Systems in the Human Services*. Philadelphia, Temple University Press, 1981.

Mott, Paul E. *Meeting Human Needs: The Social and Political History of Title XX*. Columbus, Ohio; National Conference on Social Welfare, 1976.

Paton, John A., and M.S. D'huyvetter. *Automated Management Information Systems for Mental Health Agencies: A Planning and Acquisition Guide*. DHHS Publication No. (ADM) 80-797. Washington, D.C.: USGPO, 1980.

Project Share. *Planning and Implementing Social Service Information Systems: A Guide for Management and Users*. Human Services Monograph No. 25, September 1981, Aspen Systems Corp.

Schoech, Dick J., Lawrence L. Schkade, and Raymond Sanchez Mayers. "Strategies for Information System Development," *Administration in Social Work* 5 (Fall/Winter 1981):11–26.

Siegler, Mark. "Confidentiality in Medicine—A Decrepit Concept," *New England Journal of Medicine* 307 (December 1982):1518–21.

Turem, Jerry. "The Call for a Management Stance," *Social Work* 19 (September 1974):615–23.

Youchah, Michael I., "An Introduction to Systems Analysis, Design and Implementation," in Murray L. Gruber (ed.). *Management Systems in the Human Services*. Philadelphia: Temple University Press, 1981.

**Part III
Understanding How:
Lessons from the Field**

9 The Executive in Child Welfare

Felice Davidson Perlmutter

This chapter examines the performance of child welfare executives, in both the public and private sectors, in light of the changes that have occurred since the coming to power of the Reagan administration. This administration's domestic agenda includes a reaffirmation of laissez-faire economics, the resuscitation of social Darwinism as a guide to social legislation, and a strong emphasis on divesting federal control of, and responsibility for, social programs.

Within the social services, it has been the intent of the executive and the Congress to *relinquish control* of social-service programs at the federal level; this includes control at the policy level, the administrative level, and the delivery level. The response of many localities, and the city government in the present case study, has been to *take control* of these programs. This intent reflects concern for clients, sensitivity to black and minority needs, and a desire to provide an appropriate floor of service to the consumer of child welfare services.

The element both levels have in common is the intent to implement the changes as *quickly as possible.* At the federal level it was clear that executive performance was responsive, within the context of its ideological position, to the budgetary process. The important question is whether the different ideology at the local level would allow a different leadership pattern to emerge.

We will first provide a theoretical framework for the discussion, followed by a description of child welfare in Philadelphia as background for the case study. We will then present a case study that deals with several of the administrative issues addressed in this volume. Finally, we will discuss the implications for executive leadership in both the public and private sectors. It must be noted that this discussion is designed to examine executive behavior at a particular time, in relation to a particular series of events. It is neither intended to tell the full story of an ongoing, complicated process nor to serve as an evaluation of performance.

This chapter is an outgrowth of research conducted in collaboration with Dr. June Axinn, Professor of Social Work, University of Pennsylvania.

Implementation: A Theoretical Framework

In their definition of implementation, Pressman and Wildavsky distinguish between policy and its implementation, as policy precedes and
sets the conditions for implementation:

> A program consists of governmental action initiated in order to secure
> objectives whose attainment is problematical. A program exists when
> the initial conditions—the "if" stage of the policy hypothesis—have
> been met. The word "program" signifies the conversion of a hypoth-
> esis into governmental action. The initial premises of the hypothesis
> have been authorized. The degree to which the predicted conse-
> quences (the "then" stage) take place we call implementation. Im-
> plementation may be viewed as a process of interaction between the
> setting of goals and actions geared to achieving them (1973).

While the authors separate the analysis of policy and implementation,
they are keenly aware of their interdependence, and the purpose of
the discussion is to bring them into closer correspondence.

After extensive study of the Economic Development Administration's employment effort in Oakland in the late 1960s, Pressman and
Wildavsky conclude:

> Implementation should not be divorced from policy. There is no point
> in having good ideas if they cannot be carried out. . . . The great
> problem as we understand it, is to make the difficulties of implemen-
> tation a part of the initial formulation of policy. Implementation must
> not be conceived as a process that takes place after, and independent
> of, the design of policy. Means and ends can be brought into somewhat
> closer correspondence only by making each partially dependent on
> the other (p. 143).

The process of implementation includes all actors in the system,
lower- as well as upper-level participants; consequently, one must not
examine only one sphere of an organization to see whether implementation took place. Furthermore, implementation is a sequential process
of events that "depend on complex chains of reciprocal interaction."
Pressman and Wildavsky suggest two sets of actions to achieve the
necessary correspondence between policy and program: first, it is essential to take into account the complexity and length of the interactions
required for implementation; second, it is as important to attend to the
organizational machinery necessary not only to implement a program
but also to launch it.

One final point must be made in regard to Pressman and Wildavsky's conclusions. Just as parsimony is sought in the conduct of research,

simplicity must be sought in the implementation of policy. "The fewer the steps involved in carrying out the program, the fewer the opportunities for a disaster. . . . Simplicity is, of course, not an end itself; a fast train is worse than a slow one if it takes you in the wrong direction. Simplicity can be ignored, however, only at the peril of breakdown" (p. 147).

The Child Welfare System in Philadelphia

Child welfare is a complex system consisting of an array of organizational actors operating in a highly active and interdependent field (Keith-Lucas 1974). Kadushin provides a definition of child welfare services:

> The child welfare services system is that network of public and voluntary agencies, comprising a field of social work practice, that engages in those activities concerned with preventing, ameliorating and remedying of social problems related to the functioning of the parent-child relationship through the development and provision of specific child welfare services, such as adoption, foster care, institutional care, protective services, day care, homemaker service, supportive services, etc. (1978, p. 6).

While there is variation in the extent and type of relationship between the public and voluntary sectors, there is usually a mix in the local system. The active role of the voluntary sector is historically related to the socializing function inherent in child welfare and the desire of both religious and nonsectarian groups to control that process. The Social Security Act gave fiscal responsibility to the public sector, and many counties took programmatic control as well; in some local jurisdictions, however, the provision of child welfare services was retained by the voluntary sector. Moreover, this dichotomous arrangement, with service responsibility separated from financial responsibility, remained in place in Philadelphia until 1980, when Mayor Green took office.

The Philadelphia Background

The child welfare system in Philadelphia, with its mix of public and private roles and responsibilities, was basically a stable one. While the structure was generally accepted and supported by both Republican and Democrat administrations until the election of Mayor Green in 1980, problems had occasionally surfaced in earlier decades. In 1963 a report was issued by the Mayor's Committee on Public-Private Financing of Child Care in Philadelphia (Philadelphia 1963). The report addressed the role of the city's department of public welfare in administering its child welfare responsibility. It identified administrative issues such as a central intake system, uniform fees, and determination of the rates to be paid to the voluntary agencies, and it discussed accountability mechanisms.

In addition to the discussion of these administrative concerns, the report identified six outside organizations involved and concerned with the work of the Mayor's Committee. These were the County Court of Philadelphia, the Health and Welfare Council, the Philadelphia Branch of the NAACP, the School District of Philadelphia, the United Fund of Philadelphia, and the Urban League of Philadelphia.

In 1971, the Philadelphia Area Chapter of the National Association of Social Workers requested that the secretary of the Pennsylvania Department of Public Welfare conduct an inquiry into the operations of the child welfare program in the Philadelphia Department of Welfare (Pennsylvania NASW 1971). Much controversy ensued as NASW charged that children under DPW's care, placed both in city and private settings, were often abused and ill cared for. The problems of an acute shortage of staff and adequate facilities quickly surfaced.

Yet, while the child welfare program in Philadelphia faced continuous professional, political, and fiscal problems, it was not until 1981 that a new administrative arrangement was attempted, under new executive leadership, which addressed many of the concerns identified by the 1963 report of the Mayor's Committee.

The Case Study[1]

In 1981, William Green became mayor in a period of great stress and constraint. He not only inherited many problems left by his predecessor, Frank Rizzo, but he also had to deal with a host of new problems inflicted upon the city by growing conservativism at the state and federal levels, with the attendant cutback in public monies.

The mayor swept into office with his own cadre of officials, creating a climate reminiscent of John F. Kennedy's entry into Washington. He brought into the executive branch a group of professionals who appeared to possess not only technical sophistication and competence but ideological commitments to issues dealing with equality, racism, womens' rights, the plight of the poor, and citizen review boards, among others. A feeling of optimism prevailed, and hopes were centered on the intent and capability of city government to implement a program to meet the needs of Philadelphia's complex and diverse electorate.

Wilson Goode was appointed managing director, responsible for all of the operational programs in the city, including the Department of Welfare. Mr. Goode was highly respected as a tough and competent professional whose most recent public role was as a member of Pennsylvania's Public Utilities Commission. In addition to his professional competence, he brought with him a special attribute; he had grown up poor and black in the streets of Philadelphia. His identification with the needs of the oppressed populations in the city was manifest in his public statements and activities. In addition, the appointment of Irene Pernsley as commissioner of welfare, appeared to represent similar commitments; Ms. Pernsley, a black woman, was a professional social worker long associated with public-welfare activities.

The Department of Welfare had suffered a loss of qualified leadership during the eight years of the Rizzo administration; it was not perceived as an effective program either by the professional social-work community or the administration. There were now hopes and expectations that not only would the negative image of welfare be turned around but, more important, that the performance of the department would be improved. One opportunity for this initiative was provided through the program in child welfare.

The Policy Context

As Pressman and Wildavsky have noted, implementation cannot be understood without taking the policy context into account. In Philadelphia, two conflicting policies guided developments in child welfare. First, there was the clear concern, expressed repeatedly by the managing director and the commissioner of welfare, that the interests of the children at risk were a priority, and that no child was to be hurt as a result of any changes taking place in the child welfare system. This focus on program *effectiveness* reflected a policy compatible with the values of social work, the leading profession engaged in child welfare services, and the many voluntary agencies and boards involved in this system.

Simultaneously, a second policy was enunciated dealing with fiscal priorities. Given the dramatic cuts in state funds for children's services (30 percent in fiscal year 1981), it was the intent of the managing director to stay within the budget allocations and not to allow overspending. The thrust here was for *efficiency*. It was patently clear that these two policies were in opposition to each other and it would be impossible to achieve both in an equally effective manner. Yet the executive branch assumed that both policies could be realized and proceeded immediately to implement them. Before discussing the implementation strategy, it is important to become acquainted with the central actors and interest groups involved in the process.

Critical Actors

The critical actors in this case study were the administrators in both the public and private agencies. In the *public sector,* the actors with major impact on the process, all upper-level participants, were Mayor William Green, Managing Director Wilson Goode, Welfare Commissioner Irene Pernsley, and Deputy Welfare Commissioner Francis Fisher.

The mayor, historically identified with liberal causes and closely involved with his working-class constituency, had had good communication with the social-work profession as a United States congressman. His cabinet appointments reflected a high level of integrity and competence. Having assumed the mantle of office, however, he was conspicuously absent in the governance process and did not assume a leadership role in articulating policy. Thus, when pressed to assume a leadership role in regard to *county responsibility* for the care of dependent and neglected children, with the attendant need for increased taxes, his response was "blame Governor Thornburgh, not me." When publicly reminded that child welfare was a county responsibility, he was not aware of this nor did he choose to confront the issue (March 1981 meeting with voluntary agencies).

Consequently, the managing director handled the process completely. While on a personal level he had a dual concern with program efficiency and effectiveness, in his professional role he was caught in the "executive bind" (Perlmutter 1980); at a public meeting with executives of the voluntary agencies, he stated that his responsibility was to work within the reality of the budget constraints. "We do not make policy; we manage it" (April 1981). Effectiveness thus gave way to efficiency.

This duality was operationalized by the managing director's appointments of Commissioner Pernsley and Deputy Commissioner Frank Fisher. Commissioner Pernsley was a longtime professional social worker whose career reflected a commitment to social-work values; her professional style was process oriented, with respect for the involvement and decision making of line workers, the *lower-level participants.* By contrast, Mr. Fisher was trained in management; it was his technical expertise which brought him to the department, and he obtained his knowledge of child welfare while on this job. His approach was more hierarchical, working through the organizational chain of command.

By removing himself from active involvement with child welfare policy, Mayor Green created a leadership vacuum; the goals of his reform administration were not clearly articulated by any of the other actors. Efficiency became the ascendant concern, while policy, with its underlying goals and objectives, took a back seat.

In the *private sector* the executives of several of the large voluntary agencies were mobilized to play a leadership role. There is no question that the initial impetus for this role emerged from self-interest for their agencies, for the efficiency thrust of DPW threatened their existence (Clark 1956, Perrow 1978). In the process, their professional concern for the client population helped them to become advocates for the children in the county. Again, the absence of lower-level participants must be noted.

Critical Interest Groups

Of equal importance to the actors identified above were the potential array of interest groups, both in the public and private sectors. In the *public sector*, two relevant bodies could have been concerned with policy, but because of confusion regarding their roles, they were restricted to an advisory function, largely concerned with implementation. The Youth Services Coordinating Commission was established by a city ordinance, Bill No. 665, to "plan, evaluate and coordinate, at the policy level, the delivery of services to youth in the City so as to improve the effectiveness and efficiency of those services" (section 7, (1)). Yet, its chairman was uncertain of its function in relation to the commissions' role (personal communication).

Similarly, the Child Welfare Advisory Board, whose function was to review and advise the Department of Welfare, lacked clarity about its role. The minutes of the advisory board give evidence of its confusion in discussions about the proposed 30 percent budget cut in child welfare:

> Mrs. P. [the chairperson of the board] stated that Mr. C. [Finance Committee] pointed out the problems in the budget this year very well. She questioned what the Board could do to be effective in helping solve these problems. She stated that the Board has no questions with the handling of the budget within the Department, but the Board needs to know where it fits in the matter.
>
> Mr. C. stated that it could be a question of whether this Board should go and undercut the administration. Some people will feel that this is a citizens' committee and they should say what they feel in this regard.
>
> Mrs. P. questioned if the Board would have any clout in asking

to see the Mayor and Mr. Goode in terms of what the City is providing in money to the Department. Could the Board be of help in that area?

Mr. B. [director of Liaison Services, Administrative Staff, Philadelphia County Children and Youth Agency,] felt that the City is strained to its limit in terms of money. He felt the attention should be given to Harrisburg and the State's budget. If there is any hope it should be focused there (Minutes, 1 April 1981).

The minutes thus indicate that the board was taking its cues from executive staff and abdicating its autonomous role and traditional function of advocacy. The board's role was further weakened by the poor communication it had with the Department of Welfare and especially by the lack of face-to-fact contact between its chair and the welfare commissioner.

The one active constituency from the public sector was the foster-parents' group, which had a direct stake in the process. The economies taking place were often at their expense, and consequently their self-interest led them to become strong advocates for quality care. There was little evidence of activity from the lower-echelon actors, the professional staff.

An interesting phenomenon emerged in respect to the interest groups in the *private sector*. Whereas in the 1960s a group of interested community organizations had become involved in the process, in 1981 there was a dramatic absence of those interest groups whose involvement could be expected. The professional social-work organization (NASW) and black community groups were not heard from, nor were watchdog groups such as the Committee of Seventy, the League of Women Voters, the Ministerial Associations, among others. It was our interpretation that they were all co-opted by what appeared to be an enlightened administration concerned with governmental reform.

The Implementation of Change

The Department of Public Welfare moved to take control of child welfare services in Philadelphia through a variety of actions:

1. DPW would now handle *all intake* of clients into the system whereas, previously the contracting agencies had handled their individual intake process.
2. whenever possible, services should be provided to children in their own homes, and DPW would begin to provide these *services directly* (i.e., with less contracting).
3. DPW would now develop a *uniform rate structure* to be applied

across the board to all agencies, whereas in the past the agencies had set their own rates for services.

4. DPW would *define the services* it wished to purchase, whereas before the voluntary agencies determined the services on the basis of their assessment of client need.

5. All local contracting agencies would be carefully *monitored*.

It was clear that each of these administrative actions would have a profound impact on the child welfare system as a whole as well as on each individual contracting agency. And the conflict between efficiency and effectiveness would surface throughout the implementation process.

Commissioner Pernsley's concern that implementation not be divorced from policy stemmed from her professional identification with social work and its value system. As a professional social worker, she believed it essential to involve the relevant constituents in the implementation process, in this case, the professionals and the agencies from the voluntary sector (interview, 6 April 1981). Unfortunately, this process started late in the game, after the Department of Welfare had begun to take control, in response to the shortfall of funds. Commissioner Pernsley believed there were two lessons to be learned from this process: it is important to involve the constituents as early as possible to make it a mutual problem solving process; ongoing communication between the public and private sector is essential, and this communication should not be triggered by an emergency or crisis situation.

In our view there may have been, in fact, an irresolvable problem, and the best process of implementation could not have prevented confrontation and hostility. For this was not a case of two equal opponents involved in a struggle for control; clearly, the deck was stacked in favor of the Department of Public Welfare, which had the authority, responsibility, and controlled the pursestrings. The only high card the agencies held was the capacity to deliver the services needed by the city. How far that card could take them remained a debatable issue, however, related to the issue of effectiveness.

Pressman and Wildavsky suggest that it is important to continually attend to the organizational machinery necessary to implement a program and not just to launch it. The major obstacle encountered in this case study is that the launching took place aggressively and immediately on the part of DPW, with no machinery in place to implement the program. Consequently a series of fundamental frustrations and problems arose which threatened the capacity of the total system, both in the public and private sectors, to serve the children and youth in their charge.

First, the lower-level DPW staff were neither involved in the planning nor prepared for the enormous changes put into effect by the upper-level actors. In the intake process, the voluntary agencies were expected to call in their cases to DPW intake staff, who would complete an intake form that would both open the case and allow for agency billing. This single step created an administrative nightmare, for the phones were overloaded; DPW could not even handle, on a mechanical level, the incoming calls. Thus, it took hours for the voluntary agencies to connect with DPW, and then the DPW workers were not trained to handle the process, nor did they even understand it. As a result, DPW was falling behind in its payments to the voluntary agencies for past services performed. And last, but not least, DPW's *information system* was simply not up and running; consequently, children who were dropped by voluntary agenices were still on DPW's list, while children still receiving service were not.

Second, DPW had *no baseline data* regarding their costs and, consequently, their savings. Because the department did not yet have control of the information, it would not realize its savings within the six-month period; fiscal cuts would therefore be projected onto the next six months, thus doing further damage to the system. Third, all *decision making* was centralized and no discretion left at the workers' level in regard to intake, service continuity, or service exceptions. All questionable cases had to go to the commissioner or the city manager, causing delays in what were usually urgent and pressing cases. Fourth, in regard to the new *monitoring* system, there was no official communication on procedures or expectations of performance. All appeared to depend on ad hoc activity on the part of individual staff members in individual agencies, obtained by word of mouth.

Thus, the mechanisms for taking control were far from developed, and chaos ensued, accompanied by hostility, mistrust, and a deterioration of the relationships between the public and private sectors. Pressman and Wildavsky's suggestion for simplicity in implementation, attempted here, serves to illustrate that simplicity must not be an end in itself and that "a fast train is worse than a slow train if it takes you in the wrong direction" (p. 147).

Efficiency versus Effectiveness

The implementation of the change highlighted the contradictory policies within child welfare as efficiency vied with effectiveness. In his quest for efficiency and fiscal control, Deputy Commissioner Fisher was unequivocal in his view that steps had to be taken to balance the budget, a priority that would underpin the agency's professional program. Consequently, DPW implemented various operational policies to accomplish the goal of a 30 percent across-the-board reduction (March 1981). Although the intent was to drop those services for children who were least at risk, as well as those services that were underutilized, the process was simpler in conception than in implementation. Various mechanisms were introduced: (1) intake would be closed by DPW for a four-month period; (2) youth over eighteen were to be dropped from the program; (3) a uniform rate scale was adopted, based on averaging the costs of the services among the provider agencies, and not on an analysis of the actual cost of any particular service; (4) DPW's emergency care facility was closed.

Commissioner Pernsley recognized the complexity of these moves and established eight task forces to deal with the issues. The task forces were composed of professionals from both DPW and the voluntary sector, and a great deal of time and energy was invested, with very short time frames, to accomplish their mission. Although DPW did pay attention to the work of the task forces and adjusted a few of its initial positions, the conflict between effectiveness and efficiency still continued. First, those children and youth in need of immediate care would suffer from the four-month closing of intake by DPW; second, the yough between eighteen and twenty-one who needed service would no longer be eligible; third, the new uniform fee structure did not take into account any special circumstances and/or vulnerable situations that might require more extensive and possibly costly services; and finally, although DPW decided to provide SCOH services directly, DPW staff was not trained to work with children with emotional problems or with neglected or dependent children.

At this time the executives from the voluntary sector became powerful advocates for the children. First, when DPW closed intake, the voluntary agencies accepted clients and assumed the costs. Second, the voluntary agencies fought to protect the eighteen-to-twenty-one-year-olds by pointing out that, according to Pennsylvania's Act 41 and Act 148, upon the request of the child and when so ordered by the court, the county was required to provide service beyond the eighteenth birthday for the purpose of instruction or treatment (Draft, Task Force on Services to 18 year olds, 25 March 1981); consequently the city DPW revised its position. Third, extensive work was done by the executives in interpreting the needs for a separate fee scale for special needs. Finally, the executives spoke out publically for quality service and called DPW to task for what appeared to be a lack of respect for the competence needed to provide quality care; money was the first concern. The policy conflict was dramatically evident when Managing Director Goode expressed concern with this perception and asked that he be personally contacted if a child was not properly served (9 April 1981). What was apparent was that the organization was geared for efficiency, while the upper-level *actors,* on a personal and individual basis, were concerned with effectiveness.

One solution to the efficiency and effectiveness dilemma proposed was that disagreements between DPW and the voluntary agencies concerning cases to be discontinued be resolved by three-person panels composed of one DPW staff member, one voluntary agency staff member, and one outside academic from a school of social work. Credibility would be established on the basis of the panel's neutrality. The panels were never activated, however, and ultimate decisions remained with the top-level DPW actors, again suggesting a bias in the direction of efficiency.

Thus, efficiency rather than effectiveness dominated the administrative process in this case study, in spite of the dual intent. This is a critical finding, for given the dramatic differences both in leadership and in ideology between the county level under Mayor Green, and the federal level under President Reagan, the critical question emerges: What are the implications for the social administrator?

Conclusions

There are lessons to be learned from this case study of child welfare. This chapter has emphasized the distinctions between leadership in the public and the voluntary sectors, given that each operates within different contexts and constraints. Yet, the principles for social administration may, ultimately, be generic and applicable across sectors.

First, as policy is inextricably linked to implementation, it is essential that the *policy be clearly articulated and clearly understood throughout the system.* It cannot be the property of a select few, even if at the upper echelons of the system.

Second, *implementation and the necessary organizational machinery to achieve it must be carefully tailored around the policy.* In this case study, two policies were articulated, but as discussed above, the organizational apparatus was designed to implement only the one concerned with efficiency and cutbacks.

Third, it is important to note that *in spite of ideological and professional commitments to clients in need, effectiveness can give way to efficiency in the press of fiscal constraints.* Thus, in this case study, the organizational machinery was tooled to cut back on clients and services to meet the budgetary demands. Mistakenly, the upper-level actors in the public-welfare sector promised that *personal* attention would be paid by them to any child suffering from the cuts. This ad hoc mechanism could never be effective in a large system; the problem always requires *organizational* mechanisms to meet client needs.

Fourth, the *timing and sequencing of events require careful attention, for there is a reciprocal interaction in every process that affects the product.* While simplicity is necessary, it is not sufficient; consequently, it is essential to think first and act later, not to act first and think later. Pressman and Wildavsky's instruction that the organizational apparatus must be in place not only to implement, but also to launch, a program must be heeded.

Fifth, *administrators must attend to the necessity of involving all participants in the system.* In addition to the executive suite, or upper-level participants, the involvement of staff, or lower-level participants, must be in place to insure an effective operation. This means not only that the technical or structural apparatus must be in place but that the policy must be clearly understood by all.

Sixth, *external constituencies must be involved in any shift in the social-service system.* They perform an essential function, for they represent society's concerns with populations in need. If they are not aware of the process and do not participate through their own initiative, then it is the responsibility of the social administrator to inform them of the new policy and program shifts and to give them what information they may need to participate effectively.

Finally, *social administrators in both the public and the private sectors must serve as advocates* to meet the needs of clients while responding to the total system's requirements (Slavin 1980). Richan discusses the elements available to the administrator as advocate: formal authority to act, control over resources ("money, materials, equipment and personnel"), and control over information (1980, pp. 76–79). Their use will depend on the proactive orientation of the executive. In this case study the advocacy that emerged did not stem from the Department of Public Welfare; the above elements, identified by Richan, were available but not used by the public-sector actors. The only administrative advocacy that emerged was in the voluntary sector, as many of the executives used their formal authority to act within their agencies and to mobilize resources at their disposal to further the advocacy role through their attempt to share information with the community and with the city council.

We are indeed entering a new era; the whole social-welfare system will need to evaluate its current and future stakes and structure. On the one hand, federal government is abandoning its involvement with human services; on the other, the local sector is not ready to respond to this increased responsibility adequately. This case exemplifies the enormous complexities and dilemmas in public administration and social welfare. There are no simplistic solutions or heroes. There is no question that the public sector needed to take control of its programs; there is no question that an external watchdog serves the vital function of protecting the interests of the groups served when bureaucratic requirements get in the way, intentionally or unintentionally.

This Philadelphia experience is the harbinger of things to come. Yet, even in this situation, where there was a dual concern both with effectiveness and efficiency, problems surfaced that might have been avoided through clearer administrative strategies, both in the public and the voluntary sector. It is now time for a reappraisal of the role of the social administrator. Experience from the field must be shared in order to help executives develop more effective approaches to dealing with our corrosive realities.

Note

1. This case study is based on data collected during a series of interviews with the upper echelon executives, from both the public and voluntary sectors as well as with members of the Child Welfare Advisory Board. In addition the author attended all meetings between DPW and the voluntary agencies which were held throughout the winter of 1980 and spring of 1981.

References

Clark, B.R. "Organizational Adaptation and Precarious Values," *American Sociological Review* 21 (1956):327–36.
Kadushin, A. *Child Welfare Services.* New York: Macmillan Co., 1980.
Keith-Lucas, A. "Co-planning and Advocacy in Child Welfare Services," in F.D. Perlmutter ed., *A Design for Social Work Practice.* New York: Columbia University Press, 1974.
Pennsylvania National Association of Social Workers, Correspondence file, 1971.
Perlmutter, F.D. "The Executive Bind," in F.D. Perlmutter and S. Slavin, eds., *Leadership in Social Administration.* Philadelphia: Temple University Press. 1980.
Perrow, C. "Demystifying Organizations," in R. Sarri and Y. Hasenfeld, eds., *The Management of Human Services.* New York: Columbia University Press, 1978.
Philadelphia. *Strengthening Welfare Services for Dependent and Ne-*

glected Children in Philadelphia. Report of the Mayor's Committee on Public-Private Financing of Child Care in Philadelphia, 1963.

Pressman, J.L., and A. Wildavsky. *Implementation.* Berkeley: University of California Press, 1973.

Richan, W.C. "The Administrator as Advocate," in F.D. Perlmutter and S. Slavin, eds., *Leadership in Social Administration.* Philadelphia: Temple University Press.

Slavin, S. "A Theoretical Framework for Social Administration," in F.D. Perlmutter and S. Slavin, eds., *Leadership in Social Administration.* Philadelphia: Temple University Press, 1980.

10 Aging Services and Executive Leadership

Elizabeth Ann Kutza

Over the years, many programs have developed in response to problems faced by older persons. While the decrements in functioning that accompany old age do not occur on a fixed schedule, unless precluded by death, they are inevitable. Dependency increases steadily with advancing age and is especially dramatic in the age group ninety years and over (Community Council of Greater New York 1978).

As these dependency needs increase, so do service needs. And these social-service needs are multiple and diverse, requiring both public and private intervention. Private agencies, sectarian and nonsectarian, recognized early the special needs of older persons. Between 1875 and 1919, for example, nearly 800 benevolent homes were founded catering exclusively to elderly members of particular denominations or nationalities (Achenbaum 1978). Joining these efforts were public-sector programs, most shaped by local poor laws.

As long as the elderly were cared for in private old-age homes or public almshouses, the diversity of their needs could be managed. But as the locus of services has shifted to the community, providers of service face a more difficult task of coordination. Recognizing the need to rationalize the service-delivery network within the community so as to better respond to the multiple needs of aged clients, the federal government in 1965 passed the Older Americans Act. The goal of the act was the development throughout the country of a comprehensive and coordinated service system for older persons. The relatively small ($6.5 million) program of project grants for planning, research, and training that was authorized in 1965 has grown into a well-funded ($980 million in fiscal year 1982) program of diverse services.

Through its grant-making authority, the Older Americans Act (OAA) has encouraged every state to create a department or division on aging, and further to create regional or substate area agencies on aging (AAAs). The purpose of these new bureaucratic entities is to rationalize, that is, plan and coordinate, services provided by both private and public agencies to older persons within a geographic area.

The case study that follows looks at the functioning of a few of these state and area agencies on aging and their success in developing a comprehensive and coordinated service system for older persons. The success of these agencies, or lack of it, is directly related to the nature of their mission and the authority vested in them to accomplish it. The mission of the agency, its organizational goal, is coordination, a goal that is difficult to understand and even more difficult to implement. The authority vested within these bureaucratic bodies is found in federal legislation and regulation, documents that prescribe behaviors but incorporate few incentives for compliance.

But of special significance and attention in this chapter is the role that an executive in a state or area agency on aging may play in determining success. How can a leader effect a successful outcome when faced with an ambiguous and difficult organizational goal, while operating within a constraining and sterile organizational environment? The case study that follows identifies some effective strategies.

Coordination as a Concept

Coordination is broadly supported but little understood. It is an ambiguous term having no precise definition. As Pressman and Wildavsky (1973) noted, telling a person to coordinate does not tell that person what to do. Yet coordination is thought to be instrumental in reaching desired public goals. It is cited by many as the solution to the multiple problems encountered in delivering social services.

One problem coordination is said to remedy is fragmentation of service. The usual "coordinative" strategy recommended to address fragmentation of services is increased communication among workers in the case. This strategy presumes that multiproblem clients are inundated with services not only confusing to them but inefficiently provided. Emphasis in this strategy is on cooperation among workers.

A second service-delivery problem to which coordination is deemed the answer is duplication. "Coordination" activities that address the problem of duplication of service try to facilitate joint planning among agencies. Joint planning, it is believed, will lead to a more efficient allocation of resources. Two assumptions guide this strategy: that there are hidden surplus resources that can be diverted from one service area to another, and that a cooperative planning effort by agencies will result in more rational decisions about resource allocation. "More rational" in this context means less duplicative.

Coordination, it is often believed, can also help identify and fill gaps in available service. Built upon a rational planning model, such a belief assumes that resolution of the problem of gaps in service rests upon better information. If, through coordination, the need for a particular service within the community is determined and adjudged to be absent, a plan can be set in motion that will make these services available.

A fourth problem said to be resolvable through a "coordinative" strategy is barriers to service receipt. In some cases, while services may be available, clients face barriers in procuring them. Individuals may not know about the services, may be intimidated by the process required to obtain them, or may be unable to get to where they are being delivered.

Finally, continuity of service delivery, or lack of it, may pose problems. Sometimes a desirable service package for an individual requires a serial or sequential intervention. A post-hospital discharge plan provides an illustration. In such a plan, both the frequency and type of service needed by the client would likely change across time, and their sequencing would not be random but patterned. Two approaches can facilitate continuity of service delivery. If the sequence of necessary services is fairly predictable and routine, interagency agreements or contracts are used. It is expected that such formal administrative arrangements will ease the movement of clients through all stages of the service sequence. An alternative solution to the discontinuity problem is the creation of agencies that can provide all desired services in the sequence, rather than the creation of highly specialized agencies.

Five different problems, five different strategies, all called "coordination." Their commonality is found in a formalized administrative approach to the issue. Yet this minimal commonality provides uncertain guidance to administrators expected to coordinate services.

The Case Study

Federal grants to state and local government, such as those authorized by the Older Americans Act, have been used extensively by the federal government to carry out broad national purposes. Such grants allow Congress to define the terms under which programs may win the widest possible acceptance among diverse local interests. But gaining acceptance from these interests often demands that program expectations not infringe on the prerogatives of lower levels of government. Thus, grant legislation, particularly new grant legislation, is necessarily ambiguous, inconsistent, and silent on specifics. Typically, there is only a commitment to broad goals. Many important choices are left to state and local administrators. It is expected that bargaining among the affected interests, together with "institutional learning" over time, will result in a clarification of policy purposes and provisions.

At the time of its passage, the Older Americans Act very much fit this pattern. The legislation lacked measurable objectives and, like many of the programs of the Great Society era, proposed to reach its stated aims with too limited political authority and too few resources. The original legislation established a new administrative unit at the federal level, the Administration on Aging (AoA), and provided funds to create an agency on aging in each state. Between 1965 and 1969, these agencies functioned primarily as small grant-making bodies. The 1969 Amendments to the Act, however, strengthened these state units by mandating them to plan, coordinate, and advocate on behalf of the elderly. This emphasis was compatible with the then-new Republican administration's interest in fostering efficiency in government so as to reduce costs. It was widely believed that good planning and effective service coordination would maximize the program's modest resources. Any needed new resources were to be obtained at state and local levels through advocacy, or "resource mobilization."

The 1973 Amendments to the Older Americans Act changed what had been the basic structure of the program since 1965. A presidential promise of increased funding, made at the 1971 White House Conference on Aging, compelled the Administration on Aging to develop a wider fund-disbursal strategy. Agency leadrship responded with a proposal to restructure one title under the act, Title III, in such a way as to create a new, substate level of bureaucracy, the area agencies on aging. These decentralized bodies, while accountable to the unit of state government through which their federal funds were channelled, were given a broad mandate to develop areawide plans, to expand services by pooling resources, to coordinate existing services, and, where necessary, to fund gap-filling services for the aged.

The program under the OAA therefore took on two foci: improving the existing service-delivery system through administrative mechanisms of planning and coordinating, and expanding the available pool of services through small grants to social-service agencies within the community. Today it is the former focus of activity that has gained prominence. The area agencies on aging see as their primary function the planning and coordinating of community services.

Details of the Case Study

By 1974, officials of the Administration on Aging in Washington looked across the country at the "aging enterprise" that they had created under the Older Americans Act and saw uneven progress. There was little evidence that a national comprehensive and coordinated service system for the elderly was falling into place. Some areas seemed more successful than others at achieving this goal, but federal officials wished to learn more about what they perceived as the barriers to coordination faced by state and area agencies on aging. Several research projects were funded, each directed at identifying these barriers and suggesting strategies for overcoming them. This case study is drawn from the findings of one such study (Marmor and Kutza 1975).

The purpose of the original study was to analyze the barriers state or substate AAA personnel could encounter as they attempted to co-ordinate selected federal programs for the elderly. The policy question, framed by agency personnel, asked what legislative barriers existed that would prevent state and local administrators from coordinating services for the elderly. Thus, the project began with a narrow focus on those conflicts inherent in program guidelines and regulations themselves, conflicts that might discourage or prevent an agency executive from fostering the development of an effective network of comprehensive services. The focus broadened, however, when it became apparent that the most serious barriers to the coordination of services for the elderly were to be found in the confused conception of coordination itself, and in the political and organizational realities within which state and AAA administrators worked day to day. This conclusion was confirmed through interviews with agency officials at the regional, state, and local levels, all of whom had broad experience in program administration. These respondents identified the problems inherent in the strategy of coordination and the opportunities available to effective leaders for overcoming the problems.

Implementing a Mandate to Coordinate

Having reviewed the problems inherent in defining coordination, we can now turn to its problems of implementation. While implementation of any policy is difficult, implementation of a strategy with multiple definitions and multiple goals is more so.

Agencies funded with Older Americans Act monies are mandated by the program regulations to accomplish a set of tasks defined as "coordinative." In brief, the goal of these tasks is to promote inter-dependency among other organizations. But promotion of such inter-agency interdependency is not easy and a "mutual adjustment process" is required (Lindblom 1968).

Three barriers stand out: general organizational resistance, a lack of specific incentives to cooperation, and conflicts of domain (jurisdictional, political, or bureaucratic). Strong executive leadership is needed to overcome any and all of these barriers.

Organizational Resistance

Coordination of services for the elderly over a statewide area neces-
sitates the cooperation of many existing service organizations. Yet organizations involve themselves in cooperative efforts primarily to protect
and promote their interests. Since organizations have different interests,
some will overlap supportively and others competitively. Of concern,
then, to an executive mandated to coordinate other independent agencies is how to assure these agencies that their autonomy will be preserved in areas of conflict while at the same time permitting them united
effort in areas of agreement.

All coordination, it must be kept in mind, involves a cost to participating agencies. "Organizations enter voluntarily into concerted de-
cisionmaking," Warren rightly notes, "only under those circumstances
which they perceive as conducive to the preservation or expansion of
their respective domains," and coordinated efforts may be seen by an
individual agency as a subordination of themselves to the will of outsiders (1973). When an agency's vital interests are at stake, the rationality of comprehensive and coordinated service-delivery systems is bound
to be lost on the target organizations.

Litwak and Hylton (1962) argue that a major variable that influences the success of coordinative efforts is the degree of interdependency among agencies. Low interdependency will lead to no
coordination, and high interdependency will lead to merger. Thus, the
environment within which an agency on aging is placed may determine
the extent of organizational resistance that an executive faces. And
since coordination will occur in circumstances of moderate independence, skillful executives will try to increase that interdependence.

In one state, for example, an executive of a department of aging
alerted the state department of transportation to new federal monies
soon to be made available for the provision of special services to the
elderly and handicapped. Attracted by this untapped source of revenue,
the department of transportation, in close consultation with the department of aging, applied for and received a grant. Once having received it, the transportation department continued consultation with
the department of aging executive and staff around allocation of these
funds. This was a new domain in which the transportation officials had
no expertise. Hence, a new interdependence was fostered that resulted
in continued consultation and coordination of service delivery between
two hitherto unconnected state units of government. In this case, coordination did not cost the transportation department any resources;
it brought in fresh resources.

In addition to the costs of coordination, two other organizational barriers need to be considered. First there is bureaucratic inertia. Organizations are predisposed to resist changes embodied in broad social planning goals. Such goals are formulated not to solve problems within that organization, but rather to solve those of social welfare, such as fragmentation of services (Morris and Binstock 1966). Dyer notes that for successful change efforts to go forward in organizations, there must be a strongly felt need or tension that move people to want to change (1976). The desire for coordination is rarely experienced by agencies as a strongly felt "need."

Pressman and Wildavsky have taken this idea further and suggested several reasons why participants may agree with the substantive ends of a proposal of coordination and still oppose (or merely fail to facilitate) the means for carrying it out (1973). For example, while an organization may not find the goal of coordination incompatible with its own internal goals, it may not see such a goal as falling into its perceived role and responsibility, or it may have other projects to which it has committed itself. Perhaps of most importance, coordination may fail because participants in the process may not agree on who should take the lead. A central coordinative agency, in order to be effective, must be recognized and accepted by all of the agencies whose programs would be affected. It must have organizational legitimacy.

Establishing this organizational legitimacy has been a difficult task for state and area agency executives. Some legitimacy was conferred on these new agencies by their federal mandate, but such statutory legitimacy is weak in the face of the second barrier facing OAA executives' coordinative task—lack of incentives.

Incentives

Since attempts to coordinate services for the elderly will meet with organizational resistance, widespread voluntary efforts are unlikely. Thus, inducements or incentives are required for motivation.

Since all organizations have interests they are trying to promote, appeal to these interests might induce cooperation. What, however, are the "interests" and "organizational" motives of social-service agencies? Organizational survival, maintenance, and growth may be one set, but will coordination contribute to these goals? More likely it will threaten them.

Aside from an appeal to self-interest, a second incentive to cooperation is money. The mere act of funding state and area agencies on aging will elicit compliance by these bodies to some extent, but the extent will be limited by the very limited funds available.

Conflicts of Domain

A final implementation barrier faced by executives of OAA agencies is found in jurisdictional conflicts of domain. Social services are delivered under the auspices of various levels of government (federal, state, county, township, city) and various kinds of private sponsorship (voluntary, proprietary). Services provided vary by function and clients served. This variety faces a coordinating agency with confusion over jurisdictional authority.

Executive Leadership and Implementation

"Coordination," or its absence, is commonly perceived as a problem of organizational relations, to be remedied by organizational means. Thus, the role of the leader in the organization is crucial. It is the leader, using organizational resources and overcoming organizational constraints, that can promote or impede agency goals. If the goal to be reached, as in this case, faces significant implementation barriers, then effective executive leadership marks the difference between success and failure.

In programs that lack clear policy guidance, a vigorous executive, with clear programmatic objectives, can personally overcome this lack, and a leader's freedom to do so is considerable. Yet only the exceptional leader in this case study actually set out his or her own vision of coordination. The more common experience was for the executive to rationalize his or her more limited actions through compliance with legislative mandates.

Implementation brings us to another problem. It is not the problem of which objectives to pursue and which will be most helpful in reaching a desired policy goal. Rather, the problem presented in implementation is how to influence agencies to make their activities more interdependent. Implementation requires resolving disputes among agencies in the name of coordination, and it requires substantial strategic thinking from the agency executive.

How do executives in OAA agencies overcome organizational resistance and induce interorganizational cooperation? What strategies can be used by agency executives that will help them to succeed in a situation of too little political authority and too few resources, a situation that requires them to influence other agencies? Our survey of executives who were interested in coordinating services for older persons identified three: reassurance, alliance, and support. Attention is also paid to their use of the ambiguity of the concept itself.

Reassurance

Agencies will work together on a coordinated plan of action only if that plan is consonant with their perceived interests. Yet it has been noted that identifying an agency's self-interest is very difficult. Agency personnel asked to coordinate their service with others may not primarily be asking themselves "What do I stand to gain?" but more probably may be asking, "What do I stand to lose?"

In spite of the myth to the contrary, coordination is not costless. It involves both time and resource costs. Those state and area agency on aging executives who immediately recognized the costly nature of coordination were more likely to be successful at coordination than those who behaved as though coordination was an unqualified good for everyone involved. Agencies that agree to coordinate with others run a risk, a risk they often will not verbalize, but which may lead to subversion of the coordination goal.

While social workers recognize that individuals fear change and approach it reluctantly, when these same social workers become executives of "coordinative agencies" they seem to lose this sensitivity. They often fail to recognize that changes in organizational relationships also involve risk and will be approached hesitantly. In the sample drawn for this case study, those leaders who were more sensitive to this point were ultimately more successful in developing a system of coordinated services. With great subtlety, they continually acted in ways that reassured those agency personnel who they wished to influence.

One reassurance strategy used was to redefine the goals of coordination so as to make them seem more nearly parallel to the goal of the individual agency to be coordinated. This redefinition was most effectively accomplished through one-to-one meetings in which the OAA executive met with the individual agency head on his own territory, listened carefully to his concerns, expressed understanding, and acknowledged some of the feelings of risk involved. Of equal importance during such a meeting was for the agency head to be made to feel as though his cooperation was central to the success of the coordinative effort. Bringing each agency along individually is a far more effective strategy than meeting together with all of the agencies with whom cooperation is desired. Gilbert and Specht suggest that the bringing together of a large number of autonomous and dispersed groups is more likely to result in resistance and eventual rejection of a plan of coordination because such a group meeting, instead of being reassuring, merely heightens uncertainty about the ultimate outcome of organizational relations (1977). Our respondents also emphasized the importance of never putting uncommitted people in a room together where they may discover their common opposition or worry about the project.

The main goal of the reassurance strategy is to persuade participants in the coordinative effort that the individual costs of coordination will result in mutual gain.

Alliance

Coordinative agencies such as the state and area agencies on aging under the Older Americans Act have very little authority and not much money. Thus, a major task for the executive of such agencies is to acquire the power to move beyond a limited formal charter and to influence other agencies, many larger and more powerful than his own.

One source of power has been mentioned already: technical knowledge or expertise. OAA agency executives in our sample who developed their staff's technical competence were able to influence the actions of other agencies. A data base was often the first step. While part of the mandate of state and area agencies on aging is the assessment of the health and social-service needs of older persons within the community, few agencies aggressively pursued this goal. It was thought to be too costly and to have little utility. Those executives who did accumulate a strong data base within the community, however, soon saw its utility. Having data readily available gave OAA agencies the edge they often needed to influence program development within the community. When competing claims were made on program resources, the fact that the needs of the elderly were documented lent greater weight to demands for programming in this area.

In addition to the accumulation of a data base, power was also gained within the community by those OAA executives who developed a strong and technically competent staff. Technical knowledge and expertise is power within a community, just as it is within an agency. Experts are looked toward to shape the definition of problems and their appropriate solutions. They are useful as consultants to other local groups and as suppliers of information about older persons to the general public. As these roles increase the visibility of OAA agencies, they further the acquisition of organizational power.

A second source of extended power is strategic alliances. The type

of alliance that was found to be effective by our OAA agency administrators was that with an agency at the state or local level that had
sign-off power over the projects of other agencies. In one case this was
the bureau of the budget; in another, a city planning office. These
offices not only had review power over all plans and budgets of local
agencies, but also had veto power. Alliance with such agencies allowed
OAA executives to influence the setting of criteria for final approval
of plans.

One example brought forward in this case study occurred around
community development. In a particular municipal area, all community
development plans required the approval of the planning department.
The local area agency on aging executive was able to influence the
planning department not to sign off on any plan that did not incorporate
some services to older persons. This strategy greatly enhanced the
influence of the AAA in that community.

It must be noted that this strategy, while effective, has some dangers. If every agency with a special constituency strives for sign-off
power over other agencies' proposals, a "parking lot" situation could
arise. All projects would be stalemated. However, in those instances
where the strategy was employed by the executives interviewed here,
no such problems arose.

Thus, strategic alliances can increase an OAA agency's influence
over the actions of other agencies and can provide the needed impetus
to induce cooperation and coordination among reluctant human-service
agencies.

Support

A final strategy that leaders engaged in to facilitate their mandate to
develop a system of coordinated and comprehensive services for the
elderly was the cultivation of support from political actors. Support can
mean endorsement, backing, approval, or legitimacy. Effective coordination in a state or substate area requires strong political support. In
a municipality, the mayor or city manager can intervene as the "ultimate
coordinator of all municipal departments." At the state level, strong
support and advocacy by the governor can induce other state departments to cooperate in joint programming. Vigorous local political support not only helps engender cooperation in service of the coordination
goal from those agencies to be coordinated, but it also helps OAA
agency administrators negotiate more successfully with the Administration on Aging in Washington.

Support by a political actor was enhanced in those areas where

OAA agency executives actively engaged in politicizing their constituents. Some executives took their mandate to advocate for the elderly very seriously and strove to politicize the needs of older persons through advocacy. Where this was done, political actors incurred risk by withholding their support from the agency.

Leadership Strategies with a Fuzzy Concept

Older Americans Act legislation and regulations fail to spell out specifically for OAA agency executives their authority, priorities, or objectives. Hence, executives are faced with "role ambiguity." Research has shown that when faced with role ambiguity, most executives will concentrate on administrative activities that, while relevent to their responsibility, can be achieved with a minimum amount of time and energy (Cribbin 1972). They will become "reactive" executives devoted primarily to maintaining the status quo and avoiding risk-taking situations. This is in contrast to the "proactive" executive, who is "guided by the motivation to actively influence and shape the external environment of the organization as well as its internal structure in order to fulfill the organization's mission" (Hasenfeld and English 1974, p. 155).

Executives of state or substate agencies who are proactive, while recognizing the fuzziness of the concept of coordination, see opportunity in ambiguity. They do not want further operationalization or specification of the concept. They recognize that under certain circumstances formal agreements not only are unnecessary but also are counterproductive to coordination at the client level. Formal arrangements made at the top can constrain the informal networks that get things done at the bottom. Effective leaders stress the importance of distinguishing those circumstances under which formal administrative arrangements are needed for action to occur and those under which such arrangements are disruptive of existing operational relationships within and between agencies. The provision of a coordinated package of services to older persons requires flexibility and, often, idiosyncratic responsiveness. Such responsiveness may be lost if a fixed set of preordained patterns are followed just because they have been mandated by formal interagency agreements.

Professionals in human-service agencies often develop very creative and personal solutions to vexing problems. One agency director to whom we spoke, for example, explained how she was able to persuade a local school district to make its buses available during the midday to transport older persons from their homes to congregate meal sites. This informal arrangement worked well until the state department on aging decided to make a formal agreement for such a service statewide through the department of education. Discussions of the idea led to concerns about liability, insurance rates, and financial arrangements, and these concerns led to the abandonment of the idea—even in the county where it had operated without incident.

Thus, an effective leader closely examines the informal arrangements that have developed historically both within the agency and between agencies so as to judge whether their formalization would make them more cost effective, equitable, or efficient, or whether their formalization would destroy their utility.

Creative executives also see the ambiguous directives found in the Older Americans Act as serving a latent advocacy function, a function that could not be served by more specific directives. In the minds of some, the real goal of the Older Americans Act is not "coordination" but advocacy. Prior to the enactment of the OAA, the elderly were, in one executive's words, "out of the ball game" when it came to federal service dollars. Astute state and area agency on aging executives view OAA monies as getting the elderly into the political "ball game." How? By encouraging demand. Once there is an expectation of a system of comprehensive and coordinated services, older persons will start demanding the services in the political marketplace, thus advocating in their own behalf.

Agencies funded under the Older Americans Act, because they are explicitly encouraged to advocate on behalf of the elderly, in some areas have developed into a potent political force. Executives interested in pursuing the advocacy function have educated their clients to issues that should concern them, have arranged transportation for the elderly to public hearings on important legislation, and have mobilized them to support political candidates sympathetic to their cause. Most traditional social-welfare agencies have shied away from such explicit political advocacy, but state, and especially substate, agency executives testify to the success of these tactics in getting the political marketplace supportive of spending more dollars on programs for aged persons.

Thus, coordination, an ambiguous and confused concept, faces agency executives with two choices: compliance with limited activities of administrative or architectural coordination (compliance that frequently leaves administrators feeling frustrated) or creative manipulation of the ambiguity in such a way that flexible service alternatives develop at the client-delivery level, and older recipients of service become politicized enough to advocate on their own behalf. For some executives, the ambiguous nature of the concept of coordination leads to operational difficulty or at least narrowness. For others, the same ambiguity has a subtle and usually unacknowledged utility.

Lessons for the 1980s

The cry for coordination arose in the 1960s because of a rapid expansion of social programs and a fear that they were getting out of control. As we embark on the decade of the 1980s, the social-policy environment is much different. The economy is no longer growing robustly; governmental bodies at all levels are having difficulty generating new revenues; and many feel that perhaps social programs have grown too quickly and too much.

While the social-policy environment of the 1980s contrasts sharply with that of the 1960s, one thing has remained constant: the view that coordination of social services is desirable. Whether the number of social programs is expanding or contracting, coordination is regarded as a strategy that will lead to coherence and efficiency in the delivery of these services. Thus, our belief in coordination as a strategy that will solve various problems in the delivery of social services remains unchanged.

Also unchanged in these twenty years, regrettably, is our ability to conceive of or effectively implement a plan of coordination. We are attracted to the concept but stymied by its reality. But this case study of the Older Americans Act and its implementing agencies shows us that some of these problems can be overcome with strong executive leadership. Even in the face of limited policy guidance and substantial implementation barriers, some state and agency on aging executives were able to succeed in coordinating services. Through personal and professional sensitivity, strategic thinking, and assertive behaviors, these leaders were able to promote their agency's interests and accomplish a social-policy goal.

References

Achenbaum, W. Andrew. *Old Age in the New Land: The American Experience Since 1790*. Baltimore: Johns Hopkins University Press, 1978.

Community Council of Greater New York. *Dependency in the Elderly of New York City: Policy and Service Implications of the U.S.–U.K. Cross-National Geriatrics Community Study*. New York: Community Council of Greater New York, 1978.

Cribbin, James J. *Effective Managerial Leadership*. New York: American Management Association, Inc., 1972.

Dyer, William G. *Insight to Impact: Strategies for Interpersonal and*

Organizational Change. Provo, Utah: Brigham Young University Press, 1976.

Gilbert, Neil, and Harry Specht. "Quantitative Aspects of Social Service Coordination Efforts," *Administration in Social Work* 1 (Spring 1977): 53–61.

Hansenfeld, Yeheskel, and Richard A. English. *Human Service Organizations: A Book of Readings.* Ann Arbor: University of Michigan Press, 1974.

Lindblom, Charles E. *The Policy making Process.* Englewood Cliffs, N.J.: Prentice-Hall, 1968.

Litwak, Eugene, and Lydia F. Hylton. "Interorganizational Analysis: A Hypothesis on Coordinating Agencies," *Administrative Science Quarterly* 6 (March 1962): 395–420.

Marmor, Theodore R., and Elizabeth A. Kutza. *Analysis of Federal Regulations Related to Aging: Legislative Barriers to Coordination Under Title III.* Research report submitted to the U.S. Department of Health, Education, and Welfare, 1975.

Morris, Robert, and Robert B. Binstock. *Feasible Planning for Social Change.* New York: Columbia University Press, 1973.

Pressman, Jeffrey L., and Aaron B. Wildavsky. *Implementation.* Berkeley: University of California Press, 1973.

U.S. Department of Health, Education, and Welfare. Title 45-Public Welfare, Chapter IX, Administration on Aging, Part 903—Grants to state and community programs on aging. *Federal Register* 38 (11 October 1973): 28043.

Warren, Roland, Sheldon Rose, and A. Bergunder. *Structure of Urban Reform.* Lexington, Mass.: D.C. Heath and Company. 1974.

11 The Mental Health Executive in a Context of Madness

Barbara J. Friesen and
Michael J. Austin

The stagnant economy, federal and state budget cuts, and the accelerated attack on human services from the highest levels of government have produced a crisis that pervades the social-welfare system. As in other human-services fields, mental health administrators face program reduction or elimination, loss of staff capability to operate remaining programs, and tough choices about reducing essential services and turning away needy clients.

Faced with severe program reductions and the effects of "fiscal stress (Levine 1980), there is a real danger that mental health administrators will become preoccupied with survival: choosing between cutback management strategies and fitting program pieces into an ever shrinking, shifting funding puzzle. The tendency for the original goals of organizations to become displaced by concerns about self-preservation is often accompanied by a focus on internal structure and processes, and alienation of the organization from the external environment (Blau and Scott 1962). Resource scarcity, resulting in budget cuts and other threats to organizational integrity, can accelerate this process. Concern with survival is a predictable response to fiscal stress and, indeed, an ethical responsibility for mental health administrators. The central question, however, is, "Survival for what?"

This chapter presents a conceptual framework for helping administrators to "manage madness" and to keep control over the direction of their programs; a case study of a community mental health center is used to illustrate this model for proactive administration.

Background

The administration of mental health services is complicated even under the most favorable fiscal atmosphere, given complex funding patterns and multiple mandates. The Community Mental Health Centers Act of 1963 provided federal seed money to local communities to develop a comprehensive system of mental health services. In addition to essential services (inpatient, partial hospitalization, and emergency treatment), the mandated services included prevention/promotion services (consultation and education) intended to benefit all citizens. Described by President Kennedy as a "bold new approach" (1963), the concept was visionary, involving the development of accessible, available treatment and prevention services to all community members regardless of ability to pay. The community mental health program was envisioned as a center for "mental health," in a positive sense, as well as a vehicle for providing innovative treatment services.

The complexity of the tasks faced by the mental health administrator is related to the breadth of the following system goals: *social control,* the protection of society from persons who are dangerous to themselves or others; *care and custody* of persons unable to provide for their own needs because of mental disorders; *treatment and/or rehabilitation* of persons suffering from mental or emotional disorders; and the *promotion* of mental health of all residents of a particular catchment area.

While these broad goals are complementary, they tend to compete with each other at the operational level, particularly when funds are scarce. The social control and the care and custody functions constitute bottom-line goals, because public safety and order are involved. Although these functions have traditionally been performed by the state hospital system, the deinstitutionalization process, based on the principle of providing treatment in the "least restrictive environment," has extended responsibility for these goals to many community programs. The treatment and/or rehabilitation goal has received the most attention, especially in professional training programs and "right to treatment" case law and legislation.

The promotion of positive mental health for all citizens includes research and interventions that focus on the social and environmental antecedents of individual and social dysfunction. While health promotion is not incompatible with treatment or custodial aims at an abstract level, competition for scarce funding and disparate belief systems about etiology, acceptable interventions, and appropriate domain have produced intense conflict between policy-makers and clinical practitioners (Brown 1977, Feldman 1975).

The priority given to any one of these goals depends on the shifting tides of public opinion and the vagaries of the economic environment. In operation, the four goals tend to be selected in relation to available funding and legislative mandates. Social control usually receives the highest priority, followed by the goals of care and custody and treatment. Mental health promotion is viewed as a desirable goal but is addressed only when resources are relatively plentiful.

In addition to the problem of multiple goals and scarce resources, the mental health administrator's task is complicated by a number of other conditions addressed by Feldman (1975):

1. There is a heavy dependence on public funding; hence the need to understand the political process and work closely with all levels of government.
2. Mental health organizations are multidisciplinary, professional, and highly autonomous. Therefore, they may be characterized by disciplinary rivalry and by staff loyalty to professional, rather than organizational, requirements.
3. The highly private and intimate nature of the relationship between therapist and client makes it difficult for the organization to collaborate with or intrude into the treatment process, even when warranted.
4. A highly dependent patient population presents many problems for mental health administrators and staff trying to maintain a responsible, accountable, and humane program.
5. Because the product is intangible, it is difficult to determine and measure the effectiveness of either the mental health organization or of individual staff members.
6. The diffuse boundaries of mental health services permit the mental health organization to be seen as the vehicle for meeting a wide variety of divergent needs. This may encourage unrealistic expectations from without and confusion about organizational mission from within.
7. The poor public image and stigma associated with mental health services, along with dilemmas posed by confidentiality, also complicate the mental health administrator's task.
8. There is an intangible but important need for mental health organizations to convey hope and confidence to their clients.

The challenge for mental health administration is to find ways to preserve the character, form, and ideology of community mental health programs; to prevent retrenchment to a "community mental illness" model that includes only provision of social control, custodial, and/or minimal treatment services for persons identified as mentally ill.

One response to this challenge is to serve an even wider range of community mental health needs by: broadening the base of community support through increasing the number of community members to whom community mental health services are relevant; increasing the acceptance of personal, social, and educational services, thus reducing the stigma associated with "mental" problems and programs; and improving organizational flexibility by creating and maintaining a diverse number of staff skills and program capabilities. These strategies are directly linked to such program survival questions as: What values do administrators draw upon during periods of fiscal stress? How do they conceive of their managerial leadership style during such crises? How do managers conceptualize their own managerial processes for handling difficult problems? In times of crisis, how good are their problem-solving skills and strategic-planning capacities? And finally, how well do they negotiate when the pressure is on? These questions serve as part of a framework for thinking about the tools used by mental health administrators to manage madness.

Proactive Administration

Meeting the current challenge in mental health requires forward looking, proactive leadership, as opposed to an administrative stance that is largely reactive and accommodating. Essentially, the question for the administrator is how to gain and maintain greater control over the pattern of mental health services and programs, rather than allowing them to be shaped entirely by shifts in the availability of funding (Austin and Hershey 1982).

The impact of external demands upon the mental health organization will be highly influenced by the kind of "responsive activity" in which the administrator engages. Responsive activity consists of those behaviors and processes concerned with reconciling the needs of the organization with environmental demands (Pfeffer and Salancik 1978). At least two adaptive responses account for a great deal of administrative and organizational activity: adapting and changing the organization to fit environmental requirements, or altering the environment in order to enhance the capabilities of the organization. Through this latter set of activities the mental health administrator assumes a proactive stance toward the external environment of the organization. Proactive/reactive choices are also made with regard to the internal operations of the mental health agency. It is possible to resist some cuts, to develop new markets and funding sources, to seek creative ways to use existing personnel, and to develop innovative approaches to providing services.

A framework for proactive administration is represented by the acronym, VISION, which stands for *V*alues, *I*ntent, *S*kills, *I*nnovation, *O*bjectives, and *N*egotiation. Vision was chosen as an organizing concept because one key to achieving control over program direction is an orientation to the future and a vision, or cognitive map, of what the future mental health program can and should be.

The administrator's attitudes and actions are central to this process, as s/he "sets the tone" for the organization and has major responsibility for "a program's overall focus and direction, the quality of its services, its relationship with the larger human services system, its internal management, and the organization of its fiscal affairs" (Report of National Task Force, p. 281). Although there is considerable overlap in the components of the VISION framework, each is described separately for conceptual clarity.

Values related to the provision of mental health services are influenced by the nature of wider societal concerns, such as economic growth versus stagnation, emphasis on client rights versus client responsibilities, or community interest versus lack of community interest in mental health. Mental health administrators must select from among a number of disparate value positions; for example, the welfare of clients comes first, or fiscal considerations take precedence over program considerations; accountability to funding sources is essential, or loyalty to staff is paramount; the interests of taxpayers take precedence over the service needs of fee payers.

These and many other difficult value issues suggest the importance of a periodic values clarification process for administrators, their staff, and other constituencies. Martin comments on the dilemma faced by administrators who must make choices in the face of conflicting preferences held by staff and clients and those held by the "dominant society" (1980). Because the administrator often serves as an arbitrator between these competing demands, the need to identify and reaffirm or modify the values guiding administrative practice is particularly important. A clear set of values can serve as an anchor for the proactive administrator as s/he faces a multitude of difficult pressures and decisions. Raths, Harmin, and Simon provide a useful framework for values clarification (1966).

Intent represents what Mintzberg describes as the administrator's "overall strategy," which serves as an orienting frame of reference for organizing information and making decisions (1978). Although much of this overall strategy may eventually be translated into formal goals and practices, the administrator begins with a "mental map," or set of intentions, about the preferred future direction of the agency.

An overall strategy serves as the perceptual screen through which apparent problems are translated into opportunities. From this perspective, changes demanded by external circumstances can stimulate innovations in service delivery, (as when funding cutbacks lead to new, small-scale programs or more efficient agency procedures).

An orientation to the future and the capacity to implement administrative strategies calls for management *skills* in three important spheres:

internal agency operations, external relationships, and organizational boundaries, where internal and external concerns meet.

Although management of the internal operations of social agencies has always been important, now more than ever managers must build effective programs that are also efficient and accountable. Personnel management and development, financial management, and program administration are core competencies that need to address such internal issues as revising job descriptions, establishing performance evaluation processes, developing agency staff development plans, updating salary schedules, developing cost centers, introducing performance budgeting in service contracts, and developing new service programs.

Important skills in the area of external relationships include the ability to obtain accurate information about conditions in the agency's environment, to assess the implications of that information for the agency's integrity and survival, and to initiate corrective action, either with actors in the environment or within the agency. Other externally oriented skills include the ability to interpret the agency's mission, goals, and services to various constituencies, including funding and mandating bodies, and skills in generating financial resources and other forms of support. Managing external relationships involves many diverse abilities, from negotiating contracts and other formal agreements, to building an informal network that provides ongoing access to relevant information.

The third sphere involves skills in managing the interface of internal and external processes. One important area is balancing demands emanating from the external environment, such as managing the pressures for organizational change with the needs and capabilities of the staff. Information-management skills are also part of boundary spanning and require effective systems for dissemination of information to staff as well as regularly soliciting current information about staff activities and issues. The skillful management of the dilemmas inherent in the boundary-spanning role is a crucial role for mental health administrators (Adams 1976).

Innovation refers to the general stance toward change. Rather than a troublesome process to be avoided, change is a positive opportunity to be innovative. The administrative challenge is how to lead the staff and board through a change process that is creative in modifying and developing agency goals, rather than allowing the cumulative effect of externally imposed changes to determine the nature and shape of the mental health program. Innovative planning needs to take place in the community (e.g., developing new employee-assistance programs with industry) as well as inside the agency (e.g., reorganizing the agency's structure and modifying job descriptions accordingly). Managerial lead-

ership requires an understanding of organizational change processes
(Resnick and Patti 1980) and skills in problem solving (Perlman and
Gurin 1972).

Objective refers to the translation of the overall strategy, or *intent*
of the administrator, into a formal long-range plan that is understood
and shared by relevant agency constituencies. An emphasis on long-
range planning may seem incompatible with the realities of economic
decline. Uncertainty and rapid change make planning difficult and appear to demand a crisis management approach. In fact, strategic planning can serve as a vehicle for moving from a largely reactive to a
proactive administrative stance and thereby articulate agreed upon criteria for making budget cuts. Decisions about program changes or staff
reductions made without reference to agreed upon future goals contribute to both current instability and future problems. Seemingly unrelated decisions tend to compound over time, resulting in poorly
conceived and uncoordinated program pieces. The lack of planning at
the community level in the deinstitutionalization of mental patients is
one sad example of this phenomenon. A useful framework for thinking
about strategic planning is provided by Rothschild (1976).

Special emphasis is given to *negotiation* because of the highly political nature of the mental health administrator's task (Fisher 1981).
While relating to external funding bodies, competing interest groups,
and with other human-service agencies, the administrator engages in a
number of political activities, such as negotiating with regulating bodies,
funding sources, and legislators. These activities are designed to assure
the survival and integrity of the organization while trading or giving
away as little as possible.

The connections between external negotiations, the administrator's
relationship to staff, and the internal functioning of the agency are not
always apparent. Commitments made by the administrator clearly have
repercussions for agency staff (Randall 1973). Because the administrator must be able to deliver what is promised to outside constituencies
and is dependent upon the cooperation of staff to fulfill these commitments, "external" negotiation must often be preceded and/or followed by "internal" negotiations with staff. Thus, the mental health
administrator engages in political activity both with staff and with actors
and organizations in the agency's environment.

The concept of proactive administration and the need for VISION
are joined with the realities of cutback management in the following
case study. The case situation illustrates the value issues and political
dilemmas faced by the director of a new community mental health
center who must shift from direct federal funding to state block-grant
funding.

Case Study: A Mental Health Center
Weathers the Storm

Over the past ten years community leaders and mental health professionals from a large southwestern city engaged in three major planning efforts aimed at establishing a federally funded community mental health center in their catchment area. Most of the ingredients for a successful application were in place: the need for coordinated mental health services was well documented; the catchment area qualified for special poverty consideration; and both the interest and the capability to put an acceptable plan together appeared to exist.

Each planning effort, however, was aborted before an application was submitted because agreement could not be reached about an appropriate applicant organization. Although this obstacle assumed a different form in each planning effort, the problem each time was either that local or state governmental bodies were unwilling to assume the long-term financial responsibility inherent in the status of applicant, or that private, nonprofit mental health organizations willing to serve as an applicant were unacceptable to other public and private agencies.

In 1980, interested citizen and professional leaders formed a public nonprofit corporation and embarked on a fourth planning and application process. The center board members were jubilant when they received word from the federal government that a federal staffing grant had been awarded.

An experienced social worker who had been involved in the planning process was hired as the director by the center board. Members of the board saw several advantages to hiring a director who had been involved in the planning process. Such a person was more likely to have values in common with the board, to understand the intent of the comprehensive plan, and to be able to move quickly into program planning and implementation. The new director hired several other core staff members to help develop the program, hire additional staff, and put the center plan into operation.

The first four months were very busy for the board, the director, and the center staff. Additional staff members were hired to develop and deliver mental health services. Contracts for other parts of the comprehensive program were negotiated with existing mental health agencies serving the catchment area. In addition, a multimedia campaign to inform citizens of the catchment area about center services was launched. By the end of the fifth month, the major contract relationships were in operation, and services to clients were being provided.

During this period, the director demonstrated management skills both in the internal operations of the center and in the external environment. Internally, she was primarily concerned with hiring, training, and supervising key staff and with overseeing program development and implementation. Activities directed outside the agency included negotiating contracts with other agencies and developing marketing strategies to increase accessibility to mental health services and to insure adequate client flow.

Unfortunately, the birth of the center coincided with profound changes at the federal level, most notably the shift from federal categorical to state block-grant funding. The director was very concerned about what block-grant funding would mean for her organization. Fearing loss of funds for the center, and working closely with the center board, she obtained letters from the federal, state, and county mental health agencies that recognized the efforts of center Board members and personnel to obtain the federal grant. The letters also contained various degrees of agreement that center funds should be earmarked for center use. Some board members also informally alerted their state legislators of the potential problem facing the center.

Both the director and members of the board demonstrated considerable political skill in their preparation for a period of negotiation. In anticipation of possible budget problems, they secured written agreements, cemented relationships with key legislators, and engaged in other activity designed to enhance the relative power of the agency. These activities increased the potential bargaining power of the center.

The ninety-day period during which planning for block-grant distribution was occurring at the state level was marked by great uncertainty for the director. It seemed that local planning and decision making was impossible until funding was secure. During this period, members of the board were sharply divided about how to proceed. Nearly half of the board members felt that the director should conduct "business as usual," continuing to develop and staff program components. The remaining board members were more cautious, sharing the director's opinion that it was unwise to incur further financial obligations or to make commitments for additional services until the level of funding for the center was known. After considerable discussion, the board voted to put a freeze on hiring and to suspend further program development until the funding picture was clear.

The director was more cautious fiscally and politically than some of the board members. She was concerned both with fiscal responsibility and with maintaining organizational flexibility, as long as the facts about cuts were unknown. Her attempt to hedge against possible future events was contrasted with the stance of some board members. "It's our money; we have the right to spend it." The director's skills in persuasion and negotiation were also important in convincing the board to adopt the strategy she recommended.

The axe fell on the day when the director learned that a decision had been made by state and county mental health officials to pool the center funds with other allocations to the county mental health program and to "distribute the monies equitably" among the six catchment areas in the county. Acknowledging that they had reneged on previous agreements, representatives from state and county mental health authorities explained that unexpected state revenue shortfalls had combined with federal funding changes to considerably reduce the funds available for mental health services across the state. They argued that an equal distribution of funds across catchment areas was necessary to preserve a minimum system of services countywide, and that all clients, including those in the center's catchment area, would ultimately benefit from this decision.

The director, members of the center board, and center staff members were outraged by the announcement. After the initial shock, however, it was apparent that while all people associated with the center shared feelings of anger and disappointment about the news, there was sharp disagreement about what should be done.

Several board members and many of the center staff were in favor of fighting "all the way" for restoration of full funding. They laid out a strategy that included enlisting the aid of state legislators from the district, "going public" with the issue through the media, publishing the letters from federal, state, and local officials, and organizing staff and client groups in public protests. This group's stance was essentially "all or nothing." Their position was that it was through their efforts that the money had come to the state, it rightfully belonged to the center, and they would not agree to run a watered-down, less than comprehensive program.

Another group of board members and some of the staff, including the director, identified what they saw as major difficulties with the "all or nothing" approach. Although they agreed that both a principle and a promise had been broken, they pointed out that a public adversarial process could not achieve a satisfactory outcome, no matter what happened. On the one hand, their efforts might result in a total loss of funds, if they could not garner enough support with the state Department of Mental Hygiene and the legislature. In that case, they would be unable to keep commitments made to contracting agencies or to clients they were currently serving. On the other hand, even if they were successful in obtaining a restoration of funds, the process could result in a total disruption of relationships with the county and state mental health systems, upon which they were highly dependent for important components of their comprehensive plan.

This second group felt that this would result in inadequate services for the clients in their catchment area, and they were also concerned about the effect on the countywide system of services and on clients throughout the county. This group favored taking a firm position with the state and county mental health authorities, being as persuasive as possible, but being prepared to compromise. They supported collaborative efforts with the state and county mental health systems to plan the most adequate system of services possible under the circumstances.

The situation presented both political and ethical dilemmas for the director. The major political dilemma involved the likely outcome of "biting the hand that feeds": short-term gains followed by long-term losses. The apparent ethical dilemma was particularly acute for the director. She conducted an internal dialogue as she tried to decide what was both ethically sound and administratively responsible. Considering the needs of the fledgling center alone, it seemed that her loyalty and responsibility lay in fighting to preserve the center and its comprehensive plan. Her professional values, which included a commitment to the best possible service system for all clients in the county, dictated that she adopt a perspective broader than agency loyalty alone.

The director experienced a great deal of conflict as she considered her decision. She knew her position would be unpopular with both staff and board members. Both her professional commitment to the best possible service system and her assessment of the political situation, however, helped her feel confident that she had chosen the right course.

The director's position was supported by a majority vote of the center board after many emergency meetings, much open conflict, and many sixteen-hour days. It was not an easy position to maintain, especially when two board members resigned and several staff members accused her of "selling out."

As the director reviewed the situation and listed the "next steps," she identified several areas that needed immediate attention:

1. *Relationships with the board and staff,* and the more general problem of staff morale. Basically, the director knew she had lost the trust and confidence of some members of each group. It was her

judgment that the most effective way to repair these relationships was to demonstrate that compromise was possible without severely lowering program quality or restricting comprehensivenesss. She chose this task-oriented course rather than focusing strictly on the interpersonal aspects of the situation.

2. *A strategy for negotiation* with county and state mental health authorities. The director felt that the center was in a fairly strong bargaining position: they *had* obtained the federal grant; their plan was coherent and well developed; and the letters, plus strong relationships with state legislators, constituted unspoken threats, even though the director was not inclined to invoke them.

3. *Review and modification of the current comprehensive plan,* in the light of projected funding reductions. The immediate need was to engage board and staff members in identifying which goals and program components were considered top priority in preparation for discussions with state and county mental health personnel. The director planned to argue that the promotion and prevention and the planning and evaluation capabilities of the center should not be sacrificed in order the maintain treatment services at their current levels. Promotion and prevention along with planning and evaluation constituted an investment in the future.

4. *A plan for the generation of alternatives to public funding.* Although requiring an immediate commitment of resources, such planning was also seen as an investment in the future by the director.

After several painful weeks and much active negotiation, the director received notice of an appropriation that partially restored the funding lost under the initial "equitable distribution plan." Thus, funding reductions were not as severe as originally feared.

Some services were reduced, and client demand continued to exceed the center's program capacity. Some program components were placed "on hold," and some projects were eliminated completely. Although not ideal, the board, director, and center staff were generally pleased with the results of their planning efforts.

The director was personally distressed at the residual resentment and mistrust of her which remained among some staff members, although she knew that she would never please everyone. Attacks on her professional integrity and competence during the crisis led her to question whether she was personally suited to the demands of top administrative positions. With much self-evaluation, and through discussion with other agency directors, she was able to reaffirm her commitment to mental health administration. She also felt increasingly confident that she had performed competently and professionally during a very crucial period for the organization.

Analysis

Examination of this case study within the VISION framework suggests several conclusions about the director's behavior during a period of environmental turbulence and threatened budget reduction. Clearly, the director's personal and professional *values* provided her with a framework for making choices. The most difficult process she faced was clarifying which values should prevail, for those associated with her role as director (loyalty to the center) conflicted with her broader professional perspective (preserving the best possible service system for all clients in the county). The director's assessment of the negative political consequences for the center of an "all or nothing" approach helped to resolve this apparent dilemma.

The case also illustrates the importance of the director's overall *intent,* or strategy. In this rapidly changing situation, it was necessary for the director to reformulate her intent and gain commitment to a new strategy as circumstances in the external environment were altered.

It appears that the director's *skills* in accurately assessing the need for a change in direction were stronger than her ability to manage some aspects of the internal operations of the center. Although the fiscal and political outcome for the center was reasonably favorable, the residual lowered staff morale and conflict within the board presented serious problems. While it is difficult to engage in hindsight assessment of the director's capacity to prevent the lowering of staff morale, more attention could have been given to improving the balance of internal, external, and boundary management issues.

Because of the externally precipitated crisis, the attention of the director was largely absorbed by board meetings and discussions with county, state, and federal mental health officials, with minimal personal attention to internal agency operations. Since each mental health program area was supervised by a competent manager, the director left much of the internal management to these program managers. She emphasized the importance of carrying on "business as usual" for the benefit of the center's clients.

Essentially, the director's strategy was to buffer staff from the uncertainty connected with the funding crisis so that they could give full attention to the provision of services. She did not foresee several unfortunate results of this stance, however. Her attempt to shield staff from uncertainty was accompanied by a reduced flow of information about the complexity of the problems facing the board and the director. Without accurate information, rumors based on partial information abounded, and there was a tendency on the part of staff to polarize and simplify the issues. In addition, the director's absorption with external issues and activities, and the fact that much of her work took her away from the center, led to some of the problems typically associated with those who occupy boundary-spanning roles and risked contributing to the deterioration in director-staff relations (Adams 1976). Staff members not involved in the external *and* internal exchanges often begin to question the boundary-spanner's commitment to the goals and wishes of organizational members and become fearful that she will "give away too much." Decreased trust and increased isolation of the person at the boundary are common.

While the director did not embrace the changes thrust upon the center, she demonstrated the capacity to anticipate and plan with regard to the *innovations* emanating from state and county mental health policy changes. Much of the conflict within the board revolved around the extent to which the center should adapt to these external demands and the concomitant changes, or whether the changes should be resisted at all costs. The director engaged in a combination of proactive behavior designed to resist or reduce undesirable change and reactive management focused on adapting to the realities of budget reduction. Management of the internal-change process was an area of considerable weakness.

The director had a strong commitment to planning. She recognized the need to reexamine the *objectives* of the center in the light of the policy and funding changes, and to initiate a planning process aimed at both short-term and long-range issues.

Overall, the Director appeared to be politically astute, and her external *negotiating* skills were highly developed. However, her failure to recognize the need to also negotiate with her own staff as a part of the boundary-management process created another set of difficult problems requiring managerial attention.

Summary and Conclusions

This chapter has identified some of the key issues confronting mental health administrators during a period of cutback management. Each administrator must continuously wrestle with the goals of the mental health system in his or her community and the methods for achieving these goals. At the same time, it is important to monitor actively one's administrative style, shifting back and forth between proactive and reactive postures.

We have identified VISION as the key ingredient of effective management: values, intent, skills, innovation, objectives, and negotiation. The case study illustrates the proactive posture of a center director seeking to keep a fledgling organization alive through skillful negotiation based upon clear objectives and well-grounded values.

While the future configuration of community mental health services is just beginning to emerge, it is clear that proactive administration will be needed to manage mental health services in the decades ahead.

References

Adams, J.S. "The Structure and Dynamics of Behavior in Organizational Boundary Roles." In M.D. Dunnette, ed. *Handbook of Industrial and Organizational Psychology.* Chicago: Rand McNally, 1976.

Austin, M.J., and W.E. Hershey, eds. *Handbook on Mental Health Administration.* San Francisco: Jossey-Bass, 1982.

Brown, B.S. "Conflict and Detente Between Social Issues and Clinical Practice," *American Journal of Orthopsychiatry* 47 (1977):466–75.

Blau, P.M., and W.R. Scott. *Formal Organizations: A Comparative Approach.* San Francisco: Chandler Publishing, 1962.

Feldman, S. "Administration in Mental Health: Issues, Problems, and Prospects," *Bulletin of the Pan American Health Organization* 9, no. 3 (1975):212–20.

Fisher, R. *Getting to Yes.* Boston: Houghton Mifflin, 1981.

Kennedy, J.F. "Message from the President of the United States Relative to Mental Illness and Mental Retardation." (88th Congress, First Session, U.S. House of Representatives Document No. 58). Washington, D.C.: U.S. Government Printing Office, 1963.

Levine, C.H., ed. *Managing Fiscal Stress: The Crisis in the Public Sector.* Chatham, N.J.: Chatham House Publishers, 1980.

Martin, P.Y. "Multiple Constituencies, Dominant Societal Values, and the Human Service Administrator: Implications for Service Delivery," *Administration in Social Work* 4, no. 2 (1980):15–27.

Mintzberg, H. "Patterns in Strategy Formation," *Management Science* 24, no. 9 (1978):934–48.

National Task Force on Mental Health/Mental Retardation Administration. "Report on the National Task Force on Mental Health/

Mental Retardation Administration." *Administration in Mental Health* 6 (1979):269–322.

Perlman, R., and A. Gurin. *Community Organization and Social Planning.* New York: John Wiley and Sons, 1972.

Pfeffer, J., and G.R. Salancik. *The External Control of Organizations.* New York: Harper and Row, 1978.

Randall, R. "Influence of Environmental Support and Policy Space on Organizational Behavior." *Administrative Science Quarterly* 18, no. 2 (1973):236–47.

Raths, L.E., M. Harmin, and S.B. Simon. *Values and Teaching.* Columbus, Ohio: Charles E. Merrill Publishing, 1966.

Resnick, H., and R.J. Patti, eds. *Change from Within: Humanizing Social Welfare Organizations.* Philadelphia: Temple University Press, 1980.

Rothschild, W.E. *Putting It All Together: A Guide to Strategic Thinking.* New York: American Management Associations, 1976.

12

Survival through Coalition: The Case of Addictions Programs

Harvey Weiner

This chapter presents a case study of the organizational, political, and legal strategies used in the successful effort by Pennsylvania drug-program directors to suspend new state Medicaid (Medical Assistance) regulations that imposed reimbursement restrictions on service provided to MA patients enrolled in methadone maintenance programs. Because these patients constituted a large percentage of the case loads of urban methadone programs, the reimbursement restrictions threatened financial strangulation.

While it may not be possible to completely halt the "irresistible tide" toward funding cutbacks, program executives need not passively sit back and merely wring their hands. Organizational, political, and legal strategies can be used to exert influence on legislative, funding, and regulatory bodies through the use of readily available resources: staff, board members and other community leaders, local politicians, and other interest groups.

Methadone Maintenance Treatment

Methadone, a synthetic narcotic, was synthesized by the Germans during World War II when their supply of natural opiates was interrupted. While methadone can be used medically for all conditions that require narcotics, its primary use is for the treatment of narcotic addiction. (Heroin is the most widely abused narcotic.) Methadone is used in the treatment of narcotic addicts only; it is not used to treat addiction to any other drugs.

Widespread use of methadone in the treatment of heroin addiction was pioneered by Vincent Dole and associates in the late 1960s. It is the most widely used and most successful modality for treating hard-core heroin addicts, with upwards of 80,000 patients enrolled in maintenance programs nationally (Cohen 1981, Gearing et al. 1978, Millman 1980). When an addict applies for treatment, s/he undergoes a lengthy screening process that includes a psychosocial and drug-use history, a physical examination and laboratory tests, certification of at least a one-

197

year history of addiction, and a urinalysis to verify the presence of opiates in his/her system. Program staff then review all of this data and decide the appropriateness of methadone maintenance treatment. If the applicant is accepted into the program, intake data is used to formulate a treatment plan which is discussed with the patient and modified in accordance with his/her personal treatment objectives.

This treatment plan is regularly updated, and it forms the basis of the counseling and rehabilitation services that constitute the central focus of methadone maintenance treatment. Because addiction is a biopsychosocial disorder, life-style, attitudes, personal relationships, and the like must be altered to enable the patient to cope with life without resorting to drugs. Methadone deals with the physiological aspects of the addiction, while the counseling and rehabilitation services deal with the psychosocial aspects (Weiner 1975, Weiner and Kleber 1979).

When the patient is accepted into treatment, the physician prescribes a daily dose of methadone. Minor dosage modification may be necessary initially to achieve the appropriate stabilization dose.

The unique qualities that make methadone useful in the treatment of heroin addicts include the following (Dole and Nyswander 1974, Dole 1980):

1. Methadone is taken orally in the clinic under the supervision of a nurse or pharmacist.
2. It is long acting, and a single dose can prevent withdrawal symptoms for at least twenty-four hours. Heroin and other shorter acting opiates must be taken every four to six hours to avoid withdrawal symptoms. Therefore, a single dose of methadone does away with the craving for heroin or other opiates for at least twenty-four hours. (The patient is still able to get "high" on alcohol or other drugs.)
3. Once a stabilization dose is reached, the patient is functionally normal. This is in marked contrast to the constant euphoria/dysphoria cycles that characterize the use of heroin and other shorter acting opiates.
4. The patient is involved in a program where the focus is on psychosocial rehabilitation. This rehabilitation occurs on an out-patient basis while the person is living at home in his/her community, thereby avoiding the "reentry" problems that sometimes accompany return from residential facilities.

Methadone has a high street value because it can produce a "high" in nontolerant individuals (those not using opiates on a daily basis) as well as prevent withdrawal symptoms in heroin addicts. Therefore, efforts are made to restrict take-home privileges to those patients who have made substantial progress and shown themselves to be capable of handling the responsibility of taking one or more doses of methadone out of the clinic. (It should also be noted that a high dose of methadone can be lethal to nontolerant individuals, especially children.) A "jug" of methadone (a vial containing a daily dose) has a street value of at least $25, a considerable sum of money for a low-income individual.

To prevent diversion into the illegal street market, state and federal regulations impose strict limitations in regard to take-home privileges. The primary safeguard against diversion is the programmatic requirement that most patients ingest their methadone at the clinic six or seven days per week, with take-home privileges limited to those patients certified by the program physician as having demonstrated substantive progress and a high level of personal responsibility. Simply stated, if methadone does not leave the clinic it cannot be sold or transferred illegally.

The Pennsylvania Context

The *Pennsylvania Bulletin* of 29 December 1979 contained new Department of Public Welfare (DPW) regulations for medical assistance reimbursement for drug/alcohol outpatient clinic services, to be effective 1 January 1980. While these regulations allowed more liberal payments than the proposed regulations published in the *Pennsylvania Bulletin* 3 November 1979, they nevertheless imposed a severe financial hardship on the state's urban methadone maintenance programs. It is interesting to note that the November proposed regulations elicited a number of letters from the field but no real organized opposition. Since DPW was under a legislative mandate to cut MA expenditures, the lack of organized opposition to the proposed regulations probably encouraged the belief that the substance-abuse field could be cut without arousing significant protest.

The 29 December 1979 regulations were unique, for this was the first time that reimbursement limitations were placed on psychotherapy and methadone maintenance services to MA patients. The reimbursement limitations allowed eight hours per month of psychotherapy and three methadone-dispensing visits per week for methadone maintenance patients after the first three months of treatment. As a result, the urban methadone programs with a large percentage of MA patients faced huge budget deficits, for they could no longer bill DPW for previously reimbursable services. The psychotherapy reimbursement limitation of eight hours per month was of concern to some programs, but most were unaffected because, on average, patients were seen less than eight hours per month.

Medical Implications

The Pennsylvania DPW regulations struck at the very heart of diversion prevention, for they allowed payment for only three dispensing visits per week after the first three months of treatment. Because addiction is a chronic disorder characterized by frequent relapse, methadone maintenance treatment is long term in nature. The DPW reimbursement limitation put the programs between a rock and a hard place: either programs could follow the reimbursement restrictions and provide four doses of take-home methadone to each MA patient, thereby promoting diversion and violating federal regulations, or they could continue to dispense on a daily basis and slowly bankrupt themselves. Urban programs with a large percentage of MA patients depended on MA billing for a portion of their income, and they could not afford to a lose a major portion of this income and still maintain the staffing pattern required to deliver a full range of services. The only other alternative, equally unpleasant, was to discharge large numbers of patients and continue to provide adequate services to fewer patients with fewer staff. Later, this point was effectively used to help organize community opposition to the regulations.

Another important issue raised by these regulations concerned the clinical issues that surround the prescribing of methadone. As noted previously, take-home privileges are reserved only for the most trustworthy patients who meet certain criteria in regard to progress. The recommendation of counseling staff and a prescription by the program physician are required prior to granting of these privileges. The new regulations usurped the physician's ability to use his/her medical judgment, for they included a routine prescription schedule for all patients (three times per week after three months) regardless of progress. As will be seen later, this point became the basis of an important legal issue.

Financial Implications

In Pennsylvania, DPW reimburses methadone programs for each medication visit by an MA patient. (Non-MA patients are self-pay.) This fee covers the cost of ordering, storing, preparing, and dispensing methadone, as well as all recordkeeping costs associated with these tasks. By regulation, all of these functions must be performed by licensed nurses or pharmacists.

For a large urban program, with an average of 70 to 80 percent of the clinics receiving MA, the financial loss under the new regulations would be approximately $100,000 per year. While most programs also receive program funding from city or state agencies, programs could not sustain current service levels with annual losses of this magnitude. Staff would have to be fired and clients' treatment terminated. There were no possible sources of funds to replace the loss of MA reimbursement.

It should be noted that working clients are expected to pay a fee for their services, but these fees could not be raised sufficiently to cover the MA losses. Also, city and state funding agencies were already spending all of their money in an effort to maximize substance-abuse services for a wide variety of clients. They simply did not have additional money to replace the MA losses.

When the financial and clinical implications of these regulations became clear, program directors and staff recognized the need to organize resistance aimed at suspending or revoking these limitations.

Coalition Building

In looking back, it is always possible to view events as having occurred in linear, sequential fashion according to a definite plan and clearly articulated strategies. In fact, the events occurred concurrently in anything but sequential fashion. The program directors who orchestrated much of the effort shared common goals and a common purpose. Also, frequent meetings, open lines of communication, and a sense of trust insured at least the outlines of a common strategy. But many currents were operating at once, and as could be expected, things did not always go according to plan.

The Philadelphia Forum of Drug and Alcohol Abuse Programs had served for a number of years as a vehicle for service-providers to discuss common interests and concerns. All of the Philadelphia substance-abuse program directors were members of the forum, and those whose programs contained methadone clinics began to meet on a regular basis soon after the promulgation of the new regulations. While the city's Single County Authority (SCA), the Coordinating Office for Drug and Alcohol Abuse Programs, offered valuable advice and remained directly involved throughout the battle with DPW, it was recognized from the outset that the major initiatives would have to come from the service providers. The state monitoring agency (the Governor's Council on Drug Abuse and Alcoholism) also lent some assistance, but as a branch of state government it could not actively oppose another department's effort to save money.

Identification of Interest Groups

The first coalition-building task involved the program directors themselves. All were not equally threatened by the new regulations, for certain programs had several sources of funding. Also, by age, temperament, and personality, some were more conservative than others. Most of the program directors had received their professional training as clinicians and had always worked in settings where concern for patients was uppermost.

It was difficult, at first, for the program directors to grasp the fact that DPW might only be interested in saving money, and some of the directors continued to believe that explaining the adverse clinical consequences to DPW would result in changes. As in all other situations, directors whose programs were most threatened were most anxious to move quickly and more willing to take risks. Directors whose programs were least threatened favored a cautious approach and hoped to avoid a direct confrontation with DPW, fearing possible retaliation through additional regulations, persistent audits, and the like. In particular, some of the directors felt that legal action should be a last step, for such action was bound to antagonize DPW and invite retaliatory harassment.

The first effort at coalition building took the form of having the program directors arrive at a consensus in regard to the threat posed by the regulations. Some of the more "radical" program directors cited the possibility that these regulations might represent DPW's first step against the substance-abuse field. The absence of vigorous opposition might tempt DPW to target the field for additional cost-saving measures. This argument helped convince the more conservative directors of the need for concerted action.

Once the program directors had formed a natural coalition of those who were most threatened and most willing to initiate action, the decision was made to proceed actively with the first five options presented in the next section on action strategies, and to explore the feasibility and cost of legal action.

The author was very fortunate in having dedicated and actively involved members of the Addictive Behaviors Committee of the J.F. Kennedy Community Mental Health Center's board of directors, who were committed to the continuation of the methadone program. Fortunately, many other programs were similarly blessed. It is essential for programs to have community and board support prior to any crisis. Since substance-abuse programs work with patients who are "socially undesirable" and sometimes cause problems in the community, it is incumbent upon administrative staff to involve community residents on an ongoing basis. Support is elicited by educating community members in regard to the positive contributions of the programs (less crime, professional treatment for residents with substance-abuse problems, and the like) and also by soliciting input and feedback from residents. All too often the author has witnessed situations where a crisis occurs and staff scamper around frantically seeking community support. But it's too late: the horse is already out of the barn. Organizing ongoing community input and support should be part of every administrator's agenda.

Action Strategies

Several options were discussed as possible strategies during an initial series of forum meetings:

1. Write letters to DPW explaining how clinical services would be adversely affected.
2. Arrange a meeting with DPW representatives to attempt to negotiate some compromise.
3. Have staff and board members arrange meetings with city and state legislators.
4. Meet with community leaders to enlist their support.
5. Begin to use public relations and the media to focus the issues and generate community support. These efforts would emphasize the cultural implications of this issue, as will be discussed later.
6. Initiate a lawsuit against DPW on the following grounds:
   a. Denial of treatment (patients would have to be discharged because of staff cutbacks)
   b. Interference with a physician's ability to use his/her medical judgement in regard to prescribing take-home medication
   c. Programs adhering to the dispensing schedule in the new regulations would be out of compliance with federal regulations concerning methadone dispensing.

In the letter-writing campaign to legislators undertaken by staff and community residents, it quickly became apparent that letters from staff elicited little more than a polite reply unless the staff member happened to be a constituent. Legislators correctly perceived that staff are motivated by concerns over the possible loss of their jobs. Constituents count in legislative contacts, especially those "movers and shakers" who can influence friends and neighbors to vote for or against a legislator based on his/her helpfulness when approached with a community concern.

In addition to the close working relationship between the programs and the community based on ongoing contact and shared concerns, community residents were prepared to fight for the continued existence of the methadone programs for the following reasons:

1. They perceived that patients were receiving high-quality services, and that they were genuinely being helped.
2. They feared increased street crime if hundreds of heroin addicts were discharged from treatment.
3. They were concerned about "dealing" of illegal methadone and other drugs if additional methadone was allowed to leave the clinics. (It should be noted that programmatic diligence in regard to methadone diversion stemmed partly from community complaints, which led to the closing or relocation of some methadone clinics.)

Also helpful was the use of public relations and the media to focus the issues and generate community support. At one point in the campaign, contact was made with a popular black radio talk show host, and he agreed to devote a portion of his program to a discussion of the consequences of curtailing methadone maintenance services. This was a risk, for methadone maintenance is a controversial and poorly understood treatment modality surrounded by many myths. One of the Philadelphia drug-program directors (a black physician) appeared on the radio show and did an excellent job of clarifying the issues involved in the controversy. This program was helpful in generating additional community support.

Sensitivity to the cultural implications of these regulations also helped to strengthen and broaden community support. As a result of the radio appearance and other public-relations efforts, many community residents began to view the methadone cutbacks in the broader context of denying needed services to minority populations in urban communities. Therefore, support was generated among residents who would not have spoken out had methadone been the only issue.

Fortunately, several newspaper articles in the local and national press had detailed the increase in heroin availability and addiction in large cities. The juxtaposition of decreased services in the face of increased addiction was used to good advantage.

In the company of board members and staff, the author visited three city councilmen, three state representatives, and several outspoken and authoritative community leaders. A number of other city and state legislators were contacted by telephone. As a result of these contacts, and similar contacts by board and staff from other programs, the Philadelphia City Council passed a unanimous resolution calling on the governor to take steps to rescind these regulations. Also, the state legislators contacted began to threaten DPW with action that would delay the department's budgetary appropriation.

Meanwhile, the program directors and representatives from the county's Coordinating Office for Drug and Alcohol Abuse had arranged a series of meetings with DPW executive staff in an attempt to arrive at a negotiated settlement. At these meetings, DPW's position was that they had a legislative mandate to control costs and that limitations of this type were being put into place for all health services. Also, they contended that they were not restricting the type or frequency of services, but merely setting limitations on what they would pay for. This was a specious argument, because programs barely managing to balance their budgets could not afford to provide free services.

Outcomes

The legislative pressure was very helpful in conveying to DPW executives the extent of community support for continuing these programs. In the meetings, the program directors alluded to their community and legislative support, while the DPW executives alluded to measures they could take to make things difficult for the programs. While indicating a willingness to negotiate, the DPW representatives appeared inflexible. They seemed to be interested in avoiding a lawsuit, but beyond that, their interest appeared to be simply saving money.

While the legislative contracts and DPW negotiations were proceeding, the program directors were also exploring the possibility of legal action against DPW. Following the quotation of a very high fee by a private law firm, the program directors decided to contact the Hospital Association of Pennsylvania (HAP). The directors had been in touch with substance-abuse programs throughout the state, and efforts began to build a coalition of programs (especially hospital-based programs) willing to cooperate in bringing a lawsuit against DPW. This effort was crucial, because DPW was informing legislators that this was a "Philadelphia issue" with little relevance to other programs in the state ("divide and conquer"). The formation of this coalition also had relevance to the Hospital Association of Pennsylvania, a statewide organization. Since a minority of the methadone programs statewide were affiliated with hospitals, there was some concern as to whether HAP would see itself as having any responsibility in this matter. Fortunately, a major hospital-based program in Pittsburgh decided to join the Philadelphia programs in urging HAP to pursue legal action.

In addition to the financial advantage of having the legal action undertaken by HAP, other benefits included the prestige of HAP and, most important, their expertise in handling issues of this type. It was with feelings of relief and profound gratitude that the program directors learned of HAP's decision to become involved and prepare the lawsuit against DPW. The law firm that represented HAP began to meet with the program directors to review the grounds for legal action. The directors had previously undertaken a thorough review of all existing federal regulations that would be violated if patients were given four bottles of take-home medication each week. Also, the attorneys agreed that strong arguments could be made on behalf of patients who would be denied service if programs were forced to discharge patients owing to financial hardships imposed by the new regulations.

Because the central issues had to do with the violation of federal Medicaid and FDA regulations, the attorneys decided to file suit in federal court. Four programs were chosen to bring the lawsuit against DPW. Three patients also agreed to participate as plaintiffs "on behalf of themselves and all other similarly situated persons." Physicians from the four programs were prepared to testify that the new regulations usurped their medical authority by granting uniform take-home privileges for all MA recipients. Further, physicians planned to note the danger to the public from illicit sales of methadone, as well as the danger to patients because unsupervised methadone would be readily available for abuse. The three patients were prepared to testify that they had abused heroin and were seeking or receiving methadone maintenance treatment.

Also at issue was the claim by the plaintiffs that DPW had not provided appropriate notification to MA recipients of a reduction in previously provided services. Timely and comprehensible notification is required under the federal Medicaid regulations, and the state of Pennsylvania had previously lost a legal challenge in regard to inappropriate notification to MA recipients. *(Jackson, et al.* v. *O'Bannon, et al.* Civil Action No. 500, Eastern District Court of Pennsylvania. Feb. 6, 1980.) This challenge had been initiated by mental health agencies in regard to similar limitations on psychotherapy reimbursement. This proved to be the key point: DPW had sent notification of the reduction of reimbursement for methadone maintenance and psychotherapy services, but the notice was vague and not within the prescribed time limit. DPW conceded that their notice to MA recipients in regard to methadone and psychotherapy reimbursement limitations was deficient in advance of the court date.

On 16 May 1980 the HAP attorneys, the program directors, and the DPW attorney appeared in the courtroom of Judge John P. Fullam in the case of *John Doe, et al.* v. *O'Bannon, et al.,* Civil Action Number 80-1677. The proceedings lasted less than ten minutes and Judge Fullam issued the following ruling:

> AND NOW, this 16th day of May, 1980 upon consideration of plaintiffs' Motion for a Preliminary Injunction, it appearing that plaintiffs have established a reasonable likelihood of success on the merits and that irreparable harm is likely to occur, and the defendants having conceded that the notice of change in the regulations was defective, it is hereby ORDERED AND DECREED THAT:
>
> Defendants, Helen O'Bannon, Secretary of the Department of Welfare, Gerald Radke, Deputy Secretary for Medical Assistance, and the Department of Public Welfare of the Commonwealth of Pennsylvania, are preliminarily enjoined, until further order of this court, from enforcing 55 Pa Code, §§ 1223.53 (b) and (e), insofar as it limits, reduces, or prohibits medical assistance reimbursement for methadone maintenance clinic visits and for psychotherapy treatment.

We had won! The program directors were jubilant with this victory, and they quickly shared their joy with the others who had been so much a part of the battle. Although many had said it could not be done, the program directors had shown that is was possible to fight back against onerous financial strangulation. This was a "first" for the substance-abuse field in Pennsylvania. It is estimated that the brief legal proceedings saved the Philadelphia drug program approximately $1 million annually. More important, patients could continue to receive treatment instead of facing the prospect of discharge, staff shortages, program closings, and the like.

The situation has now been resolved with the publication of new DPW regulations that allow reimbursement for up to seven days per week of dispensing. At the same time, DPW has reduced the number of reimbursable therapy hours per month from eight to six. As noted earlier, the latter change does not pose a serious financial or clinical problem, for most patients are seen, on average, for less than six hours per month of psychotherapy.

Implications and Recommendations

Every situation is unique, and a major advantage in the Pennsylvania situation was that it occurred before the firestorm of recent funding cutbacks. This enabled the program directors and board members to capture the undivided attention of legislators and community leaders. The climate is different today. With cutbacks occurring in so many health and social-service areas, legislators are now deluged with requests from constituents in regard to a host of different services. Nevertheless, it is possible to draw some conclusions from the Pennsylvania experience. These recommendations will be presented in two parts: those related to coalition building, dealing with the primary actors and interest groups; and those related to action strategies, dealing with timing and risk taking.

Coalition Building

Many health and human-service executives come from a clinical background where concern for patients is uppermost. As a result, it is almost reflexively assumed that others share this concern. This erroneous assumption led to unnecessary delay in Pennsylvania, for several program directors initially thought DPW simply misunderstood how methadone programs function. They felt that DPW would lift the reimbursement restrictions once they understood the clinical issues involved. This view proved to be completely in error. It is important to recognize that the priorities of funding and regulatory agencies may not be centered around the best possible care for patients.

As a corollary to the above, many health and human-service executives tend to be "negotiators"; they customarily try to achieve a consensus when conflicting opinions exist in regard to clinical and programmatic issues. The initial response on the part of the Pennsylvania drug-program directors was to attempt to negotiate with DPW in regard to the reimbursement limitations. Even after several futile meetings demonstrated that the objective of DPW was to save money wherever possible (i.e., where there would be no legal or legislative challenge), some program directors were reluctant to pursue legal action. Instead, they preferred to go through the motions of making the rounds of legislators and writing letters to reiterate the same points. One almost got the impression that some executives felt that undertaking legal action was in bad taste. Nonsense: closing programs and discharging patients is the ultimate in bad taste. When faced with opponents who are playing hardball, one should respond in kind.

In regard to contacting legislators, constituents count, community consequences count, and patient discharges count. Professionals who are perceived as motivated in part by the fear of job loss may be accorded a polite reception, but they will have little impact unless they are voting constituents. In one instance, the author was visiting a city councilman along with a staff member who lived in the community. This staff member had a reputation of being able to get out the vote in local elections. When he mentioned using his influence in the upcoming elections, the councilman practically snapped to attention. While the author's letters and visits to politicians were politely received, the real response came when concerns were expressed by constitutents representing their communities.

Coalition building is often based on a perceived threat as well as on the goal of achieving common objectives. While the common objective was the maintenance of established treatment services for heroin addicts, the perceived threats for the various groups included fears regarding job loss (progam directors and staff), concerns about drug dealing and increased crime (community residents and board members), and possible loss of votes (legislators). In attempting to organize coalitions, it is important to utilize the perceived threats to various participants in addition to stressing their common goals.

Public relations and the media should be used to focus the issues and generate community support. As noted earlier, a black radio talk show host proved very helpful in publicizing the problems and issues posed by the new regulations.

It is important to be sensitive to the possible cultural implications of particular issues and to be prepared to utilize these concerns to strengthen and broaden community support. As noted earlier, many community residents began to view the methadone cutbacks in the broader context of denying needed services to minority populations in urban communities.

Action Strategies

At some point negotiators must become decision-makers, and actions must be undertaken even though they carry some risk. While clarity is required in regard to potential consequences, executives need to be prepared to change their customary style, even though it may result in some risk and discomfort. This, after all, is what we tell clients every day.

It is essential to pursue several strategies at once and be prepared to switch quickly as opportunities present themselves. As with life itself, undertakings of this sort rarely proceed according to plan. In the Pennsylvania situation, the progam directors recognized that legal action represented a gamble that might not succeed. Fortunately, the foundation had already been prepared for legislative and community action if the legal challenge failed.

One must be bold and creative. As noted, situations like this require strategies and actions that are atypical for most health and human-service professionals. For example, in the midst of the legislative contacts a legislator from Philadelphia publicly announced that he planned to organize his constituents to blockade all of the city's methadone clinics unless DPW relented. The program directors had not been consulted in advance, and they reacted with justified alarm at the prospect of two thousand heroin addicts facing small groups of citizens blocking access to methadone clinics. Frantic efforts were undertaken to reach this legislator. Much to the relief of all concerned, he indicated that his threat was merely a ploy to increase pressure on DPW.

A critical factor is a sense of timing. In Philadelphia, some program directors were prepared to dash out immediately and threaten, sue, and so on once the regulations appeared. Others were never prepared to initiate any meaningful action. A certain sense of flow must be established so that the broader coalitions (board members, community residents, legislators, and the like) are all moving in the same direction at the same time. As with sex, a sufficient state of general arousal is desirable, but prematurity can have negative consequences.

It is helpful if the issues have emotional as well as intellectual impact. This is particularly important in dealing with the broader community, for it enhances the possibility of generating support beyond those immediately affected. In Philadelphia, issues related to street crime, drug dealing, and the cultural implications of the cutbacks aroused concern among community residents.

One must feel free to move beyond the established, structured, bureaucratic way of doing things. As noted above, the providers decided to go around established regulatory agencies and pursue their interests independently and directly. Also, several nontraditional approaches were effectively utilized.

Finally, one must maintain a sense of optimism! A pervasive mood of pessimistic fatalism seems to characterize the health and human-services field, particularly at the administrative level. Lethargy and failure to mount effective opposition may be viewed as weakness and invite further cutbacks.

Summary

This chapter has presented a case study of the successful effort by Pennsylvania drug program directors to suspend the state's Medicaid reimbursement limitations for methadone maintenance and psychotherapy services. Following a description of the organizational, political, and legal strategies employed, guidelines were offered for those facing similar funding and/or regulatory battles.

In the final analysis, an element of luck is necessary for the successful outcome of such an undertaking. For example, the Pennsylvania Department of Welfare was involved in a number of other issues (including the introduction of a computerized billing system) which may have prevented their executive staff from devoting full attention to this dispute. There is no doubt that DPW could have continued the fight had it chosen to do so. For example, it could have issued new regulations and sent appropriate notification to MA recipients. From the perspective of the program directors, it might have been difficult to maintain the necessary legislative momentum, for cutbacks in other services (particularly education) were beginning to cause great concern in Philadelphia.

With President Reagan's New Federalism it becomes increasingly important to form coalitions that can effectively advocate for services at the state and local levels. In the near future, issues regarding funding, program priorities, service delivery, and the like will be decided by state and local legislators. Where national groups and institutions have been relied upon to present the view of various service components in the past (NIMH, NIDA, NIAAA, etc.), the new direction of government power mandates stronger and more effective political activity at the state and local levels. As demonstrated in this paper, a heartening aspect of this shift is that it is always easier to gain a sympathetic hearing and demonstrate the influence and voting power of constituents at these two levels.

In the final analysis legislators need votes to get elected. Also, most legislators share a humane concern for the well-being of their communities and constituents. It is up to us to reach them.

References

Cohen, Sidney, *The Substance Abuse Problems*. New York: The Haworth Press, 1981.

Dole, Vincent. "Addictive Behavior," *Scientific American* 243, no. 6 (December 1980):38–154.

Dole, Vincent, and Marie Nyswander. "Rehabilitation of Methadone Patients," *New York State Journal of Medicine* 74, no. 7 (July 1974):1415–24.

Dole, Vincent, and Herman Joseph. "Long Term Outcome of Patients Treated With Methadone Maintenance," *Annals of the New York Academy of Sciences* 31 (29 September 1978):181–89.

Gearing, Frances, Dina D'Amico, and Frieda Thompson. "What's Good About Methadone After Ten Years?" In Arnold Schechter, ed. *Drug Abuse: Modern Trends and Perspectives*. New York: Marcel Dekker, Inc., 1978.

Jackson, et al. v. *O'Bannon, et al.* Civil Action Number 80–500, Eastern District Court of Pennsylvania, 4 February 1980.

John Doe, et al, v. *O'Bannon, et al.* Civil Action Number 80–1677, Eastern District Court of Pennsylvania, 16 May 1980.

Millman, Alfred. "A Fifteen Year Study of Addiction Treatment Successes and Failure." In Russell Faulkinberry, ed. *Drug Problems of the 70's: Solutions for the 80's*. Lafayette, Louisiana: Endac Enterprises, 1980.

Pennsylvania Bulletin 9, no. 44 (3 November 1979).

Pennsylvania Bulletin 9, no. 52 (29 December 1979).

Weiner, Harvey, "Methadone Counseling: A Social Work Challenge," *Journal of Psychedelic Drugs* 7, no. 4 (October–December 1975):381–87.

Weiner, Harvey, and Herbert Kleber. *Basic Administration Principles for Drug Abuse Treatment Programs*. Medical Monograph Series, National Institute on Drug Abuse, 1, no. 3 (1979).

13 Professional Dissonance in Public Welfare

Willard C. Richan

How do social-work administrators reconcile the conflict between the expectations of their professional community and those of the welfare bureaucracies that employ them? This chapter examines the responses of a group of administrators to such a dilemma. All were employed in administrative positions by a state welfare system that enacted a welfare "reform" proposal vigorously opposed by the state chapter of the National Association of Social Workers (NASW), and which these administrators were expected to help implement.

As professional employees of service bureaucracies, all social workers face potential conflict between professional duty and organizational loyalty. That this problem has been a major preoccupation of the social-work profession for more than a quarter of a century is attested to by the steady outpouring of books and articles on this subject. The pioneering article of Ohlin, Piven, and Pappenfort (1956) on dilemmas among probation and parole workers was followed in 1960 by Rapoport's more general treatise on stress in the social-work profession and Gottlieb's (1974) depiction of a "welfare bind." Worker stress and burnout have been attributed in part to conflicting expectations (Harrison 1980, Maslach 1978). Recent primers for line workers on changing the organization from within (Brager and Holloway 1978, Patti and Resnick 1980) echo this same concern with professional and organizational conflict.

For social workers who are administrators, the issue is further sharpened by conflicting interests and their more exposed position. Caseworkers may betray their professional credo or defy organizational mandates in relative secrecy, but administrators' choices are quickly known throughout the organization and may even make page one or the six o'clock news. The shrinking job market in the human services is further restricting administrators' options.

The relationship between the social-work professional community and social-welfare organizations is complex and often ambiguous. Sometimes the two systems reinforce one another; sometimes there is tension between them in certain respects but not in others. Rarely are the differences between them presented with such stark clarity as occurred in the case to be presented.

Professionals in Organizations

While in a numerical sense social work may have been the "dominant" profession in public welfare, including public assistance, it has never attained the kind of power ascribed to the medical profession in health-care settings by Friedson (1970). Public-welfare social workers are generally subordinate to political appointees and specialists in fields such as public administration and accounting.

Much of the literature on social-work professionals as employees emphasizes the importance of the work setting in shaping their orientation and behavior (Billingsley 1964, Richan 1973); nor should this be surprising, since it is the agency that retains tangible sources of power over the career of the worker, long after departure from social-work school. In the absence of legal regulation of social workers, the professional community per se has virtually no sanctioning power. But even where licensing prevails, this is primarily focused around technical competence and deals with only the most explicit sorts of ethical violations. Hence, to all intents and purposes, reinforcement of professional principles in the worker must rely upon internalized sentiments and the influence of the professional community.

The tensions created when professional values conflict with organizational ones are dealt with in several ways; the theory of cognitive dissonance provides a framework for analysis.

Cognitive Dissonance

Cognitive dissonance is a state in which "an individual simultaneously holds two cognitions (ideas, beliefs, opinions) which are psychologically inconsistent" (Abelson 1969, Festinger 1957). Since dissonance is uncomfortable, the actor seeks to resolve it by changing one or both cognitions. For instance, a social worker who has scruples against taking punitive action against clients, but finds it necessary to do so in order to remain employed, may change his or her view of such work in order to make the situation more tolerable. In the case of a value conflict, as in the present study, the person must define the situation so as to retain self-esteem (Rokeach 1968), that is, justify the behavior.

The definition of the situation, a framework for interpreting events, can be handled in various ways. The writer has identified three dimensions of definition: selection, perceptual orientation, and evaluative orientation.

Selection

Selection involves focusing attention on certain elements in a situation and excluding others. Through the selective adaptation of *suppression,* the actor may avoid potentially threatening content. Abelson cites the tendency of persons caught in a dilemma between different beliefs to deny the presence of one or the other (1959). For example, an administrator, shown evidence that a presumably exemplary worker has been extorting money from clients, might block out the information. A person addicted to smoking may "tune out" when exposed to information regarding its harmful effects. The same phenomenon has been seen in Germans who blocked out knowledge of the extermination of Jews under Hitler.

Welfare bureaucracies provide a ready means of selection through specialization of function and insulation of one unit from others. Administrators may claim that a particular issue is outside their jurisdiction. By extension, issues raised by the professional community can also be defined as outside one's area of concern, or one may deny awareness of the professional stance on an issue.

Perceptual Orientation

Perceptual orientation provides the basis for interpreting events, for understanding what is going on. Through the use of the perceptual adaptation of *distortion* the actor is allowed to place events in an acceptable intellectual framework. The person retains awareness of what is happening but places a construction on it which "makes sense." Some Hollywood writers who informed on their friends before congressional red-hunters later asserted that this had not harmed the persons so named (Navasky 1980, pp. 279–313). Some of Milgram's subjects went to considerable lengths to convince themselves that their "victims" were not hurt by the alleged electric shocks, or that token gestures of help by them somehow mitigated the effects of the shocks (1965).

Welfare administrators required to carry out policies that are potentially harmful to clients are often encouraged to use distortion by agency rhetoric suggesting that policies are in fact beneficial to all concerned. In the present study, the state administration had sought to sweeten the welfare-policy scheme by proposing that a large part of the expected savings should be used to increase the grants of the remaining recipients and provide job training. Thus, the "truly needy" would in fact be better off if the measure passed. A second kind of distortion fostered by welfare bureaucracies of all kinds is the belief that one cannot influence events, and hence must learn to live with "reality."

Evaluative Orientation

Evaluative orientation sets the standards against which events are to be judged; the adaptation of *revaluation* provides an acceptable moral framework for choices. Thus, for example, the actor may perceive events accurately but modify the value context. "Blaming the victim" is an illustration of this mechanism (Ryan 1971). Some Hollywood writers interviewed by Navasky asserted that the persons on whom they informed deserved what they got because they had brought the trouble on themselves or had been willing tools of Communism. Some of Milgram's subjects became angry at their "victims" for submitting passively to the alleged electric shock (1965).

    Another way of recasting events in an acceptable moral framework is to associate them with a higher order of values (Abelson 1959). Many Milgram subjects, while uncomfortable with their role, felt called upon to serve the cause of science, just as some Hollywood informers asserted that they were moved by a sense of patriotism.

    The devaluation of welfare clients as being untrustworthy and generally unworthy is constantly reinforced by welfare rules and guidelines. The preoccupation with cheating by clients permeates virtually every activity in which welfare staff members engage. Thus, the professional social-work presumption of recipient dignity and worth is steadily eroded in the working environment of the welfare bureaucracy. So it would be surprising not to find professional administrators resorting to this kind of adaptation when faced with dissonance between professional and organizational mandates. A second means of justifying actions that appear to be antiprofessional is to devalue the professional community itself, or its official spokespersons, as naive. This may be coupled with a belief that the general society is being harmed by the excessive demands of a poverty-stricken minority; thus, one has a higher duty, despite professional tenets to the contrary.

    An additional factor in coping with dissonance is social support. The belief that peers share the same views acts to reduce stress (Blau 1960, Gottlieb 1974). Administrators who believe their co-professionals agree with them will be under least pressure to engage in the three defensive adaptations described above.

The Case Study

In the midst of high and growing unemployment, the governor of a large state in the Northeast proposed the exclusion of persons defined as employable from the general assistance roles. As a proposal by the state administration, the plan had the strong public support of the welfare secretary, who lobbied actively for its enactment by the state legislature.

From the outset, the state chapter of NASW played an active role in the fight against the measure, bitterly condemning the proposal as inhumane. Its stance was consistent with the stated position of NASW on public-assistance policy and social-work professional values generally.

The Code of Ethics of NASW in effect at the time of this controversy states: "Social work is based on humanitarian and democratic 'ideals' " and "requires of its practitioners . . . compassion [and] belief in the dignity and worth of human beings." It cites as the primary obligation of the social worker "the welfare of the individual or group served" (National Association of Social Workers 1970). The NASW goals for public social policy have asserted "the right of all Americans to an adequate income" and consistently espoused a public-assistance system "based on financial need as the only criterion of eligibility," which assures "that no one because of socioeconomic reasons or the lacks and deficiencies in other income provision arrangements shall be without a decent level of income" (National Association of Social Workers 1969 and 1980).

Thirty persons in senior-level positions in the state welfare agency, selected to reflect various administrative levels and a diversity of specialization, were interviewed regarding their views on the governor's welfare proposal. Although some of the administrators in the study were not members of NASW, all had been professionally socialized in graduate schools of social work. Both the professional literature and the standard-setting organization in social-work education consistently emphasize the professional obligation to respond to human need (Briar 1977, Brieland and Atherton 1975). From these transmitters of social-work values, the message is clear: Depriving poor people of subsistence without regard to the availability of work is not consistent with professional values.

These administrators were thus placed in a bind between professional and organizational expectations. It would be difficult for any of them to be unaware of the conflict. Given the nature of both formal and informal communication systems in this state agency, the welfare secretary's advocacy of the welfare "reform" was well known to staff throughout the organization. The NASW chapter took pains to make its opposition known through both the chapter newsletter and the news media.

Professional subservience in the agency was intensified by the fact that the state agency had, for several years, been engaged in a conscious process of "declassification," that is, eliminating professional educational requirements for many positions, as well as replacing many social workers with nonsocial workers. Had it not been for civil service rules, the ranks of the social-work professionals would have been decimated at an even faster rate than they were. Thus, there was a high degree of job insecurity, intensified by the trend, national as well as local, away from support of social programs.

All of the above factors would be expected to militate against active resistance by the social-work administrators in this case study to the agency's position in favor of the welfare plan. And if the response was to remain in the potentially conflictual situation, then an accomodation could also be expected.

Attitudes toward the Welfare Reform Scheme

As discussed earlier, the literature on social-work professionals emphasizes the importance of the work setting in shaping both orientations and behavior. In regard to *orientations,* the administrators in this study retained their professional values. Not only did twenty-one of the thirty administrators disagree with the policy as a matter of principle, but they also perceived that they reflected the predominant sentiments of workers in the agency, despite the official support of welfare reform at the top. It should be noted that the five who actually spoke in favor of the principle of eliminating employables from the welfare rolls acknowledged that they reflect a minority view of the social workers in the agency. Thus, as opposed to the official espousal of welfare reform, the administrators who participated in this study were getting a very different message from the informal system around them.

But, in support of the literature vis-à-vis *behavior,* the readiness to condemn the policy did not carry over into overt steps to fight it. Only five respondents took any action that could be interpreted as opposition to the policy; in most cases, this consisted of sharing information with outside groups known to be opposed to the policy, thus "giving ammunition to the enemy." In some instances, respondents went to considerable lengths to justify this activity, saying they felt it was "appropriate" (legitimate).

All but two of the administrators who reported experiencing some degree of stress regarding the welfare reform issue were opponents of the reform. One veteran employee of the agency, who described the policy as "unconscionable. . . . a three-decades step backwards," had considered leaving the department altogether but eventually remained; a second administrator simply "withdrew" (felt no more personal investment in the agency); a third respondent wanted to speak out publicly in opposition but felt constrained to remain silent, while another, who was asked by superiors to make recommendations regarding the policy, declined to do so because of utter opposition to its basic intent. Yet, at the same time, most of these individuals avoided taking any action that could be construed as disloyal to the agency, even though asked to do so by professional colleagues. Although the administrators felt trapped, only one even contemplated leaving the agency on this issue.

The concept of cognitive dissonance will be used to examine the mechanisms employed to resolve the tensions created for administrators caught between their professional values and their bureaucratic roles.

Coping with Dissonance

Through a content analysis of the interviews it was clear that twenty-six of the thirty administrators used one or more of the mechanisms for reducing cognitive dissonance.

Suppression was clearly the major form of adaptation, observed in seventeen cases, and primarily used by the opponents of the welfare policy. It is interesting to note how this was played out. Through the mechanism of suppression, respondents denied awareness of the profession's stance on the issue of eliminating employables from eligibility for assistance, although the chapter's explicit opposition had been widely publicized in the state. One respondent, a current member of the state chapter, initially declared, "I am not aware of the NASW chapter position on this question," but then showed by his responses to questions that he was indeed conscious of the group's opposition.

If one does not have to acknowledge that a conflict exists between professional tenets and the policies one is required to implement (or at least be implicated in) as part of the welfare bureaucracy, it is possible to reduce the issue to a matter of personal opinion rather than a potential violation of a professional commitment.

Selection was also evident in cases where respondents focused away from the issue of depriving employables of assistance. Since the legislation contained sections dealing with AFDC reform and a workfare program for those remaining on the rolls, a few respondents shifted the discussion from the question of eliminating employables from the rolls to sections of the bill dealing with workfare, child care, and job training.

One administrator with major responsibility for putting the policy into effect declared, "Our job is to implement agency directives. I have no personal view on this. There is a horrendous amount of work involved in getting it into effect." If this respondent had any misgivings about the policy itself, they were not acknowledged. Others, whose function did not involve the administration of money payments directly, also professed noninvolvement in the implications of the welfare reform scheme.

The second most used adaptation was that of *revaluation*. The application of normative standards that serve to justify one's position was observed in one-third of the respondents. The administrators who did *not* oppose the governor's welfare proposal, those who failed to support the professional social-work stance, were significantly more likely than opponents of the policy to use revaluation. Their response was to devaluate the welfare recipients and/or the professional community.

One administrator who approved of the welfare reform plan spoke of her recent disillusionment about welfare recipients. "In the last couple of years I have been disturbed by what I have seen," she said. "Something had to be done." Another who was ambivalent about the legislation said, "People want to get things without having demands made upon them." And others made reference to "cheating" and to "lazy" people in the case load. In other cases the comments were couched in professional language. "Casework training has taught us what motivates people, but we seem to have forgotten that . . . people respond to rewards and punishment." "People need to be pushed to be independent." "In the past, social workers were materialistic, thought you must give something. Now the idea is to help people help themselves."

In some instances, the professional community rather than the client population was at issue. "The profession continues to live in the past," said one administrator. Another declared,

> What concerns me is the social work professional ethic. If we are to take moral stands, the world will pass us by. I am troubled by some things I've read in NASW publications. There is an absence of thought and consideration of realities.

It is conceivable that revaluation was not involved here. Rather, these respondents may have consistently held such negative views, with no feeling of cognitive dissonance, hence no need to reduce it. There are two reasons to doubt this interpretation. One is the observation that respondents who devalued the clients or the professional community also used suppression or distortion, suggesting that dissonance was indeed a factor. Second, nonopponents of welfare reform were significantly more likely than opponents to have changed their position toward support of such policies during their careers. This finding supports the notion that social workers have started from a common base predominantly opposed to this kind of policy, but some have moved toward a more approving stance. A number spoke of having gained a different perspective in the past few years, a period that coincides with a generally more hostile climate to the welfare population. This came through forcefully in the case of one administrator who had worked in general assistance since the 1960s, but whose cynicism regarding clients had developed in the past few years. Assuming that welfare recipients were no more virtuous, on the average, in the 1960s than the late 1970s and early 1980s, it appears that other factors in this administrator's experience had been at work.

By contrast, the predominant reaction of the opponents was to criticize the failure of others to fight the legislation more vigorously, or to defend their own lack of active opposition to a policy that they acknowledged was detrimental. "Why didn't people call me? People called on the abortion issue . . . Why didn't people call me on [welfare reform]? Thirty calls on abortion, zero on [welfare reform]. Where was the United Way?" Others claimed that the administrators were not as free to express themselves as those on the outside and asserted that if they did not implement the policy others would.

It is perhaps not surprising that those who approved of the governor's welfare proposal or were ambivalent about it were the most likely to use revaluation. By dissociating themselves from the value stance espoused by the social-work professional community and its institutions, they could justify their position on the policy. Judging from the fact that they were also less likely than opponents to report experiencing stress regarding the welfare-reform issue, it appears that they were more successful in resolving whatever cognitive dissonance may have been present.

The *perceptual adaptation of distortion* was the mechanism least used by this sample; only five administrators reinterpreted the factual situation in this way. A typical reaction was the belief that the effects of the policy would somehow be averted, either through alterations in the implementation phase or later reversal in the legislative or legal arena. For example, one administrator said, "If you stay around here

long enough, things go around in circles—things turn around;" Few
respondents questioned the hardship that the policy would cause to at
least some poor people. But one administrator declared, "It forces
people to live with their families. They will get food stamps and medical
[assistance]. The families will have to support the incidentals." This
assertion flew in the face of the fact that large numbers of persons had
no families; for them the effects would hardly be "incidental."

The Administrative Bind: Implications for Action

What about the dominant group of administrators who shared the
profession's opposition to the policy but felt constrained to remain in
the system and help with implementation? They faced a kind of dilemma
that is common in many parts of the human-services enterprise and is
likely to intensify in the coming years as shrinking budgets and a conservative political climate take their toll. How can administrators be
helped to cope more effectively with this problem?

Acknowledging reality. It will be recalled that the most frequent adaptation to cognitive dissonance in this group was suppression. While
it may reduce stress for the individual, this form of adaptation makes
the administrator less able to cope effectively with conflicting expectations. The official institutions of the professional community have an
important role in helping social-work administrators deal with reality.
For instance, any waffling or ambiguity on the part of professional
organizations in regard to social-work values or their implications for
policy and practice is likely to be seized upon by many administrators
faced with conflicting agency expectations.

Fear of retaliation by the agency did not appear to be the primary
reason why opponents of welfare reform did so little to stop it. In fact,
many commented on the freedom of expression within the agency.
Instead, there was a deep-seated belief that one was professionally
obligated to support and carry out agency mandates, however distaste-
ful. Said a strong critic of welfare reform:

> There is a point up to which people can express their views. Then,
> once the decision is made, you must comply if you are going to stay
> as a member of the staff. If people cannot live with it, they should
> get out if they want to retain their integrity.

This raises an issue of professional priorities. Historically, loyalty
to the agency was indeed viewed as one's primary professional duty

(Rapoport 1960). But in the late 1960s, NASW declared that the social worker's responsibility for the welfare of the clientele took precedence over all other obligations, including that to the employing agency (Ad Hoc Committee on Advocacy 1969). If social-work administrators are to be advocates for the people they serve, they should understand this order of priorities.

So the social-work community needs to make clear to its members the official tenets regarding professional standards of conduct as well as substantive policy concerns. Yet more is involved in dealing with denial and distortion than presenting a consistent professional face. It seems clear that many respondents in this study were closing their ears to a widely broadcast message. Nor should we expect that exhortation in social-work school and the official pronouncements of the profession would be enough to influence administrators' actions. Rather, it is necessary, in view of the exposed position of social-work administrators, to find ways of building in support and protection.

Protection of profession autonomy. Needless to say, professional mandates remain on the level of exhortation unless there is machinery to support and enforce them. Several years ago, in the heyday of political ferment and advocacy in social work, NASW strengthened its machinery for protecting its members in their dealings with their employers. In the current period of retrenchment, it is harder for the professional association to provide this sort of support, especially with respect to administrators. But this is essential if the profession expects its members to meet their professional obligations, and administrators need to be made aware of this kind of resource.

NASW has explicit policies on ethical conduct, the right (and responsibility) of social workers to be advocates for their clients, and personnel practices by agencies. There is adjudication machinery through which such policies can be given tangible meaning. A legal defense service has been made available to NASW members in recent years. These structures have been utilized in the past, in some instances to protect administrators against punitive action by their employers (See, for example, *NASW News* 1972.)

Realistically, few administrators will place their trust in such formal machinery unless it is augmented by other forms of protection. The most meaningful supports of this kind lie within the collectivity of social-work administrators themselves.

Mutual support among administrators. If they are to develop any sense of security, social-work administrators need opportunities to come together and give one another mutual support and counsel. In the large welfare bureaucracy in this study, administrators had a great deal of contact with other senior staff and had, in effect, developed their own in-house reference group. While sufficient to reinforce their stated dislike for the policy, it did not move them to become active opponents. Many social-work administrators lack even this kind of support from professional peers.

Of the administrators in this study, 70 percent spent little or no time outside of working hours with other social-work professionals. Nearly 40 percent had at one time been NASW members but had allowed their membership to lapse, and a similar proportion had dropped out of the American Public Welfare Association (APWA), the other major professional association for public-welfare workers. Several respondents, including both opponents and nonopponents of the welfare policy, said they no longer thought of themselves as social workers. In effect, they had withdrawn from the professional community. In view of this degree of professional isolation and the pressure from the organization, the opposition of so many administrators to agency policy is particularly impressive.

Peer solidarity has several functions. On the most practical level, organizations are hesitant to retaliate against persons who have a supportive constituency. Demoting or reassigning a troublesome individual can usually be rationalized with appropriate labels from the professional jargon, but this becomes more difficult where group interests are concerned. Second, one's conviction in the rightness of what one is doing can be eroded rather easily without a supportive reference group.

On the positive side, group support enhances one's leverage for bringing about change or, as in this case, resisting it. Aside from what has already been said, the reasons for this are clear. Coalitions of this kind multiply individual administrators' access to information and expertise, as well as access to powerful allies.

So it is especially important that social-work administrators be aided in developing close relationships with professional colleagues, both within and outside of their agencies.

Political sophistication. Finally, administrators' ability to affect policy depends on their expertise in an area that may seem on the surface to be outside of their special domain: political influence. It is an area of content notably missing from most management training programs. Social-work administrators frequently rise through the ranks, in which case their only professional training may have been in direct service delivery. Among the administrators interviewed for this study, nearly two-thirds had majored in casework, group work, or other direct-service skills. Only one had majored in administration. Thus, they had little preparation for dealing with the power dimension of their role other than what they might have picked up on the job.

The typical way of dealing with this situation is for the administrator to be "a-political," concentrating primarily on survival skills. This may serve the individual well in the narrowest sense of that term—in survival within the organization—but in the larger view, it can be self-defeating for the administrator and the agency as well. Slavish obedience to directives from above allows an organization to rigidify, with the professionals inside transmitting only the "good news" to their superiors. The system is then ill-prepared to deal with the conflicting forces in its environment.

Conclusion

The issue examined in this study was posed more starkly than is usually the case; the professional social-work community was outspokenly critical of a policy the agency was promoting just as publicly. Frequently the professional community and the bureaucracy share common objectives and assumptions, or their differences are blurred by the ambiguities inherent in so much of human-service work. In this case, the strong public stand of the state NASW chapter and the governor's personal political stake in the outcome of the controversy left social-work administrators within the agency little room for maneuver. But while the administrative bind may not always be sharp, the elements discussed here are probably present in most such situations.

All three cognitive adaptations—selection, perceptual distortion, and revaluation—were evident in the responses of the administrators interviewed, and two of them, selection and revaluation, were most used and were related to the respective stances of individuals in relation to the conflict between professional and organization allegiance. From a professional standpoint, the revaluators—those who rejected the professional value stance in some manner—appear to be the most problematical, for they were the ones who experienced the least stress, and thus had resolved the dilemma most successfully. Insofar as an administrator aligns himself with the agency outlook and is comfortable with this resolution, there is little motivation to change.

But this group was also significantly more likely than others to have changed their views toward approval of the welfare policy in the course of their social-service careers. This indicates that it may be possible to "reach" this population if it is done early enough. The most intensive period of professional socialization is during the years in social-work school. Forty percent of the administrators in this study said their perception of "the social-work professional stance" on the welfare-reform issue was acquired either thorugh social-work or the professional literature. All this suggests a critical role for the schools and the professional associations in determining administrators' perception of what is "professional," in addition to helping them to acquire the necessary political tools. Admittedly, this will not prevent capitulation to anti-professionalism in the organization, but the investment in trying at least to reduce it is well worthwhile.

References

Abelson, R.P. "Dissonance Theory: Progress and Problems." In R.P Abelson et al., eds. *Theories of Cognitive Consistency: A Source Book*. Chicago: Rand-McNally, 1969.
———. "Modes of Resolution of Belief Dilemma," *Journal of Conflict Resolution* 3 (1959):343–52.
Ad Hoc Committee on Advocacy. "The Social Worker as Advocate: Champion of Social Victims,' *Social Work* 14, no. 2 (1969):16–22.
Billingsley, A.W. "Bureaucracy and Professional Orientation Patterns in Social Casework," *Social Service Review* 38 (1964):400–407.
Blau, P.M. "Orientation Toward Clients in a Public Welfare Agency." *Administrative Science Quarterly* 5 (1960):341–61.
Brager, G., and S. Holloway. *Changing Human Service Organizations: Politics and Practice*. New York: Free Press, 1979.
Briar, S. "Social Work Practice: Contemporary Issues." In *Encyclopedia of Social Work*. 17th Issue. Washington, D.C.: National Association of Social Workers, 1977.
Brieland, D., and C.R. Atherton. "Social Work and Society." In D. Brieland, L.B. Costin, and C.R. Atherton, eds. *Contemporary Social Work: An Introduction to Social Work Social Welfare*. New York: McGraw Hill, 1975.
Festinger, L. *A Theory of Cognitive Dissonance*. White Plains, N.Y.: Row, Peterson, 1957.
Friedson, E. "Dominant Professions, Bureaucracy and Client Services." In W.R. Rosengren and M. Lefton, eds. *Organizations and Clients: Essays in the Sociology of Service*. Columbus, OH: Charles E. Merrill, 1970.
Gottlieb, N. *The Welfare Bind*. New York: Columbia University Press, 1974.
Harrison, W.D. "Role Strain and Burnout in Child-Protective Service Workers," *Social Service Review* 54 (1980):31–44.

Maslach, C. "The Client Role in Staff Burnout," *Journal of Social Issues* 34 (1978):111–24.

Milgram, S. "Some Conditions of Obedience and Disobedience to Authority," *Human Relations* 18 (1965):57–76.

NASW News. "Berkan Appealing Dismissal as County Director; May go to State Court." 17, no. 5 (August-September 1972), p. 4.

National Association of Social Workers. *Code of Ethics* (Amended). Washington, D.C., 1970.

———. *Revisions in Goals of Public Social Policy.* New York, 1969.

———. *Compilation of Public Social Policy Statements* (Revised). Washington, D.C., 1980.

Navasky, V. *Naming Names.* New York: Viking Press, 1980.

Ohlin, L.E., H. Piven, and D.M. Pappenfort. "Major Dilemmas of the Social Worker in Probation and Parole," *NPPA Journal* 2 (1956):211–25.

Patti, R.J., and H. Resnick, eds. *Change from Within: Humanizing Social Welfare Organizations.* Philadelphia: Temple University Press, 1980.

Rapoport, L. "In Defense of Social Work: An Examination of Stress in the Profession," *Social Service Review* 34 (1960):62–74.

Richan, W.C. "The Social Work Profession and Organized Social Welfare." In A.J. Kahn, ed. *Shaping the New Social Work.* New York: Columbia University Press, 1973.

Rokeach, M. *Beliefs, Attitudes and Values: A Theory of Organization and Change.* San Francisco: Jossey-Bass, 1968.

Ryan, W.F. *Blaming the Victim.* New York: Pantheon, 1971.

Index

About the Contributors

Michael J. Austin is Professor and Director of the Center for Social Welfare Research, School of Social Work, University of Washington.

Joseph J. Bevilacqua is a Commissioner, Department of Mental Health and Mental Retardation, Richmond, Virgina.

Richard K. Caputo is Director of Research, United Charities of Chicago.

Barbara J. Friesen is Assistant Professor, School of Social Work, Portland State University.

Murray L. Gruber is Professor, School of Social Work, Loyola University of Chicago.

Burton Gummer is Associate Professor, School of Social Welfare, State University of New York at Albany.

Ernest M. Kahn is Associate Director, Philadelphia Federation of Jewish Agencies.

Elizabeth Ann Kutza is Associate Professor, School of Social Service Administration, University of Chicago.

Roger A. Lohmann is Professor, School of Social Work, West Virginia University.

Thomas Meenaghan is Professor, School of Social Work, Loyola University of Chicago.

Felice Davidson Perlmutter is Professor, School of Social Administration, Temple University.

Willard C. Richan is Professor, School of Social Administration, Temple University.

Mark J. Stern is Associate Professor, School of Social Work, University of Pennsylvania.

William J. Vosburgh is Professor, Graduate School of Social Work and Social Research, Bryn Mawr College.

Richard Weatherley is Associate Professor, School of Social Work, University of Washington.

Harvey Weiner is Director, Addictive Behavior Programs, John F. Kennedy CMH/MR Center and Clinical Associate Professor, Hahnemann Medical College.

About the Editor

Felice Davidson Perlmutter is Professor of Social Administration and Chair of the Graduate Program in Administration and Planning, School of Social Administration, Temple University. She is the author of several books, including *Leadership in Social Administration* and *A Design for Social Work Practice*. Her articles have been published in *Administration in Social Work, Social Work, Community Mental Health Journal*, and *American Journal of Orthopsychiatry*, among many other publications. Dr. Perlmutter serves on the editorial boards of several professional journals and has been a consultant to human-service agencies in the public and voluntary sectors.